Ritual and Economy in Metropolitan China is essential background for understanding how traditions modernize within and through global processes. It is essential reading for understanding Shenzhen's emergence as China's fourth city by making salient how South Chinese villagers repurposed family identities and kinship networks to become successful entrepreneurs.

—*Mary-Ann O'Donnell, co-editor of 'Learning from Shenzhen: China's Post-Mao Experiment from Special Zone to Model City'*

This is a stimulating study of the cultural underpinnings of urbanisation and economic development in the People's Republic of China, using the case-example of the southern metropolis Shenzhen. The authors' unusual combination of economic, sociological and anthropological approaches offers novel perspectives for specialists in all these fields, and for scholars in Chinese Studies more generally.

—*Philip Clart, Leipzig University*

A great deal of social science scholarship on China gets caught up in a false dichotomy of Chinese exceptionalism vs. 'Western' social theory, resulting in studies that focus on either how much China differs from 'the West' or on how China serves as a site where abstract 'Western' theory yields 'Chinese characteristics' on the ground. *Ritual and Economy in Metropolitan China* is one of those rare and rewarding studies that succeeds in transcending this dichotomy by laying the groundwork for a genuine 'global social science'. Through a rich and highly grounded exploration of ritual practice and the ritual economy in Shenzhen, the authors demonstrate effectively that our taken-for-granted assumptions about social theory can be enriched and broadened by paying some attention to practices in places less heard from in the Western canon. A fascinating account that reaches far beyond the 'China studies' field.

—*Tim Oakes, University of Colorado at Boulder*

Ritual and Economy in Metropolitan China

This book focuses on Shenzhen, one of China's most globalized metropolises, a leading centre of high-tech industries and, as a melting pot of migrants from all over China, a place of vibrant cultural creativity. While in the early stages of Shenzhen's development this vibrant cultural creativity was associated with the resilience of traditional social structures in Shenzhen's migrant 'urban villages', today these structures undergird dynamic entrepreneurship and urban self-organization throughout Shenzhen, and have gradually merged with the formal structures of urban governance and politics. This book examines these developments, showing how important traditional social structures and traditional Chinese culture have been for China's economic modernization. The book goes on to draw out the implications of this for the future of Chinese culture and Chinese economic engagement in a globalized world.

Carsten Herrmann-Pillath is a Professor and Permanent Fellow in the Max Weber Centre for Advanced Cultural and Social Studies, Erfurt University, Germany

Guo Man is an Associate Research Professor in the School of Economics and Management, Harbin Institute of Technology, Shenzhen, China

Feng Xingyuan is a Professor and Executive President, Cathay Institute for Public Affairs, Beijing, China

Routledge Studies in the Growth Economies of Asia

139 Innovation, Investment and Intellectual Property in South Korea
Park to Park
Ruth Taplin

140 A Microcredit Alternative in South Asia
Akhuwat's Experiment
Shahrukh Rafi Khan and Natasha Ansari

141 Development Agenda and Donor Influence in South Asia
Bangladesh's Experiences in the PRSP Regime
Mohammad Mizanur Rahman

142 How China's Silk Road Initiative is Changing the Global Economic Landscape
Edited by Yuan Li and Markus Taube

143 Trade Unions and Labour Movements in the Asia-Pacific Region
Edited by Byoung-Hoon Lee, Sek-Hong Ng and Russell Lansbury

144 International Entrepreneurship
A Comparative Analysis
Susan Freeman, Ying Zhu and Malcolm Warner

145 Ritual and Economy in Metropolitan China
A Global Social Science Approach
Carsten Herrmann-Pillath, Guo Man and Feng Xingyuan

146 Cyber Risk, Intellectual Property Theft and Cyberwarfare
Asia, Europe and the USA
Ruth Taplin

For more information about this series, please visit: www.routledge.com/asianstudies/series/SE0133

Ritual and Economy in Metropolitan China

A Global Social Science Approach

Carsten Herrmann-Pillath, Guo Man and Feng Xingyuan

Routledge
Taylor & Francis Group
LONDON AND NEW YORK

First published 2021
by Routledge
2 Park Square, Milton Park, Abingdon, Oxon OX14 4RN

and by Routledge
605 Third Avenue, New York, NY 10017

First issued in paperback 2022

Routledge is an imprint of the Taylor & Francis Group, an informa business

British Library Cataloguing-in-Publication Data
A catalogue record for this book is available from the British Library

Library of Congress Cataloging-in-Publication Data
A catalog record has been requested for this book

ISBN 13: 978-0-367-56372-1 (pbk)
ISBN 13: 978-1-138-39197-0 (hbk)
ISBN 13: 978-0-429-42243-0 (ebk)

DOI: 10.4324/9780429422430

Typeset in Times New Roman
by codeMantra

Dedicated to the memory of Fei Xiaotong and his contribution to global social science

Contents

1 Introduction

China has been emerging as a world economic power and is increasingly perceived as a 'systemic challenge' to advanced Western economies. For decades now, economists have pondered what the peculiar features of the 'socialism' or 'market economy' 'with Chinese characteristics' are. This includes fundamental questions such as whether China is 'socialist' or 'capitalist', or whether it represents a new systemic type, often labelled 'state capitalism'.[1] Given the fact that the Chinese Communist Party maintains the rhetoric of reforms and transformation even after 40 years of permanent institutional change, one difficulty seems that almost all features of the system may prove to be transient. However, there are elements which are beyond dispute, for political and ideological reasons, barring a collapse of One-Party rule, such as the pivotal role of state ownership in certain industries. Yet, how these features interact with other elements of the system remains difficult to assess, and after all, the precise nature of the interaction between party, state, and society is just at the heart of the troubles in dealing with the perceived systemic challenge.

This book focuses on one apparently defining feature, land ownership and its economic, social, and cultural ramifications in the megacity of Shenzhen: In socialist China, land is publicly owned, in two forms, collective ownership in rural areas and state ownership in urban areas. Hence, urbanization of rural areas comes along with complex changes in the structure of property rights as unbundled spectra of various partial rights, which generates a distinct dynamic of social and even political changes, though in the context of stable state ownership of land. We believe that the key to understanding the Chinese system can be found in improving our knowledge about how such a dynamic works on the micro level: in this case, how land ownership interplays with public administration, business, and social groups in emerging new forms of economic organization and patterns of social interaction. However, in doing so, we cannot claim to present a general picture of the Chinese system. But we argue that this special case may give us insights about certain principles and the logic of how the system works in a specific setting. This follows the tradition of Chinese institutional economists in the 1990s who argued that given the complex and transitory nature of the system, the case study approach is most recommendable.[2] If we want to think about the system in toto, this fits to a view that approaches it as a multi-scalar, diversified, and complex structure bound together by certain basic principles and less by institutional integration.[3]

We add another idea that has been also ventilated in the recent Chinese literature and has been programmatically pursued by the historian Philip Huang for many years.[4] Our problems in dealing with China may not only reflect the complexity of Chinese transition, but also deficiencies of social science theories that in the past were mainly developed in analysing Western societies. We agree with that view and believe that these deficiencies are already visible on a conceptual level, probably even on the level of social ontology: Thinking in terms of a 'system' is a case in point, because the term suggests a degree of functional integration and institutional coherence and uniformity that may project false expectations about the Chinese practice and performance.

In the context of economics, two issues loom large. The first is the conceptual and therefore also analytical separation between state and market, and the second is the relationship between market transactions and other types of social relations. Economists typically assume that there are neat conceptual borders in both domains. However, this is not a 'naturally given' fact, but mirrors a certain way how the actors in advanced Western societies institutionally create and maintain those borders, which in many instances may be porous in the real world.[5] Since these institutions are based on certain theories that inform their design, we surmise that the theories become performative: That means, the theories determine institutions which shape practices that in turn conform to the theoretical predictions.[6] What if there are alternative theories that create different forms of performing the economy?

If we talk about 'theories' here, in the first place we have social science theories in mind, but clearly the argument extends to all kinds of ideas about the economy in relation to other domains that are maintained by the actors in the economy.[7] That means, we must not only consider scientific theories, but causal beliefs and conceptual categorizations in general: For example, what are the ideas that entrepreneurs maintain about the economy, how do these result into actions which create a specific pattern of institutionalized processes in the economy that in turn confirm the expectations that entrepreneurs form about the economy? And after all, both can relate to each other: For example, the idea of a 'free market' is a concept with intuitive meanings in Western societies which is formalized in neoclassical economics, thus creating the conceptual borderline to 'government'. In China, right from the days of the first Chinese classic on the economy, the 'Guanzi', the market was seen as being an integral part of the state, and hence economics was conceived as a part of statecraft that does not need to be approached as an autonomous domain of knowledge: China did not produce an Adam Smith, despite having achieved a high level of sophistication in managing the economy.[8]

Let us give an example how this general methodological concern applies in our book. A celebrated distinction in the social science is between weak and strong ties as properties of social networks that embed markets.[9] The theory states that strong ties are less conducive to generating new information in network interactions. Only weak ties can achieve that, because they connect people in very different environments and with different backgrounds. Mathematical network theories define these weak ties as 'random'. It seems natural to think that markets are mainly driven by weak ties, for that reason, and because markets themselves systematically create forces of random encounters among people. More fundamentally, strong ties may even stay in tension with the demands for rational and profit-oriented action on the marketplace. Hence, there is at least the implicit assumption that markets and closer social interactions are separate domains in society. Now, a Chinese sociologist, Zhai Xuewei, raised a simple question when studying Chinese social networks: If ties are weak, how can we trust that the new information is reliable?[10] Obviously, the implicit assumption in the weak tie argument is that there are exogenous determinants that safeguard the quality of the information independent from the agents that engage in the relationship, such as institutions or values, given that the very definition of 'weak tie' implies that the belief that the information is truthful cannot be grounded on personal trust. Zhai argues that this is exactly the reason why Western social scientists struggle with the notion of 'guanxi' as a network formation. *Guanxi* connect people with weak ties but create a bond that commits them to certain actions that are trustworthy. For example, if *guanxi* are generated via a surname association that theoretically would include millions of individuals, they can build on a cultural frame that fosters mutual trust. Accordingly, the strong/weak duality is broken: There is a third type of network connection which combines features of both, such as among individuals with the same surname who meet in arenas where surname is mobilized to create connections. One the one hand, the individual with same surname is a stranger (weak tie), but at the same time, an emotional closeness is suggested rooted in values of kinship (strong tie).

As this example shows, the Western theory of networks needs to be improved by adding a type of network interactions which can be theorized in terms of Chinese indigenous notions of networking, with straightforward translations into generic concepts.[11] This is one case in point for what we define in our book as 'global social science approach'. A global social science activates the potential of indigenous concepts about social action, relations, and structures for generating truly universal theoretical concepts in social science, and of course, establishes what could be called a 'post-colonial' recognition of indigenous social science, as in our example, introducing Zhai's ideas in the argument of this book. Our book builds on previous work by one of us which argues that one essential difference between a 'Chinese' and a 'Western' social theory is that the former assigns a central role to the concept of ritual.[12] *Guanxi* are supported by certain types of ritualized interactions. As we argue in Chapter 2, ritual was a concept that stood at the centre of Confucian theories about social order and was an essential feature of real-world institutions in old China. One manifestation is the 'ritual economy': the merging between ritual actions with economic actions, such as in the domains of kinship and popular religion. The eminent 20th-century Chinese sociologist, Fei Xiaotong, confronted the Chinese 'ritual order' with the Western 'legal order', 'rule by ritual' versus 'rule by law'.[13]

The straightforward question is: Is ritual a concept that can give us better access to Chinese realities than other theories? And if this is the case, should we reassess the status of 'ritual' as a theoretical concept in global social science? Indeed, ritual is a neglected theoretical concept in Western social sciences, in the sense that it is not a foundational term. One reason for this is that most thinkers believe that with the process of modernization and secularization, ritual has become marginalized or confined to specific types of action, such as in religion. Accordingly, and endorsed by Fei Xiaotong himself, we would assume that as China modernizes, the ritual order crumbles. In fact, Chinese modernizers in the 20th century actively and even aggressively battled against ritual, such as the ancestral cult.

This book takes an empirical observation as a starting point: We observe the renaissance of ritual in modern Chinese society, even actively promoted by the Communist Party, salient, as in the case of the ancestral cult, in the reconstruction of ancestral halls with high public visibility. This goes hand in hand with a growing interest in the corresponding social theory, namely Confucianism. Many entrepreneurs publicly express interest in Confucianism, and some organize reading classes in their companies. What does that mean? If ritual is still relevant as an indigenous concept for understanding China, does that also imply that ritual must assume a different position in generic social science theories, thus eventually also transforming the lens through which we look at Western societies? Is ritual just a phenomenon specific to China, or does the Chinese case demonstrate that there is a blind spot in established social science theories?[14]

We pursue both dimensions of this question in our book. We take on the lens of ritual to better understand certain phenomena in China, and we claim that this supports the case for upgrading the status of ritual in social science theories. Our choice of Shenzhen as the empirical case for our research is motivated by the idea that Shenzhen, by all means, can be regarded as belonging to the avant-garde of modernization and globalization in China, that is, a leading case of what we refer to as 'metropolitan China'. Therefore, if we diagnose a revival of ritual *even there*, this is highly relevant for defining a research agenda also for the rest of China. Shenzhen is a perfect laboratory for testing our ideas about China, and the merits of alternative theoretical frames. At the same time, with the rise of Shenzhen as a global city, this enriches the cultural diversity of globalized modernity, and correspondingly encourages us to rethinking theoretical approaches to understanding modern societies in general.

If we diagnose deficiencies of Western theories, we think of the dominant views. In fact, there are approaches that push ritual to the centre of analysis. One is informed by game theory, arguing that ritual is the essential means to create and maintain common knowledge in social interactions.[15] In this book, we follow the theory that was developed in much detail by Randall Collins, which generalizes over certain ideas first articulated by Durkheim.[16] As we show in Chapter 2, this theory provides powerful conceptual and analytical means to access Chinese realities. Therefore, we believe that studying Shenzhen can also contribute to current debates among different social science theories, endorsing some, and weakening the case for others. This is our contribution to developing a truly global social science. In the context of ritual, the Chinese case reaches farther than the issue of social interactions, because ritual is traditionally seen as the core governance mechanism also in the relationship between state and society. We surmise that this creates distinct forms of what Philip Huang dubs the 'statification of society' and the 'societalization of the state', which gives fresh insights for assessing related ideas beyond Chinese studies, in particular, Migdal's concept of 'state-in-society'.[17]

That said, most of the book is spent on presenting empirical details about various aspects of ritual in the context of the Shenzhen economy. During the past five years, the authors collaborated in various settings in research on family business and business associations in the Pearl River delta. After the publication of Herrmann-Pillath's book on 'China's Economic Culture', Guo Man, a long-time Shenzhen resident and former PhD student of Herrmann-Pillath, agreed to launch a project on urban villages and lineages in Shenzhen further pursuing the argument of that book. Feng Xingyuan, an authority on the rural economy of China at the Chinese Academy of Social Sciences, Beijing, later joined in adding his expertize on associations and family business. In the past three years, apart from continuous ongoing empirical work by Guo Man residing at Shenzhen and teaching at Harbin Institute of Technology, Shenzhen campus, the authors joined for three fieldwork activities per year, two to three weeks each. Some results were published in academic journals.[18] This book offers a complete and systematic picture of our results, presenting a much more elaborate theoretical frame, additional information, and many themes that were not treated in previous publications. Each chapter starts with a theoretical reflection about basic notions in Chinese studies and how they might inform general theoretical concepts guiding our analysis. In the conclusion, we pull all theoretical arguments together in sketching a theory of ritual that combines with Collins' theory, but also goes beyond.

Chapter 2 develops the theoretical argument, first in submitting the case for adding ritual to our fundamental theoretical toolbox, and next in outlining our theory of choice, Randall Collins' 'interaction ritual chains', and relating this to the notion of 'ritual economy' as familiar in Chinese studies. Chapter 3 presents the core empirical reference, urban villages in Shenzhen, and our corresponding theoretical concept, the 'ritual space'. We mainly analyse two villages in more detail, Fenghuang in Bao'an district, and Xiasha in Futian district, to illustrate the general point that we make in Chapter 2: Urban development of Shenzhen is shaped by the ritual spaces of former villages in its territory. This starts out from the observation that the traditional Chinese village is a ritual unit of space, culture, and social structure, centring on various ritual artefacts such as temples and expressed by regular ritual activities. We show how the face of the city has been increasingly shaped by these underlying ritual spaces. This roots in the growth of urban villages on the territory of the original villages and the growing clout of village communities in influencing further redevelopment. The central ritual institution is the lineage: Many villages in the Shenzhen territory are single-lineage villages, which explains their resilience under conditions of extremely rapid economic growth and structural change. Therefore, a marker of ritual space is the ancestral hall, which often combines with a temple open to the public. We expand this view to include other ritual aspects, such as *feng shui*, in influencing urban design.

Accordingly, Chapter 4 focuses on the lineage and its organizational complement, the Shareholding Cooperative. Originally emerging as an almost subversive organizational means of villagers to keep control of their property rights on land, they have morphed into parafiscal units of urban management and administration, thus creating fuzzy borders between government, business, and kinship groups. We look at one shareholding cooperative, Fenghuang, in much detail and explain why it should be regarded as part and parcel of the local ritual economy. This is salient in the many ways how traditional lineage rules influence management and organization of the cooperatives in modern transformations, such as regarding inheritance of shares. One important insight connecting with Chapter 7 is that the shareholding cooperatives are now tightly integrated with party control yet remain partly autonomous as business units.

Chapter 5 widens the perspective and looks at the activities of entrepreneurs in mobilizing ritual in business, a phenomenon for which we coin the specific term of 'ritual entrepreneur'. This includes the activities of lineage leaders who may become influential entrepreneurs in shaping urban redevelopment projects in the interests of the village community, with Xiasha as a prime example, and its resurrection and transformation of the traditional 'common pot' feast. However, we also look at other activities which take place against the background of the government policy of activating culture for developing Shenzhen as a 'global city'. Often, ritual entrepreneurs become active in tourism and leisure projects, or they engage in promulgating traditional values in consulting activities, and so on. Further expanding the scope of the argument, we approach the distinct phenomenon of 'shanzhai' industry as a form of how ritual is manifest in business, in the sense of reflecting a specific form of business networks manifest in performing the *shanzhai* economy.

One argument in this chapter is that ritual entrepreneurs create arenas where trust emerges between individuals engaging in business. Therefore, Chapter 6 analyses associational life in Shenzhen, focusing on those forms where ritual comes to the fore, such as surname associations and extraterritorial chambers of commerce, both deeply rooted in Chinese tradition. One of our cases is the Huang at Xiasha, who are strongly engaged even in the international context in fostering surname-based networks and promoting related traditional concepts of descent and distinct values. Often, place of origin is enmeshed with subcultural identities, such as the Meixian extraterritorial chamber which is a Hakka association. Another important phenomenon complicating the analysis of ritual space is that often urban villages may be dominated by one group of immigrants from other places of China, even adding occupational specialization, such as Hunan taxi drivers.

Chapter 7 introduces the notion of cultural governance that has become prominent in Chinese studies recently. Shareholding cooperatives can be regarded as an institutional manifestation of cultural governance, as they invoke and endorse traditional values which are disseminated among the residents in their areas, such as at the public schools which offer mandatory 'national learning' 'guo xue' classes. Cultural governance is enmeshed with the emergence of new elites, such as the villagers-turned landlords or the array of developers and construction companies, often controlled by immigrant Chaoshan entrepreneurs. A complex entangled web of relations between government, business, and specific social groups emerges that excludes large groups of Shenzhen society from participating in urban management, mostly the migrant workers with only temporary residence permission. In this web, the party plays a leading role, less via direct intervention, but via leadership by authority and status distinctions.

Chapter 8 reflects upon our results in starting out from Max Weber's grand narrative about Western modernization as the rise of capitalism and rational bureaucracy, a process of rationalization and disenchantment. For Weber, China was the antipode of the West, a most extreme case of 'irrational' organization of society, despite her civilizational achievements. Huang argues that this reveals a white spot in Weber's theory, lacking an ideal type of substantive rationality. We pursue this argument in various dimensions, such as in the context of urbanism, where Weberian rationalism inheres the Hausmannian tradition in rationally creating efficient urban structures by means of radically eradicating evolved structures. We argue that the case of Shenzhen allows for developing a truly global social science, which builds on theories and concepts of medium range that emerge from the interaction between generic theorizing and empirical work on the ground, akin to the evolutionary trajectory of Shenzhen urban design and architecture driven by the polarity between modernist utopias and the existing villages.

Although we present rich empirical material, it is difficult to generalize, despite the fact that most of our empirical observations have been also made by other researchers, and thus have been corroborated in many ways.[19] Certainly, we do not even claim that what we report is representative of Shenzhen economy and business, such as with reference to the large listed high-tech companies. However, we claim that the ritual economy is an important factor in Shenzhen economic life, and that its impact may reach far, such as in terms of framing social values and public imaginaries, or in terms of sustained complementary social structures. For example, although ritual practices of original villages are certainly peripheral to the mainstream Shenzhen ITC industry, they are crucial for maintaining the social fabric which makes affordable housing and living conditions possible for millions of migrant workers who work in these industries and provide complementary services for the white collar middle class who populates the Starbucks and the upscale shopping malls. And we definitively argue that the ritual economy reveals mechanisms that are generic in the Chinese context, and thus will be manifest in other forms in other contexts. To a certain extent, the conditions in Shenzhen replicate the dualism between two types of economy that Hill Gates identified 30 years ago in her historical research on the Imperial economy.[20]

In sum, the Shenzhen case is special, both because of the institutional nature of the megapolis emerging from a SEZ and because of the strength of traditional communities. One cannot project this case on other parts of China, although there are also regions where similar interaction between rural communities and modern business may emerge in the context of fast urbanization. However, Shenzhen is a model in two senses. First, it may become a template that might be copied at other places, as it often happens in China. Second, it can be translated into an analytical model by which we can better understand China.

Our work received support by many individuals and organizations. Especially, we are grateful to partial funding by the China Development Institute and the encouragement by its director, Professor Fan Gang. The basics of our book had been outlined in a report prepared for the CDI.[21] Many individuals were willing to spend their time for interviews, experts, lawyers, businesspeople, and villagers. Yet, some of our topics are difficult to touch in the context of formal interviews. The researcher must move like fish in the water, constantly being alert for valuable information popping up at casual meetings and conversations, including, of course, one of the favourite pastimes of all Chinese, the joint lunch and dinner. Much information is accessible via observing what people do, not what they say. We are lucky that today 'doing' often involves the internet, hence resulting in a rich and growing panorama of the role of ritual in modern Chinese society.

We dedicate this book to Fei Xiaotong, who was one of the founders of Chinese sociology and anthropology. For two decades, in the prime of his life, he could not further pursue his brilliant career started at the LSE in the 1930s after returning to China to contribute to his motherland. Fei advanced the view that the fundamental difference between Chinese and

Western society is ritual, and his theory of Chinese society was combined with a distinct view on Western society that differs substantially from Western self-descriptions. Therefore, he was one of the first who contributed to the creation of a truly global social science. This remains a promise only. We hope that our book is a modest contribution to that project.

Notes

1 Naughton (2017); on state capitalism, see Orenstein (2011).
2 Zhang (1996).
3 Zhang and Peck (2014).
4 Huang (2019) presents a comprehensive survey of his work.
5 According to Searle (1995, 2010), we therefore talk about 'mind-dependent facts', hence social ontology.
6 The concept of performativity has gained considerable traction in institutional economics and economic sociology today, for a survey, see Boldyrev and Svetlova (2016). One of us has contributed to this development, Herrmann-Pillath (2012, 2013).
7 Callon (2007). Therefore, the literature on performativity ties up with developments in political science that reinstated the role of ideas in political processes, see Béland and Cox (2011).
8 On the various dimensions of this issue, see the volume edited by Campagnolo (2016).
9 Granovetter (2005).
10 Zhai (2011).
11 Interestingly, a related debate currently takes place in archaeology regarding networking practices among Greek cities, see Williamson (forthcoming 2020).
12 Herrmann-Pillath (2017).
13 Fei (1947). Barbalet (2020) discusses Fei's contribution with special reference to *guanxi*.
14 Seligman et al. (2008) raise a similar question, also referring to ritual in other cultures, such as Jewish.
15 Chwe (2001). This is one of the theoretical references in Herrmann-Pillath (2017).
16 Collins (2005).
17 Migdal (2001).
18 Guo and Herrmann-Pillath (2017, 2019), Herrmann-Pillath et al. (2019), Herrmann-Pillath and Guo (2019a,b).
19 Important contributions include Wang (2016), which touches upon many of our topics, though without our systematic theoretical focus, the collection of papers on Shenzhen O'Donnell et al. (2017) and the various papers by O'Donnell resulting from her two decades-long research on Shenzhen, the anthropological work of Trémon (2014, 2015a, 2015b) and numerous collaborative work that is often realized by researchers from Hong Kong and Shenzhen, such as Po (2008, 2012) or Lai Yani and colleagues.
20 Gates (1996).
21 Accessible via Research Gate, Herrmann-Pillath (2018b).

2 Ritual theory and the economy

1 The view from China: The unfortunate marginalization of ritual in modern aka 'Western' social science

The central theoretical concept in this book is 'ritual'. We employ this term in a deliberately ambiguous way: On the one hand, we use it as a general theoretical term in the social sciences, and on the other hand we refer to the Chinese concept of ritual 'li' 礼.[1] This is a creative ambiguity, because in reflecting upon the Chinese meanings and manifestations of ritual, we introduce a 'view from China' on the generic theoretical concept. As a result, we expect that the empirical phenomena that we investigate in our Shenzhen cases also help to advance general social theory and economics: This is the 'global social science' approach.

In classical Chinese philosophy, the concept of 'ritual' was a cornerstone in Confucian thinking about human life and the core concept as far as the practical consequences are concerned for designing, establishing, and maintaining social order. In the writings of the leading Chinese anthropologist and sociologist of the 20th century, Fei Xiaotong, ritual was conceived as a third type of social order ('li zhi' 礼制) as compared to 'rule of law' and 'rule by men'.[2] However, Fei believed that ritual order was specific to Chinese rural society and will wither away in the transition to urban modernity.

The emphasis on ritual emerged in China very early in Pre-Imperial times and was elevated to a key philosophical term by Confucius.[3] At that time, the competing philosophy of Legalism 'fajia' 法家 emerged, too, which had a lasting impact on the organization of the Chinese state.[4] Different from the Western idea of 'rule of law' that was created during the enlightenment, Legalists approached law as an instrument to enforce sovereign rule ('rule by law'), based on the belief that human nature is opportunistic and amoral, and therefore needs to be governed by a system of rules enforced by punishments. In Late Imperial times, legalist administrative practice was certainly a pillar of state power, yet Imperial ideology highlighted the role of ritual, and ritual was enforced and implemented on all levels to enact Imperial rule.

When comparing this constellation with absolutist Europe, the role of ritual in expressing and enacting the power of the King or Emperor was certainly as salient as in China, and ritualization of power kept its strength at least until the demise of most monarchies in the wake of World War I, though it became a core feature of fascist rule as well.[5] However, there were two fundamental differences between China and Europe. The first is the institutional separation between the religious and the political domain, and the second is the role of ideas as unfolding in philosophy and related intellectual domains, such as in legal thinking.

In Europe, important domains of ritual were governed by the church, down to the level of the grassroots communities, where rituals of the annual agricultural cycle and of life cycle transitions were as essential as in Chinese villages.[6] The separation of church and state contributed to the slow retreat of ritual as a core means of legitimizing and expressing state power, although secular rituals, especially military ones, partly took the place of religious rituals. An important driver of this separation between church and state in the ritual domain was the Reformation: The Reformation took Catholic ritual as a major object of its intellectual attacks, and the invention of new ritual practices proceeded partly in terms of rationalizing life of communities and establishing a ritual frame for a major concern of the Reformation, that is, establishing a direct relationship between the individual believer and God. These developments were an important part of the process of secularization and 'excarnation' of Western civilization, of which the retreat of ritual in public life was an important indicator.[7]

In philosophy, this was undergirded by the intellectual movement of the Enlightenment in its various European forms, such as the French, the Scottish, or the German. The individual and its inner world were accentuated as the locus of autonomy and freedom, and dumb following of rituals was just seen as an expression of individual immaturity.[8] Simultaneously, Western thinkers focused on law as the central means of rational governance of society, rooted in certain anthropological assumptions about natural rights of individual human beings. These Western ideas were avidly received by Chinese reformers in the late 19th and 20th centuries, and accordingly, traditional ritual became a target of vitriolic attacks, especially in the fight against backwardness and 'superstition' in the rural areas. Yet, Maoism invented new forms of ritual, partly even with a religious, if not outrightly magical dimension, which were mostly discarded after 1978.[9] Thus, on the surface, in modern times we can diagnose a convergence between Western and Chinese stances towards ritual.

The obliteration of ritual is one aspect of the general pattern of secularization and rationalization in modern societies, as reflected in their modernist worldviews. Accordingly, ritual does not have an important status as a theoretical notion in Western thinking, certainly not in philosophy, but also not in the social sciences. In the latter, we can identify three major fields where ritual remains important as a theoretical notion.

- The first, and obvious one, is the study of 'non-modern' societies or modernizing societies, where rituals enshrine what is loosely defined as 'tradition'. Ritual remains an essential concept in anthropology, which may also transfer its expertize on ritual on research on modern societies, yet that does not mean that ritual becomes a core theoretical term in the study of modern societies.[10]
- The second, equally obvious one, is the study of religion, where ritual remains an important medium of religious action also in the present and across all forms of religious activity.
- The third is the microsociological analysis of ritual in theories of social interaction, mainly in the tradition of Ervin Goffman.[11] This is important, as in this area the concept obtains almost universal scope, as all kinds of actions even in modern societies may manifest ritual aspects in this sense, such as consumer behaviour, music festivals, daily routines, or corporate culture.

Hence, we diagnose a tension. The third view on ritual implies a very different concept of ritual than from which we started out: Ritual is a specific type of human behaviour, and therefore universal. It may be even seen as biologically determined, as ritualization of behaviour is a universal feature of animal life.[12] If this is true, why is ritual not a central concept in modern sociology? The major reason seems to emanate from the historical sketch: Ritual is not seen as a major macro-structural aspect of modern societies but as limited to certain social domains or specific forms of individual behaviour.

We think that one deeper reason for this tension is the partial neglect of material aspects of social life in modern social theory. This is not the place to explore this issue in detail, thus we just notice that this is recognized in recent calls for a 'material turn' in sociology or even a 'new materialism'.[13] We only want to highlight one field where this is most obvious, the field of cultural analysis. And even narrowing down further, we concentrate on economics, because economics should be the field where material aspects may be less ignored, and because this book concentrates on the economy and economic behaviour. If we recognize the materiality of human life and social interaction, we become more sensitive to the role of ritual in shaping behaviour and social structures, since a defining feature of ritual is being external, public, and embodied in physical actions and artefacts. We switch our attention from internal drivers of social phenomena, such as values and beliefs, to external drivers: In the excarnated view on society, the latter are simply expressions of inner states, but we can also switch our direction of causal analysis and interpret external phenomena as drivers of inner states.[14] Then, ritual theory becomes thoroughly externalist in approaching the relationship between ideas, values, beliefs, and all other kinds of mental phenomena, as which culture is often approached in modern theories: For example, the influential economics and management approach to culture by Geert Hofstede speaks of 'mental programming'.[15] Indeed, ritual theory explores how this programming is materially enacted, resulting in a reductive elimination, or at least marginalization, of inner mental states as prime drivers of action.

2 Ritual and the production of culture

Whereas ritual does not exist at all in economics as a theoretical term, culture has experienced a comeback in the recent decades.[16] Previously, economists were exclusively focused on institutions and law, but today they recognize the pervasive impact of culture on both institutions as frames of actions and on actions proper. However, culture is mainly defined in terms of beliefs and values, that is, inner mental states of individuals. External and material aspects of culture are neglected or just relegated to the status of external manifestations of culture.[17] Accordingly, rituals as cultural forms are not in focus of economic research. One exception is the concept of routines in evolutionary economics, which is mostly related to organizational practices and less to society at large.[18]

The prevailing idea that culture is a manifestation of inner mental states overlooks the essential fact that inner states and practices are inextricably related to each other, and that practices often create the forces that trigger inner states and the following actions.[19] In addition, this view cannot convincingly explain why and how all members of a group might share the same inner states, mostly pointing towards socialization across generations.[20] However, a hallmark of modern societies is the recognition of the creative autonomy of successor generations; so why should certain cultural phenomena persist at all?

In the context of culture, ritual can be reinstated as a macro-concept in social theory: Ritual is the activity that produces and reproduces culture in a group. This view was seminally introduced by Durkheim, though somewhat confined to specific forms of ritual, especially in the religious domain.[21] Yet, Durkheim also offered a broader conceptualization of religion as a means to create and sustain the identity of a group. Hence, two aspects of Durkheim's analysis remain valid for our approach: First, rituals serve to create and reinstate the shared identity, if not solidarity of a group, and second, this happens via the mediation of emotional states, which Durkheim referred to as the 'effervescence' of the ritual event.

Obviously, the Durkheimian view does not extend to including the Goffman-type of ritual, which mostly seems to lack the components of effervescence in a group event and of the mobilization of strong emotions. The broader conception of ritual appears to include forms of ritualization of behaviour which even would lack a strong emotional foundation, as it seems to be expressed in routines, that is, almost automatic behaviour without any emotional engagement. Yet, this perception is partly misleading as the emotional component of ritual can also become explicit in violations of ritual expectations. For example, a greeting may be entirely automatic, but if it fails to be produced, it can cause strong emotional reactions, such as embarrassment and anger. Hence, we diagnose a range of forms of ritual, yet suggest a common theoretical foundation for all these forms in terms of fundamental mechanisms and functions, which remains informed by Durkheim's seminal ideas.

The topic of culture is extremely broad, and we cannot discuss this here. Thus, we start out from one of the established definitions in the context of economics suggested by Beugelsdijk and Maseland: 'we loosely define culture as those behavioural and ideational structures that are deemed essential to the constructed identity of a community'.[22] This definition is narrower than many other definitions of culture, because it centres on group identity.[23] This excludes many uses of culture, such as when doing a cultural analysis of epistemic stances, unless they also play a role of forming, sustaining, and expressing group identity. We think that these broader uses blur the distinction between culture and other analytical categories, and that they become under-specified in terms of the relationship between the individual and the societal or group level. In the Beugelsdijk and Maseland definition, this relationship is defined via the concept of identity: The individual relates with the group in sharing the identity with other members of the group. Culture is at the same time manifestation of this identity, as it is the medium by which it is produced and sustained.

However, it is not clear how this works. This is where the concept of ritual becomes essential. Ritual is the type of action that produces and reproduces culture. In other words, ritualization of behaviour is a major manifestation of culture. This elevates ritual to a core term of general social theory, together with culture. On a most general level, culture can be approached as common knowledge shared by all individuals of a group which generates compatible mutual expectations of behaviour and which is embodied in behavioural patterns. Ritual as a pattern of behaviour produces and reproduces this common knowledge.[24]

On a most general level, this view eschews the dominant internalist view of culture in favour of the externalist view. The externalist view has been shaping anthropology over many decades after the emergence of the discipline, mostly in the research practices of ethnography. In these views, culture includes the whole range of material artefacts and practices of a group, thus becoming all-inclusive. Most economic uses of culture, being internalist in essence, ignore these aspects completely in concentrating on beliefs and values. Therefore, the externalist view has direct consequences for economic methodology: Artefacts and practices become major objects of research, which implies the introduction of standard methods of anthropology, such as detailed ethnographic accounts. This is what we refer to as 'material turn' in the economic analysis of culture. The material turn goes hand in hand with a different approach to reconstructing inner states as values and beliefs, which has also been defined classically in anthropology, namely as interpretive 'thick description' which aims at revealing the meanings of observed patterns of action.[25]

The material turn has important consequences for understanding the relationship between culture and economy, because it attracts attention to the economy of cultural production. One of the surprising aspects in the recent cultural turn in economics is that most economists treat culture as exogenous, also suggested by the construction of their preferred quantitative methodology, that is, econometrics.[26] Although this is not true for the subdiscipline of 'cultural economics', this mainly focuses on the creative and cultural industries, and mostly does not define an economic approach to culture in general.[27] One reason is the 'dematerialized' concept of culture as far as the generic concept is concerned. In contrast, the material turn that we suggest implies that we expand the view beyond the scope of cultural industries and look at activities of 'making culture' or 'doing culture' across all social domains. This includes the cultural industries as a major domain where this happens, for sure. This perspective is most fruitful when considering the case of China, where much of generic cultural production is today cast into the frame of cultural industries, such as in the context of tourism, however, for political reasons.

If we link ritual and culture on a fundamental conceptual level, the economic aspect looms large in the production of ritual, as this involves the use of material resources and time. Again, we need to distinguish between different types of ritual. If we concentrate on ritual aka ceremonial events here, for the sake of presenting our theoretical argument, this refers to the costs and benefits of conducting rituals. This includes, for example, providing for the stages where rituals are conducted, paying for the production of ritual artefacts, or the opportunity costs of time of participating at rituals, perhaps also including paying for ritual specialists. From that point of view, as in cultural economy research, ritual is directly connected to the economy, both markets and public actors, such as the government. This is even more evident when we consider the rituals of consumption, such as ritualized displays of luxury goods at certain occasions, such as a film festival, as a modern ritual in the media industry. In other words, the producing and enacting of ritual is an economic process of its own kind in the technical sense, and many forms of economic action are factually ritual actions. For example, modern professional sports often combine both aspects, such as the Olympic Games.

But there is also the opposite direction of analysis: Uses of culture in economics include the idea that culture is a major medium which enables and sustains economic interactions.[28] This is often tied to the transaction cost approach, implying that culture is a determinant of transaction costs, in the broader sense also including organizational costs. In the latter context, the conceptual reference is 'corporate culture', which is a major topic in the management sciences.[29] Corporate culture creates identities of organizational members and thereby affects organizational performance, such as the motivation to cooperate. Corporate culture is often explicitly tied to practices aka rituals that produce and sustain it. There are various meanings and cross-connections of that concept, as it can refer to the idiosyncratic corporate culture of an individual company, or shared properties across a group of companies such as corporate cultures of investment banks or family business, or national characteristics such as Japanese corporations. In these contexts, culture is not necessarily approached as a positive determinant of performance, such as when family culture is sometimes seen as impeding innovation.

With reference to markets, culture is approached as a positive factor mainly in the context of trust: Shared culture creates trust among agents, and therefore reduces transaction costs. The archetypical example is the culture of immigrant and diaspora communities that thrive in a culturally different environment, such as the Chinese in Southeast Asia.[30] This view directly ties up with the definition of culture we follow, as culture mainly works via shared identities vis-à-vis other groups. This is a very significant perspective, as it helps to avoid the essentialist fallacy in reifying groups as fixed and stable collectives, such as 'the Chinese'. What counts is the relationship between shared culture as manifest in shared rituals and a flow of interactions that are enabled in this medium, which is at the same time co-produced by this flow. This view connects ritual theory with another foundational term in the social sciences, which has recently resulted in a certain convergence of methods in sociology and economics: networks.[31]

3 Ritual and networks: The theory of interaction ritual chains

When relating culture to markets, we need an intermediate theoretical concept which allows to conceptualize and analyze the flow of actions by which both are co-produced. This is networks. Markets are approached as embedded into social networks, and these in turn manifest boundaries and structures shaped by culture defining the identities of network members, and which is produced and reproduced by ritual.[32] This is another venue of the material turn, since networks are material phenomena in terms of interactions among network members, and network analysis is action-centred, not value-centred. It is important noticing that these interactions need not be fully congruent with market transactions. The point about network analysis is that the market interactions relate with other types of interactions, which defines the core concept of 'embeddedness'.[33] This is the point where rituals come to the fore. Whereas the market transactions in the narrow meaning can be purely instrumental and generic, such as haggling over the conditions of a contract and finally signing it, this can relate to other interactions, such as an accompanying sequence of meetings over dinner or at the golf course. These interactions may have properties of ritual, although business negotiations themselves are often also governed by rituals (think of the archetypical haggling at the bazaar).

As a result, we can directly relate ritual analysis to the network analysis of culture. Specifically, this means that we look at a special kind of network interactions that involve ritual actions. Based on what we said previously, this includes the following phenomena.

First, ritual network interactions involve certain artefacts which are standardized across a wide range of interactions, both synchronically and diachronically. The notion of 'artefact' is a broad one and includes, for example, standardized gestures such as body movements of greeting and of course, all kinds of other artefacts with a generic component. For example, gifts are artefacts and can be highly diverse in principle, but are often standardized (such as the notorious bottle of *Maotai* in Chinese business gifts). Further, the artefactual component, most importantly, also includes the stage or venue where the ritualized interaction takes place (such as the expensive restaurant or a religious site). 'Synchronic' refers to standardization within a group, 'diachronic' to standardization through time. A major effect of this is that expectations of proper actions anchor in the repeated use of similar artefacts, which is a major manifestation of ritualization.

Second, rituals involve practices and artefacts which are deemed valuable, even if, as said previously, this may only be salient in case of the violation of ritual expectations. The notion of 'value' may directly connect with market valuation, such as in the case of the previously mentioned bottle of *Maotai*. However, value is often tied to other social domains. This is where the connection to Durkheim becomes more salient, since one important social domain is religion, hence specifying the notion of value as 'sacred'. This directly establishes connections between the various field of current research on ritual, especially religious studies and economics.[34] In empirical terms, this means to investigate into the role of religion in enabling and sustaining ritual interactions that in turn impact on economic actions. It is of utmost importance to realize that this view departs substantially from most approaches to religion and economy, which are deeply shaped by Max Weber's approach that adopts the internalist view, that is, emphasizing inner states of mind (classically dubbed 'spirit'). In ritual analysis, what counts is the creation and maintenance of sanctity by means of ritual, in principle independent from inner states.[35] In other words, inner states become endogenous to ritual interactions. This allows for neutralizing the distinction between 'authentic' and 'instrumental' uses of ritual. For example, a purely instrumental ritual action on one part of the participants may combine with authentic beliefs of other participants, thereby perpetuating the role of ritual in the group independent from individual motivations. What unifies the group is coordination of practices, not beliefs as inner mental states. And after all, the instrumental use of ritual presupposes that ritual is taken seriously even by those who exploit it.

Third, rituals, as being material phenomena, can be the object of reflective action, referring to the notion of instrumental uses that popped up in the previous paragraph. The exogenous treatment of culture in economics excludes what anthropologist have emphasized over decades, namely that culture is the object of strategic manipulation, intentional design, and all types of instrumentalization, especially in the context of power hierarchies.[36] If we link culture and ritual, this is easy to accommodate, because ritual is an object that can be handled in a quite literal sense. This avoids the troubles that accompany much analysis of phenomena, such as 'cultural revival' that raise the question of authenticity. In ritual analysis, authenticity as referring to inner states is a secondary matter.

In sum, we argue that culture, ritual, and networks are the fundamental concepts of our theoretical framework. We are lucky that we do not need to invent the wheel anew when further detailing our approach. One of the rare approaches in modern sociology that centres on ritual in the sense developed so far is Randall Collins' theory of 'interaction ritual chains'.[37] This theory provides a more detailed conceptual framework for our analysis and for our empirical strategy (see Figure 2.1).

Collins' approach differs from the economic approach in taking a 'situation' as the starting point, and not the individual. Individual agency is seen as emerging in interactions, which however are driven by individual actions that aim at harnessing 'emotional energy' in social relations. One reason of this reversal of analytic decomposition is that agency always relies on collective scaffolds created situationally and on shared understandings of a situation. For example, in a business interaction, mutual trust is essential to reach a satisfying result for both sides; in this sense, building the mutual perception of trustworthiness is a collective effort, even if at the same time strategic and instrumentalist considerations reign over the specific tactical moves.

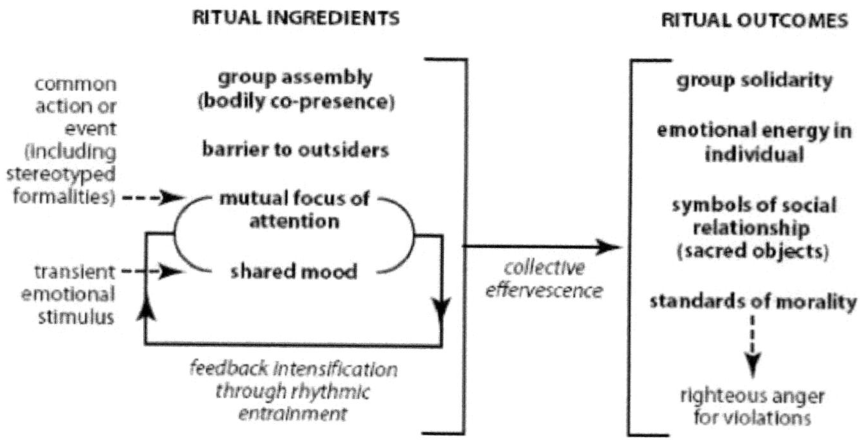

Figure 2.1 Overview of the theory of 'interaction ritual chains'; copyright Randall Collins, reproduced by permission of the author.

There are a few basic conditions for achieving this kind of coordination. The first is physical co-presence. Even in the time of the internet and videoconferencing, it is a well-known fact both empirically and theoretically that until now, no technological mediation can substitute for the complex transmission of implicit information via body language in the broadest sense, including subtle aspects such as the coordination between gestures and spoken word. Therefore, the basic unit of analysis is a co-present group, with the dyad as the minimal group. However, Collins argues that there is even an individual level of analysis via the internalization of experiences and expectations, and even an extension of ritualization to inner mental states, such as inner speech, rehearsals of experiences, and so on. Many ritual practices also originate in the group context, but are conducted individually, such as when managers develop practices of daily exercises, which appears to be a behavioural standard in a group that defines itself as high-performing, disciplined, and as concerned about maintaining high levels of capacity to perform.

One precondition of the emergence of a group is mutual focus. Mere physical co-presence is not enough, such as a crowd of strangers rushing on the sidewalk. A group emerges when individuals focus attention on what the other individuals are doing and when they coordinate their own actions with them. For example, a conversation is a primordial and most universal form of a group emerging by mutual focus. In human societies, this emergence is channelled and structured by a wide range of practices and conventions, such as the implicit rule on how to converse in the flow of mutual changes of the positions of listener and speaker. One important consequence of mutual focus is that the group creates a boundary between insiders and outsiders: Think of conversations at the break of a conference, where the crowd divides in groups of various sizes and conventions of politeness govern the movements of individuals across groups.

In such practices, the emergence of shared emotional states is essential. For example, a transient group at the conference may develop a shared feeling of interest in a topic that is demonstrated via facial and gestural expressions, or may share the feeling of relaxation by laughing about a joke. This is one of the many forms by which 'emotional energy' is produced and exchanged in a group, and which may lead to a range of consequences. For example, an individual may succeed in getting recognition by others, which may translate into enabling her subsequent role as a leader in suggesting a new research initiative.

Many processes of group formation go beyond the transient structures of conversations, and ritual is the scaffold on which that is based. Indeed, a scientific conference may be conceived as a ritual event of its own, and not without reason many people think that the coffee breaks are the most important part of it. In other words, ritual as embodied in standardized practices and organizational efforts in conducting rituals is the means of creating the conditions of the emergence of groups. It is important emphasizing that this effort can fail: There is no mechanical process that guarantees that a ritual event will indeed lead to the formation of shared productive states of a group. This implies an important corollary: There is no one-to-one relation between generic states of groups and the specific ritual form that can generate these states; however, the ritual forms as such create a distinctiveness that constrains arbitrary forms of social interaction. For example, and highly significant in our context, trust in social networks is a generic potential state of a group, and it does not matter whether this emerges in a religious ritual context or a sports event. But if in a specific society the standard form how this is enacted is the religious form, an individual cannot arbitrarily choose the sports event as alternative and must invest into the capability to engage and participate in the religious practice. In this sense, the mechanism of generating trust is both universal and specific to a group context. In other words, rituals manifest a wide range of functional equivalences across societies, without being substitutes in the specific context of a specific society. This is what constitutes the 'cultural specificity' of ritual. Cultural diversity is not a phenomenon on the level of generic phenomena, but of the ritual forms, and the ritual forms are not arbitrary, because they require specific social skills and capacities to participate. Intelligent social actors are aware of this fact, and therefore are also able to exploit and manipulate rituals in a strategic way. This is the reason why often critics of the cultural approach claim that phenomena in question (such as the infamous Chinese *guanxi*) are not culturally specific, yet others maintain that the practices differ, and in fact practitioners may fail to reproduce *guanxi* practices in an appropriate way.

One important feature of ritual is what Collins calls rhythmic entrainment. 'Rhythm' is a notion relative to the time span in which activities are regularly conducted with extremes such as, on the one hand, the rhythm of speakers switching roles in a conversation or, on the other hand, the annual meetings of an association. Rhythm is an important condition enabling coordination, shared attention, and all relevant forms of readiness for subsequent actions.

The result of successful ritual is collective effervescence. This Durkheimian term needs to be relieved from its aura of exceptionality: It simply means a state of emotional arousal that is shared in a group. As mentioned, a private conversation can manifest effervescence in this sense, if individuals share the enthusiasm about an interesting topic. But many rituals, of course, also involve the narrower Durkheimian form of effervescence, such as a religious festival or the Super Bowl.

In general, rituals produce a certain set of outcomes. The first is group solidarity and coherence. This builds on emotional energy produced by the ritual event. For example, the excitement of participating together with other fans at a soccer game produces the emotional basis for feeling as a part of the community of fans, which translates into a wide range of related activities throughout ordinary periods, such as putting a fan bumper sticker on the car and talking about the club at every possible occasion. One important aspect of emotional energy is its unequal distribution: In many ritual activities, certain individuals will gain disproportionally high emotional energy, which is manifest in adopting leadership positions. This also applies for the simpler context, say, of conversations: An individual may be extrovert, attracts the sympathy of others, and receives more attention and respect than others, which translates in building high personal reputation. In more formal ritual contexts with organizational structures, those individuals may assume formal leadership positions, such as becoming president of an association.

Successful rituals may also become creative in producing new artefacts that further structure and focus ritual activity. For example, a group may develop new practices in the context of regular meetings, such as identifying a specific restaurant as the regular site and with the restaurant mentioning this on a plaque (think of the Lion's club). Many of these practices also create distinctions to other groups, that is, mainly serve as markers of group identity. This is highly significant in the context of well-established results in social psychology that even arbitrary markers of group identity can create the emotional forces of in-group solidarity and out-group discrimination.[38] This is an example for ritual externalism: The practice and the artefact create the condition for the emergence of mental and emotional states. One correlate of this is the emergence of norms of proper behaviour and the readiness for moral aggression against violators, which is a crucial factor in stabilizing cooperation also in contexts where emotional commitments may be weak. That is, in states of low emotional commitment, the expectation of sanctions will also keep opportunistic actors in line.

Now, if we look at certain domains of society in more detail, these may not be shaped by one type of ritual exclusively. To be sure, a tightly knit religious community may be an example for full-scale ritual integration of the group across almost all domains. But most groups manifest only partial ritual integration, such as the soccer fans who do not necessarily subordinate all their life concerns to soccer and their fan club (although some may indeed go very far in this).

For our analysis, it is most important to realize that many rituals are parts of larger social networking structures, without being themselves the dominant ordering principle. This is true even for potentially totalizing rituals, such as religion: A businessperson may actively take part in religious rituals but would not necessarily subordinate business to religion. Yet in many ways, the religious rituals affect the business activities. For example, being an active member of a certain religious group may create trustworthiness, or the group as such enables in-group networking with high levels of trust, even though the transactions remain purely profit-oriented. In the latter case, the solidarity is not manifest in altruistic acts towards in-group business partners, but in the higher level of trust. That means rituals serve as arenas and focal events in the wider process of network formation in

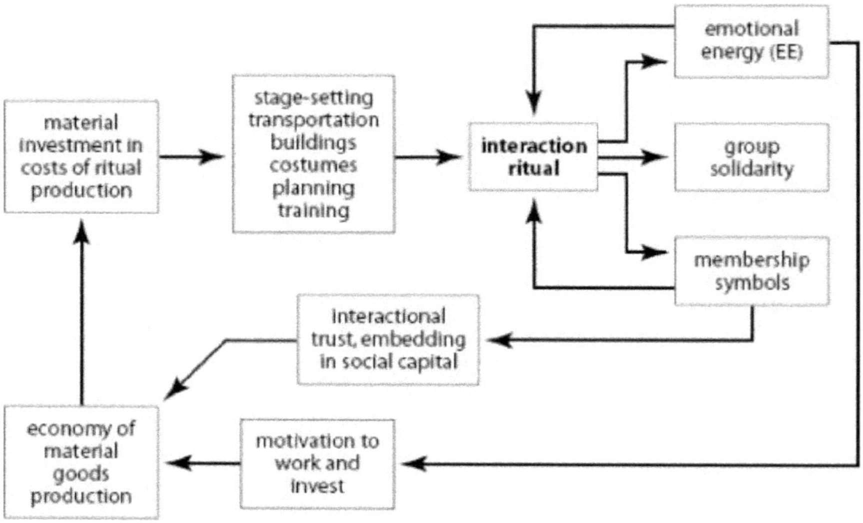

Figure 2.2 Rituals and markets; copyright Randall Collins, reproduced by permission of the author.

society and business. To repeat, in the externalist view, this does not imply that they are ephemeral and superficial as they are necessary conditions of successful performance.

Another very important aspect of Collins' theory is the explicit link between ritual and markets (Figure 2.2). As we said previously, many forms of ritual directly consume resources and are therefore related to markets and production. However, Collins adds an important twist to this in arguing that ritual is also an essential determinant of valuations of economic goods: From that perspective, ritual is primordial to markets.

One way to substantiate this argument is to modify the standard economic theory of preferences and to put positional or status goods at the core. This is an old argument in economics going back to Adam Smith, but has never obtained the central place in preference theory, presumably because of the far-reaching consequence for the standard welfare reasoning about markets.[39] This does not matter in the current context, suffice to notice that once we assume that preferences are deeply shaped by concerns about status, ritual comes to the fore as central activity in defining and expressing status. From that viewpoint, for example, luxury goods consumption is a social ritual. There are important aspects of ritual consumption across many domains, even in the poorest societies, such as expenditures for life cycle events such as weddings. Even in the realm of apparent privacy, rituals may govern the domestic consumption of goods such as wine in proper glasses. Industries such as car production are governed by a whole complex of societal rituals that establish the image of cars and which are strategically managed via advertisement.

In general, lifestyle consumption appears to be governed by consumption rituals in many ways. In many contexts, lifestyle consumption creates forces of implicit group identity, such as the shared lifestyle and professional ethos of financial professionals at places such as London or Frankfurt. Driving certain cars or owning certain watches are markers of 'membership', which in turn create the condition for certain forms of solidarity, partly based on reputation in the group that allows for sanctions of deviant behaviour. As a consequence, a whole range of service industries, real estate companies, and luxury goods producers is affiliated with the ritualized lifestyle of a 'global city' today, thus being a driver of economic production and prosperity and also of cementing inequalities.[40]

One way to explicate this relationship between markets and ritual is the well-established notion of social capital. Social capital is produced via the production of in-group and out-group borders and of status differences, or the control of access to high-status positions.[41] In this view, social capital is a club good shared by members of the group, but can also be individually exploited. Rituals are both a means of creating or sustaining social capital and of signalling it.

Before turning to the Chinese case in more detail, let us conclude this overview of Collins' theory with some remarks on why and how the theory is congenial with certain views about Chinese social interactions and networks, which however seem to suggest that these are culturally specific. Collins' theory implies a very different conclusion: It suggests that the Chinese case is generic in terms of ritual theory, and that the supposed difference to 'Western' networks reflects the failure to properly take account of ritual when analyzing the latter. This example substantiates our claims in Section 1 that indigenous Chinese concepts can also shed light on phenomena in Western societies, if we interpret them as suggesting certain generic theoretical stances among the many alternative theories available in established social science. In other words, the conjunction of Chinese concepts and Collin's theory results in a 'global social science' approach.

The case in point is 'guanxi' 关系, the Chinese form of social networking, which has been a topic for thousands of scholarly articles, books, and is also a familiar topic in applied cross-cultural business.[42] This notion will also be prominent in this book, but combined with Collins' theoretical framework. The following features of *guanxi* have emerged in that literature:

- *Guanxi* are egocentric networks that have a 'rhizomatic' structure, which means they are not hierarchically centralized and manifest fluid forms of overlap and interferences across many subjects, thus also generating fluid group boundaries.[43]
- *Guanxi* manifest a peculiar fusion of instrumental and emotional dimensions of interaction, building on the recognition of shared properties

of individuals. Often, the latter is ground in a ritual context, such as ritually affirming shared identities as a classmate. Emotional loading is itself ritualized in the shape of public recognition as the moral obligation to mutual exchange of reciprocal benefits ('renqing' 人情), which differs from inner-felt emotions of a private and more idiosyncratic kind ('ganqing' 感情).[44]

- Therefore, *guanxi* are manifest in reciprocity, though of a long-term kind. In other words, *guanxi* are networks of mutual credit and debt in terms of *renqing*, and direct fulfilment of reciprocal obligations would destroy the basis for the long-term stability of the relation.[45]
- One essential element in *guanxi* is the mutual recognition and 'giving' of face, which implies that networks often have the dimension of status differences, in the sense that *guanxi* overcome these differences while also recognizing the face of the high-status member.[46]
- *Guanxi* clearly have the function to produce, allocate, and exploit social capital, mainly in the pursuit of the interest of its members. With regard to Collins' framework, it is essential to recognize the role of rituals. This qualifies *guanxi* as a more specific form of 'li shang wang lai' 礼尚往来, that is, the proper handling of mutual obligations in social interactions.[47]

If we look at the narrower expression of *guanxi* in the business context, rituals include practices such as dining in expensive restaurants and subsequent nightlife activities.[48] Their ritual nature is evident in the standards that govern these practices, such as the use of only specific brands of liquor as gifts exchanged on that occasion, and the role of certain venues or dishes as signalling 'face giving' to special guests of the dinner. The emotional dimension is salient in the often illicit forms of behaviour, such as touching or even crossing the borderline to prostitution in Karaoke parlours. The shared experiences create shared emotions of cooperation in transgressing certain norms, and thereby foster mutual trust and commitment (in an almost exclusively male group).

This example almost ideally fits the Collins model, especially regarding the close interaction between markets and ritual. *Guanxi* rituals create groups that cooperate in the long run in the business context, without necessarily moving into the narrower domain of corruption as a spot transaction: Hosting an expensive dinner for an official may not aim at getting a certain benefit next day, but serves to create a productive relationship for future needs, that is, the product is social capital formation. This may be seen as 'corrupting', but does not necessarily move into the domain of criminal action at the ritual scene. *Guanxi* enable business activities and at the same time, they directly relate with a wide range of industries that produce the ritual goods that are necessary to enact *guanxi*, such as the arenas (e.g. expensive restaurants), gifts (such as expensive *Maotai*), or the status goods displayed by the individuals (such as the Rolex watch). *Guanxi* are not merely instrumental though, because they are only stable if they are emotionally grounded, especially in terms of creating a shared identity and commitment to the long-term obligations. In this sense, we can qualify them as establishing a moral economy of cooperative social capital production and utilization.[49]

Evidently, the example of *guanxi* cannot only be straightforwardly analysed as an archetypical 'interaction ritual chain' in the sense of Collins; but this observation also shows that the difficulties of social theory with *guanxi* do not result from their being culturally specific, but from the neglect of ritual in general theory formation. Collins' theory resolves this conundrum: All the constituent elements of Collin's theory have direct complements in the standard conceptualization of *guanxi*, such as emotional grounding and situated effervescence, instrumental uses in market contexts, production of shared identities, and so forth. Hence, the indigenous concept assumes also the status of indicating how to theorize about ritual and networks in generic terms. Does this also apply for the Chinese notion of ritual in general? Here, it is important to look at the ways how ritual is theorized in Chinese studies as a concept specific to China.

4 Ritual economy and ritual entrepreneurship in China

We start with a principled methodological point that has emerged in Chinese studies in recent decades. This is the juxtaposition between the internalist and the externalist perspective, which is manifest in Chinese studies as confronting 'orthodoxy' and 'orthopraxy'.[50] This mainly relates to the domain of religion, which, however, appears 'diffuse' in the Chinese context,[51] as religious practices are not tied to formal denominations and a canon of sacred texts and rituals, thus blurring boundaries to other domains, such as between kinship and religion.

The central point in distinguishing orthodoxy and orthopraxy is the claim that in the Chinese context, inner beliefs do not count in establishing proper religious attitudes, but mainly conformity with ritual practices. Specifically, this relates with ritual governance in the Empire, which focuses on proper conduct of certain rituals, both without covering the entire range of rituals and without governing proper belief. By implication, the same ritual practices could combine with various other practices that allowed for a much wider range of variety, and could go along with different beliefs (such as whether the ancestral tablets would only represent ancestors or indeed embody ancestors, a metaphysical issue that, in other context, divided Christianity in the Middle Ages). However, there was the notion of 'authenticity' 'cheng' 诚 of ritual practice, referring to the display of effort and attentiveness in conducting ritual.[52]

Against the background of the previous section, we can offer another interpretation of this duality: We do not interpret this as a cultural difference between China and the West, but as a biased projection of Western stances towards ritual that are themselves culturally rooted, namely in the excarnation and individualization of views on social interaction and relations. That means the Chinese view of orthopraxy involves the externalist approach to ritual that we present as a correction of common assumptions in social science theory. In other words, Chinese practice, as reflected in Chinese conceptions of ritual, is a manifestation of generic forms of ritual. Or, in other words, the Western view which has attained cultural hegemony in the social sciences is in fact a special case, whereas the Chinese case represents the generic constellation. Such a radical shift of perspective has been also articulated in the work by Seligman, Weller, Puett, and Simon, who also invoke indigenous Chinese views on ritual to elaborate a general and revisionist view on ritual in general social science.[53]

The implication is that we must avoid a misplaced 'cultural' explanation of certain Chinese practices, but at the same time need to recognize that different ritual practices go along with cultural differences that are created by those practices, as argued previously. Part of what has been identified as 'Chinese culture' in the past reflects a biased understanding of ritual in the generic sense. As we shall see, this is important to avoid unjustified claims on cultural specificity, such as Chinese networking practices, while at the same time allowing for diagnosing empirically valid differences on the level of observable ritual behaviour.

Interestingly, and significantly, similar analytical problems have emerged in understanding the relationship between the ritual domain and the economy in Imperial China. These issues had assumed immense political relevance in the Chinese catch-up policies and forced modernization of the 20th century. Max Weber's view on cultural constraints on endogenous modernization and transition to capitalism in China were closely related to the idea that the Confucian emphasis on ritual maintained a type of 'magical' thinking which impedes rationalization (the Confucian 'Zaubergarten', 'enchanted garden'; we come back on this in Chapter 8).[54] Basically, this idea, even if not directly tied to a reception of Weber, shaped much of modernist thinking of intellectuals and the political avant-garde of 20th-century China: Ritual was seen as being inimical to economic development, such as specifically in the belief that surplus was mainly wasted in display of ritual and not invested into useful activities.[55]

Recent research in social and economic history has changed this picture radically, enshrined in the notion of 'ritual economy'. This refers to the utilization of ritual forms for organizing economic activity.[56] There are several aspects here that are also important when analyzing conditions in contemporary China.

It is true that ritual activities consume resources, but of course this also generates income for those individuals that provide for the materiality of ritual, such as the carpenter who works in the construction of a lavish ancestral hall (which corresponds to Collins' view on ritual and markets). In old China, many ritual activities had at least indirect economic value in expressing the leadership role of a certain group in society, that is, forming the basis for the accumulation of valuable social capital that could be harnessed in business. This must be seen against the background of intense competition between families over access to resources. Ritual often was an essential means which enabled the pooling of resources (such as joint investment into an ancestral temple of a lineage), which then could be also invested in other economic activities. For example, although the main income may rest on land, surplus may be invested into other activities, too, such as establishing a marketplace.[57]

Further, ritual forms evolved into templates for other forms of economic organization.[58] This is especially true for the organizational differentiation of the large extended family, the lineage, into sub-branches that may hold their own estates with a specific form of governance, that is, shares of lineage branch members, boards, and often professional managers. There were many organizational forms which followed these templates, such as when lineage members founded special trusts to raise funds for festive activities, also including specific economic activities. There was a vast associational domain beyond kinship that also activated ritual motives and practices, such as native place associations.[59]

In this context, it is important noticing that the lineage was by no means a monolithic form of kinship organization. There were important differences between North and South China, and many variants also in the core areas of lineage organization, that is, South-Eastern China. On the one extreme, there were tightly knit patrilineal communities that centred on landholdings, but there were also loosely structured kinship groups located at different places which sustained their shared identity by means of joint rituals. In this context, the distinction between lineage and clan is significant, with the clan denoting a larger group often with fictitious shared descent, and eventually shifting towards the looser structure of the surname association in modern times.[60]

Ritual also served as a social glue that kept the strata of officials and businessmen together against the background of the shared ideology of descent.[61] Very few individuals could actually achieve the status of an official, and lineages developed strategies of social mobility and maintenance of status in investing into individuals with chances to succeed, for example, starting out from lineage-funded schools. Since for these efforts economic resources were indispensable, it is wrong to posit a fundamental division of interests between the two groups. Ritual practices of affirming group identity served to overcome the forces of differentiation, and hence provide for an open socio-economic structure that also recognized the social status of merchants.

Many ritual activities and artefacts also directly served economic functions. The deeper structural manifestation is the congruence between ritual hierarchies and spatial hierarchies in the Chinese marketing system as classically analysed by Skinner.[62] Local and regional markets were always ritual centres, too, in both the senses of the Collins model: First, ritual activities could provide the arena for market activities, such as temple fairs and other events. Second, there was a whole range of ritual services and production, such as ritual experts or craftsmen producing ritual artefacts.

To sum up, the concept of 'ritual economy' refers to the functional convergence of ritual and economy in many specific ritual activities (other examples include the signalling of claims on inheritance in funeral ritual). Another way to analytically diagnose this relationship is the so-called 'religious markets model' that was developed in the context of modern religion in the US and was also applied in China, past and present.[63] The topic of religion is important for our empirical argument, because many of the phenomena that we describe in Shenzhen are on the fuzzy borderline to religion because they involve rituals.

The religious markets model projects the model of markets and economic organization on religion, in the sense that on the religious market, supply and demand for religious services meet and exogenously given religious needs are satisfied. Now, in old China, as in new China, the hypothesis may hold that governmental governance and containment of large-scale autonomous religious organization created the institutional condition for the emergence and sustenance of vibrant religious markets. Beyond the confines of what government always defined as 'evil beliefs', many providers of religious services could become active, and individuals had many choices how to fulfil their religious needs.

Beyond the famous characterization of Chinese traditional religion as 'diffuse', it is therefore analytically clearer to refer to ritual 'politropy'.[64] This means, various ritual practices serve different categories of religious needs, such as concerns about good life and health on the one hand or life cycle events on the other hand. For example, for funerals people may approach a Buddhist priest, whereas for health a Daoist practitioner may be solicited. Chinese popular religion was and today re-emerges as a complex amalgam of multifarious practices manifest in specific ritual forms.[65] It is also important to distinguish larger domains of ritual, especially popular religion, kinship, and ancestral worship, and divination and 'feng shui' 风水 practices. Regarding the latter, often a distinction to religion is drawn, as the *feng shui* master is conventionally seen as an expert and professional skilled in detecting and interpreting the cosmic forces that flow together at a specific place, and which themselves are conceived as having quasi-physical nature. Similarly, health practices such as *Qigong* are partly non-religious, in the sense of claiming quasi-scientific epistemic stances and rigour of method. However, all these practices involve a strong role of rituals that eventually determine decisions of individuals, such as where to locate a building.[66]

The fuzzy boundaries between religion and other social domains which are mediated by the unifying notion of ritual can be also observed in distinguishing between culture and religion, which transpires in the difficult issue whether Confucianism is a religion or a philosophy that plays a defining role for conceptualizing Chinese culture.[67] This is also pertinent for understanding the relationship between culture and economy. In the 20th century, in the domain of business a special type of entrepreneur emerged that has been christened the 'cultural entrepreneur'.[68] This includes two wider classes of entrepreneurial activity, which, however, converge in manifesting engagement for the transformation and renovation of Chinese culture: One category is the cultural industries in the broadest sense (publishing, media, arts, and so forth), the other is to conceive entrepreneurial activity as a contribution to cultural reconstruction, starting out from interpreting one's own career as entrepreneur as culturally creative, also in the individual sense. For example, in Republican China, a cultural entrepreneur would conceive launching new hygiene products as a contribution to civilizational progress and at the same time would engage himself as poet or artist.[69]

We suggest that the 'ritual entrepreneur' is a specific manifestation of cultural entrepreneurship in China. Ritual entrepreneurs actively engage in the reconstruction and renovation of ritual, and they invest in ritual as both a contribution to society and as a means of entrepreneurial goal achievement, such as in activating ritual for the accumulation of social capital. In Imperial China, the ritual entrepreneur was a person who strove for reputation and legitimacy in adopting ritual roles, such as becoming a leader of ritual entities like temple associations, and in aligning himself with the public authorities, such as receiving the status of an official as bestowed by the Imperial administration.[70] One important aspect of ritual entrepreneurship is the promulgation of certain forms of moral economy and business ethics.

This leads us to a final aspect of ritual economy, the merger between economy and the public domain. This has been grasped in the term 'culturalism' as applied to Imperial China.[71] This refers to the fundamental pattern of governance in old China that combined weak bureaucratic integration with relatively strong efforts to homogenize culture, mainly via homogenizing elite culture by means of the examination system and via standardizing rituals. A unified culture was conceived as a means to shape and channel societal self-organization. Intermediary social strata, such as 'Confucianized' merchants, played a pivotal role. Indeed, culturalism may be interpreted as a Confucian approach to government, and Confucianization was a major goal of culturalist practices. For example, officials spent much effort in publishing guidelines for lineage ritual, including very practical aspects of lineage organization, also including economic management.[72]

To summarize this section, there is a rich literature on the economic role of ritual in China which can be straightforwardly interpreted in terms of Collins' theory of ritual. This offers a fresh perspective on the issue of culture and economy in China: Could we specify this in terms of a continuity of forms of ritual economy? This is one central question that we pursue in this book. On the one hand, we argue that a generic theory of ritual such as Collins' is powerful to analyse certain phenomena in modern Shenzhen economy and business. On the other hand, we think that we can build on 'family resemblances' with the Imperial ritual economy to better understand the distinctiveness of ritual in Shenzhen today. Both points converge in the claim that a 'ritual economy' is part and parcel of economic modernity in Shenzhen, and that this is not simply manifesting resilience and revival of 'tradition', but is the active recreation of ritual exploiting the imaginery of traditional Chinese culture, mobilizing generic mechanisms of ritual, networks, and economic performance as theorized by Collins.

5 Consequences for research strategy and method

The theoretical framework outlined so far has several implications for method. The most fundamental one is that we need to combine detailed empirical description with a strong interpretive approach, as pursued in 'thick description' championed by Clifford Geertz.[73] That means on the one hand it is important to describe and diagnose ritual in as much detail and scope as possible. This differs from the standard economic approach to concentrate on statistical databases, surveys, or more recently on experiments to investigate into cultural phenomena as defined in terms of values and beliefs. Ritual analysis requires approaching ritual practices in the field and identifies their case-specific contextualization. The latter means to engage in interpretation, and this can only be empirically vindicated in dialogue with the actors of ritual, both directly and in accessing the whole range of discourses about specific rituals, which today take place in all kinds of media, such as WeChat.

That means the prime method of ritual research is the case study along the lines of anthropology. However, there remains a distinct difference between economics and anthropology in terms of approaching the 'case'. The anthropologist would always strive at experiencing the full context of specific topics in terms of long run field research with a strong component of participant observation, ideal-typically represented by the village study which aims at achieving a full-scale view on the local community and all possibly relevant contexts. In economics and business studies, the 'case' rarely involves this kind of effort, but investigations concentrate on the specific topic, and then analyze ramifications often based on other types of material, such as statistical data. For example, when studying family business, the economist would rarely spend a year at one single company. However, it also deserves notice that in modern economy and business, actors are often reluctant to allow for this kind of very intensive and even intrusive research.[74] That means, even though the anthropological field study is the gold standard for research in phenomena of the ritual economy, this is almost impossible to achieve, given the type of actors and activities and, after all, the current political restrictions on fieldwork involving sensitive issues such as religion.

Another important implication for method is to connect current observations with historical information. In standard economic analysis of culture, it is often difficult to specify the causal channels of transmission of values and beliefs that connect past and present. The case of ritual is different, since we adopt the externalist view: We can directly identify historical continuities by diagnosing the stability or revival of ritual practices. However, this needs to be combined with interpretive caution, since the same ritual may have very different meanings and functions in the past and the present. Obviously, this creates many difficulties for achieving unequivocal interpretations, as we have seen in the discussion of the ritual economy: Interpreting past ritual practices as having economic functions was a major shift in recent historical research. There are many important issues where interpretive ambiguities loom large, such as gender.[75] Since we also face interpretive troubles in the present, this creates the possibility that we have a range of possible historical trajectories that connect alternative interpretations past and present while referring to the same empirical facts about rituals.

This problem is especially virulent when considering the meta-narratives of modernization, tradition, and cultural change, and the fact that they are not only constructed on part of the scientific observers, but also the subjects themselves.[76] The highly contentious role of ritual in the recent intellectual and social history of China creates many difficulties in achieving a proper interpretive stance. For example, many Chinese intellectuals tend to sideline popular religion as a social phenomenon, and often the status of religion is hidden under the label of 'local customs'. But this attitude is itself a result of past intellectual exchange with the West, and hence reflects a peculiar stance towards modernization in relation to certain religious practices.[77] Even Western observers might therefore have difficulties in properly discerning the religious nature of certain practices, since they maintain a biased view on what constitutes 'religion'.

At the same time, the concept of 'local custom' currently serves as integrative interpretive framework to combine ritual and economy in the context of tourism and leisure activities. This implies that the same practice can integrate many different interpretive stances, such as those held by local officials or by citizen-practitioners.[78] But for researchers, it is very difficult to reveal the true stance, because everybody is aware of the value loadings of the practices: A local official will rarely recognize and endorse the religious nature of ritual, and even the practitioner may be cautious in doing this. Hence, the researcher may need to rely on direct observation of manifest behaviour, and then interpret this in certain ways. Indeed, actors in the field may often not be willing to talk openly to the researcher about these matters and would even refrain from using certain words. Therefore, it may be more helpful to look at their actions. One new source of information is very useful, this is the internet, because here action combines with written texts. We often have observed that subjects may neutralize or marginalize a certain field of action, but simultaneously engage in internet-related activities in that field. Therefore, in our book, we make heavy use of internet sources to contextualize our field observations.

To conclude, research in the field of ritual in China today is detective work, often based on circumstantial evidence, on indirect observations, and reluctant comments by participant actors. This is true even though rituals are manifest in actions and artefacts, hence easily observable. But this often appears like the salient evidence of the crime, the broken window, the corpse of the victim, the fingerprints. The 'Whodunnit?' remains a tricky question, and we may end up with charging the wrong people with the deed. Yet, if we combine information from many sources and across many domains of action, an authentic and comprehensive picture emerges that is Shenzhen's ritual economy. This picture is ours though, and must be treated as a theoretical hypothesis of 'medium range', not as an empirical fact sui generis.[79] We will discuss these methodological issues further in the final chapter of the book, and now want to invite the reader to the field.

Notes

1 In Chinese, there are two concepts that reflect the semantic ambiguity of the English 'ritual'. Ritual, especially in the plural, may refer to the specific actions and artefacts in doing ritual, which is often translated as 'yishi', 仪式'ceremony'. *Li* includes this aspect, but also the behavioural stances and the systematic totality of a social order created by rituals. Ceremonies are public and formal, whereas *li* also covers norms of proper social interaction in everyday life.
2 Fei (1947). Fei has been very influential in suggesting the concept of 'differential mode of association' 'chaxu geju' 差序格局 as a theoretical model of Chinese social structure.
3 For a thorough philosophical comparison between classical Chinese philosophy and Western philosophical traditions, see Hall and Ames (1998). The ancient Chinese literature on ritual is also invoked by Seligman et al. (2008) to develop a general theory of ritual.
4 MacCormack (2006).
5 A classical analysis of rituals in expressing and manifesting the power of the French emperor in the Ancien Régime is Elias (1969).
6 A fascinating difference between Europe and China is that the Church in Europe imposed ritual forms of family life that radically transformed extended kinship, whereas in China Confucian ritual mostly conformed to those practices; see Goody (1983).
7 The term 'excarnation' is used by Charles Taylor (2007) in describing and analyzing these changes.
8 These developments are overviewed in Stephenson (2015). For a more principled argument on this, see Seligman et al. (2008).
9 The religious and ritual nature of Maoism is highlighted in Goossaert and Palmer (2011).
10 Classics include Geertz (1963, 1973) and Turner (1967).
11 Goffman (1967).
12 Stephenson (2015) emphasizes this aspect.

13 Influential contributions are Pinch and Swedberg (2008) and Bennett (2010).
14 Seligman et al. (2008).
15 Hofstede et al. (2010).
16 There is now a very rich literature on culture in economics overviewed by Beugelsdijk and Maseland (2010) or Alesina and Giuliano (2015). However, in management sciences, culture always was an important topic, with classics such as the updated Hofstede et al. (2010).
17 The value-based approach joins economics and management sciences, partly because both often refer to empirical value studies. That means both disciplines tend to ignore anthropology and its ethnographic methods; exceptions include some authors in the Austrian school of economics, for example, Storr (2004).
18 D'Adderio (2011).
19 There is a long tradition in philosophy that leads back to Hegel and which highlights this dialectical relationship between action and inner states, such as American pragmatism (Dewey, Mead, and others); see Herrmann-Pillath and Boldyrev (2014) and Joas (2011).
20 Tabellini (2008).
21 Durkheim (1915).
22 Beugelsdijk and Maseland (2010: 11)
23 This problem haunts anthropology since its inception, with many definitions of culture literally covering everything that appears specific for a certain community as compared to others, such as the design of vessels, culinary practices, or beliefs about the weather. The literature fills libraries, and there was a time when anthropologists even thought that the concept should be discarded; Brumann (1999).
24 This has been analysed in game theory by Chwe (2001). It deserves emphasis that 'knowledge' is not conceived as a mental state here, but as being distributed in social groups that are collectively engaged in ritual, following Hutchins (1995).
25 The classic is Geertz (1973).
26 This is the centrepiece of Jones' (2006) seminal critique of culture in economics.
27 Towse (2010).
28 For example, and more specifically, culture is conceived as a medium of the formation of social capital, and social capital is a central determinant of enabling successful economic interaction; see Beugelsdijk and Maseland (2010).
29 Classics include Schein (2017).
30 There is a very rich literature on networks and economic interactions, with seminal contributions such as Rauch and Casella (2001) and overviews such as Jackson (2014). The connection to Chinese studies has been established by Landa (1994, 2016).
31 For an overview, see Jackson (2014).
32 This idea is elaborated in various approaches to social networks in sociology, such as White (2008) or DiMaggio (2011).
33 Granovetter (1985, 2005).
34 There is growing literature on the economics of religion; see the seminal survey by Iannaccone (1998) and McCleary and Barro (2019).
35 Seligman et al. (2008).
36 Zweynert (2009).
37 Collins (2005).
38 Taijfel's seminal and famous experiments on insider bias and stereotyping have generated a substantial literature also in economics; see, for example, Chen and Li (2009).
39 Since Veblen (1899), economists have investigated the central role of status in consumption, but the idea never reached the core of the theory of choice. There are different concepts, such as 'positional goods', and the question is whether they are treated just as special cases or as a universal feature of choice. Important

recent contributions include Hirsch (1976), Frank (1985), or Hopkins and Kornienko (2004).

40 Sassen (2018).

41 The literature on social capital is voluminous. We follow the exposition in Lin (2001). Sociologists mostly refer to Bourdieu here, including his concept of 'cultural capital', but we do not want to delve into wider theoretical debates in this book. Lin's theory is especially compatible with Collins' framework and with social network theory. Another highly relevant contribution is Burt (1992, 2002).

42 For surveys on the *guanxi* literature, see Gold et al. (2002), Chen et al. (2013), and Bian (2018).

43 Yang (1994).

44 Classical accounts of this are Jacobs (1982) and King (1994).

45 This goes back to the Chinese notion of reciprocity, seminally treated in Yang (1957).

46 These aspects are emphasized by Chinese researchers, such as Zhai (2011).

47 Chang (2010).

48 Osburg (2013).

49 *Guanxi* are a form of 'nurturing' yang 养social relations (Stafford 2000). On the intricate issue of differentiating *guanxi* and corruption, see Qi (2013).

50 This distinction has been seminally introduced, but independently, by Watson and Rawski (1988) and Schmidt-Glintzer (1983).

51 Yang (1961).

52 Sutton (2007). It is important to distinguish this notion of 'sincerity' from the use in Seligman et al. (2008), although the underlying phenomena are the same. Seligman et al. use 'sincerity' as 'authentic expression of inner beliefs', which might therefore better called 'authenticity' to distinguish from the Chinese term. 'Sincerity' of ritual action does not refer to the meaning of the ritual as intended by the individual practitioner, but to her or his effort and zeal in 'doing the ritual'. That means somebody can be 'sincere' in doing the ritual, even if she does not believe in its specific meanings.

53 Seligman et al. (2008).

54 Weber (1991). Weber remains relevant today; see, for example, Landes (2007).

55 Riskin (1975).

56 Faure (2006), Yang (2007). For a more detailed treatment of the following, see Herrmann-Pillath (2018a).

57 Siu (1989).

58 Zelin (2004, 2009).

59 Sangren (1984).

60 Cohen (1990) and Zheng (2001). We will discuss this in much detail in Chapter 4.

61 Ebrey and Watson (1986).

62 Skinner (1964).

63 Iannaccone (1991), Yang (2006, 2011), Lu et al. (2008). For substantial critical comments, see e.g. Liang (2014).

64 The notion of diffuse 'originates from Yang (1965). On politropy, see the rich and seminal argument in Chau (2011, 2012).

65 Clart (2012), Chau (2019).

66 The complex patterns of various ritual domains in religion and beyond, which partly reflects the projection of Western conceptions of religion on China, are comprehensively treated in Goossaert and Palmer (2011) and Chau (2019).

67 Sun (2013).

68 Rea and Volland (2015).

69 Lean (2015).

70 A fascinating example are the Chinese businessmen in late 19th-century Hong Kong who strove for official recognition by the Emperor (Chan 1991).

71 Levenson (1968).
72 Faure (2007).
73 Geertz (1973).
74 For an exemplary discussion of these methodological and practical challenges, see Osburg (2013). The methodological differences also come to the fore in specific fields such as research into family business (Stewart 2013), which are also important for studying the Chinese ritual economy.
75 Siu and Chan (2010).
76 An example is the traps of orientalism and reverse orientalism, as in the debates about 'Confucian capitalism', Yao (2002). For a lengthy discussion of these issues, see Herrmann-Pillath (2018a).
77 Lagerwey (2010).
78 Siu (1995), Kang (2009), Bruckermann (2016).
79 On the general validity of this methodological perspective in Chinese studies, see Little (1992).

3 Ritual spaces of Shenzhen

1 What is a ritual space?

Ritual is an activity that takes place in space and time.[1] In the social domain, space and time are not continuous but are structured by ritual: Rituals take place at certain locations and impose a rhythm on the flow of time. Space and time are interrelated via ritual artefacts, in the sense that artefacts are always located and handled in space and they often have the property of durability through time, although the corresponding ritual actions are transient. A ritual action as such may just happen and end, but the artefacts involved stay, thus creating connectivities through time. There is a type of artefacts that defines locations, often over very long time spans, such as temples, thus creating a potential for the sustainability of ritual action in the longer run: Artefacts are externalized memories of ritual. More specifically, artefacts create affordances that motivate, trigger, and sustain ritual actions: Time gets structured via repetitions of ritual actions.

Structuring time and space by rituals is often manifest in coherent conceptions of the temporal flow of ritual: A pre-eminent example in all human societies is the annual cycle of festive celebrations, originally matching the natural sequence of seasons in agricultural production, in this sense producing a primordial form of ritual economy. Space is structured by ritual too, such as designing a public square and a church in a way to enable the proper conduct of ritual. In this chapter, we study ritual spaces of Shenzhen, manifest in a multiplicity of ritual spaces created by communities living in the megacity and embodied in artefacts that are often remnants of the past, including one essential phenomenon: the land on which native rural communities dwelled over decades, often centuries. Ritual spaces centre on ritual places.

We define a ritual space as a space that is demarcated and structured by certain ritual artefacts and ritual activities and that is congruous to the entire set of physical entities that make up a certain area in the space-time continuum. That means the ritual space overlays with other aspects of space which do not have ritual functions and meanings. In an urban environment, a certain location is shaped by functional needs of urban infrastructure and logistics, yet, at the same time, emanating from the existence of a ritual artefact, the location obtains ritual significance, even though most observable processes and events may not be related to ritual actions at all. For example, in Shenzhen many former villages erect *torii* to mark the entry to the village territory even if no functional border exists, but some villages also erect a turnpike to control traffic.[2] The ritual space is a semiotic construct created by ritual; at the same time, it is a material structure embodied in the artefacts and their effects on the environment, which can also affect other functional properties. For instance, if a temple is located at a certain place, this causes adaptations of other elements of urban infrastructure, but also offers opportunities for activities which may not be directly related to the original rituals involving the temple: a temple might be combined with a public space that can be devoted to certain ritual activities on holidays, but can be used otherwise for most of the year, as a rallying point of bustling leisure activities. This fact may easily distract attention to the underlying ritual nature of the place, even in terms of public assertions about purpose: In Shenzhen, ritual actors may legitimize their action mainly by economic interest and marginalize ritual meaning to avoid political tensions with official secularism in China. However, it is commonplace in Chinese popular religion that many ritual artefacts may lay dormant most of the year, only activated on certain sacred occasions. Yet, that does not deprive them of their ritual significance beyond the period of intense ritual activation. Indeed, many visitors of a place marked by a ritual artefact may not be aware of its ritual significance, just treating it as a remnant of the past.

This implies that the ritual space has a virtual dimension, in the sense that it even might not be visible under ordinary circumstances. Hence, a better characterization would be that the ritual space is a spatial network created and instantiated by ritual that organizes affordances for ritual action. One important example is the kinship-related rituals that involve the native places of people who migrated to other regions.[3] In this case, for example, a kinship group located in Shenzhen may conduct pilgrimages to a location in Jiangxi province, which defines a ritual space of very large reach, but of course that would not mean that the entire region covered by this activity belongs to the ritual space of Shenzhen. Yet, in terms of the spatial network this is true, and it can be traced by the movements of people, which might also signal their ritual significance of various symbols, such as markers on cars. The spatially distributed artefacts create a network of affordances for ritual mobility in a group of actors.

That means if we consider a certain ritual place in Shenzhen, such as an ancestral hall, it is of paramount importance to approach this as a node in a spatial network that connects this place with other places, and thereby marking the ritual space. There are two criteria that allow identifying this spatial network. The first is history. A place may have a history that connects it to other places, for example, via migration events in the past. However, to count as a ritual space, this history must have a ritual meaning that is evoked in the historical accounts by people engaged with the place today, and not just by historians. This is clearly the case if the migration event is not simply a movement of various disconnected people without shared characteristics, but is referred to the genealogy of the emigrants, tracing the place of origin also to a common ancestor. As we shall see, this is often the case in Shenzhen villages. The second criterion is ritual activities in the present that connect various places. Typically, this combines with the previous point, as in the case of pilgrimages, but not necessarily. This may happen, for example, when a certain temple at another location attracts fresh attention by devotees, and people start to visit, without a previous history of similar practices. This phenomenon is now widespread in China, for example, when local authorities and business invest into the creation of tourist attractions with the potential for ritual activation, not just existing religious sites, but often newly created locations with cultural and historical significance.[4]

As a consequence of these observations, we need to recognize that there is never only one ritual space, but a huge multiplicity of overlapping and criss-crossing spaces that, in the most extreme view, are defined by the total number of egocentric spatial networks involving ritual artefacts and becoming manifest in the individual ritual actions that can be aggregated according to certain criteria into collective phenomena. This radical individualization of ritual space reflects the fact that eventually individual families have their own histories, that individuals may have their own ritual preferences for certain places (e.g. visiting certain temples), and so on. This is another manifestation of the politropy of Chinese ritual practices and the absence of a homogenous institutionalized public religion.

Although this is perfectly true, this cannot be made empirically operational beyond individual case studies on individuals as ritual actors. In order to get empirically manageable results, we can focus on two criteria:

- The first criterion is the existence of ritual artefacts that are focal points for egocentric networks and therefore create a force of convergence across a larger number of those networks. For example, a temple may attract many visitors with various backgrounds and motivations, but they share at least the orientation towards the temple. The larger the number of shared artefacts in such egocentric networks, the stronger the convergence of networks as collective phenomena. This is important when considering the evolution of ritual spaces: For example, a village may build a new temple that is launched as a tourist attraction as well and eventually may become a rallying point of a much wider range of ritual activities beyond those of the original villagers.[5]
- The second criterion is reference to a group that conducts shared rituals. This is most evident, because one defining feature of rituals is to express group identity. As we discussed in the theory section, and is especially true for China, rituals may be shared in an orthopractic way,

> without necessarily implying shared beliefs. One specific aspect is rituals that directly define groups in terms of spatiality: This is the ritual reference to a shared place of origin. This differs from the place of origin of kinship groups ('xue yuan' 血缘) and directly emphasizes spatial criteria ('di yuan' 地缘). An important example is business associations that refer to the shared native place of members independent from original kinship relations at that place.

Thus, the methodological implication is to identify relationships between certain artefacts and groups that establish ritual reference to those artefacts. This relationship is performative, which implies that causality works in both directions. Groups use artefacts to express their identity, and artefacts create shared identities. This is reflected in the prime importance of orthopraxy: In orthopractic actions, the artefacts and externalized rituals have autonomous causal powers – affordances – mediated via the actors, which may maintain very different beliefs and objectives when interacting with the artefacts.[6]

It is important noticing that individuals may belong to different groups, even though on the surface we would deal with one group. An important example is the single-lineage village, where we can distinguish at least three groups centred on different rituals: One is the village community, the other is the local kinship group, and the third is the surname group (often referred to as 'clan').[7] At a closer look, these groups may be structured by different rituals. For example, whereas the lineage may centre on the ancestral hall, the surname group may centre on place of origin, which effectively reveals that we deal with two different groups here, one local, the other even extending as a transnational surname group. The village community focuses on the temple and the other on place-related artefacts (such as the Earth God).

When discussing ritual spaces in Shenzhen, the role of the village is essential. Therefore, it is necessary to understand the ritual and expressively religious nature of the traditional village.[8] If we confine ourselves to the conditions in Guangdong, the village differs in one essential respect from the virtual nature of ritual spaces discussed so far: The village territory as a totality is a ritual space or it is an integrated ritual place, with many constituent and even continuously connected sacred places that in totality make up the ritual space (see Figure 3.1). That is implied by the important role of *feng shui* activities for all activities that involve the location of artefacts, such as buildings, temples, or cemeteries with gravesites. The artefactual structure of the village reflects the whole historical sequence of locational decisions that involve *feng shui*, beginning with the origin of the village by the first settler. That means the village is a nested reflection of *feng shui* flows that permeate the territory. These flows involve also those artefacts that are not primarily defined via *feng shui*, but by other beliefs such as the temple, the location of which, however, was determined by *feng shui*.[9]

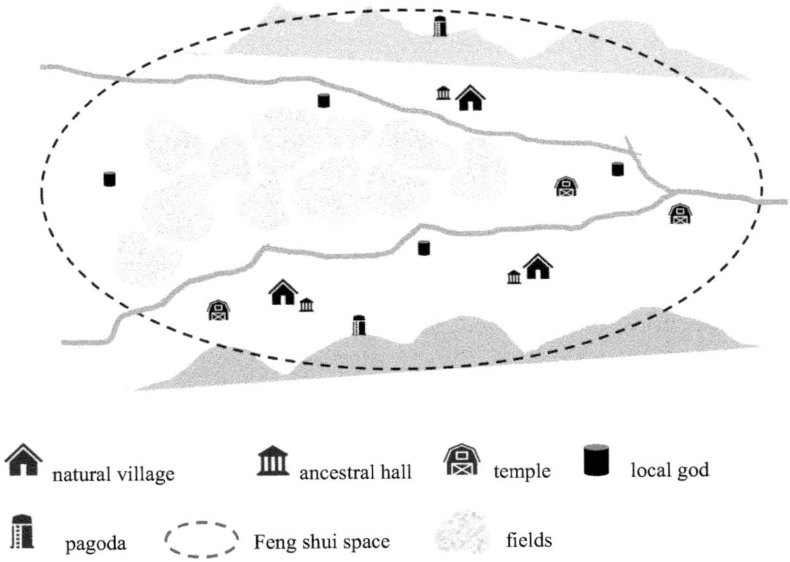

Figure 3.1 The ritual space of the traditional Chinese village (stylized and modified after Lagerwey 2011).

Another reason why the village territory is a total ritual space is that it is shaped by the location of central religious sites. The most salient spatial form is the walled Hakka village ('weilongwu' 围龙屋) in the Pearl River region, which is walled off from the surroundings with convergent circles oriented to the ancestral hall in the middle. In the Shenzhen area, however, many villages of the original settlers, the so-called 'guangfu' 广府 people, were also walled compounds (a famous example is Hubei Ancient Village at Luohu).[10] But even for the case of looser structured villages, the location of religious sites defines its ritual space as one homogenous and unified spatial structure. In popular religion, this is also reflected in some idiosyncratic aspects of temple rituals even if the temple may be devoted to a standard god such as Tianhou, which reflects the village community as being different from others: For example, the temple in one of our cases, Fenghuang, also includes an altar that is devoted to the local deities, which is effectively regarded as most important by the villagers.[11] In addition, certain religious sites directly reflect the nature of the village as being part and parcel of the territory of the Chinese state, traditionally as the Empire 'under the Heaven', most directly in terms of the Earth God shrine. Finally, there are many local gods and deities to which altars and other artefacts such as steles may be devoted and are dispersed over the territory.

Finally, we must mention another fact that defines the village as a continuous ritual space: This is that every family, sharing contiguous territorial borders with other families by its ownership of land, is a basic ritual entity, with family shrines and daily ritual routines such as burning incense and offering fresh fruit at the altar. In a single-lineage village, these elementary ritual units are connected via the shared genealogy, which, however, does not nullify their ritual autonomy. These practices survive under the conditions of modern Shenzhen: Many native villagers live in apartments which include an elaborate ritual interior, such as a protective altar at the entrance, an altar devoted to the deceased father, an altar devoted to the Stove God, and so on.[12]

Ideal-typically, the traditional village would reveal its dual nature as a co-resident community and as a kinship group in terms of the duality of village temple and ancestral hall. This duality becomes more visible if the village is a multi-surname village, and thus may feature various ancestral halls. But even in the case of a single-lineage village, lineage branches and even wealthy families may build separate halls. In Figure 3.1, a ritual space is shown that is shared by several hamlets, each of which would be inhabited by one lineage or surname, and which correspond to the 'natural village' in modern administrative language; the entire space would correspond to a so-called 'administrative village'. The division between the hamlets is manifest in the separate ancestral halls and some local gods mainly worshipped by the lineage members, probably related to some historical event in lineage history, and larger sites of worship such as a Guanyin temple or pagodas devoted to major local gods that are visited by all villagers.

To summarize, ritual space is a central feature of traditional Chinese culture and popular religion, especially in village life. However, as a result of the modernization efforts of the 20th century, often accompanied by aggressive destruction of ritual infrastructure, ritual spaces have been shrinking and vanishing in many regions of China. This is especially true for cities, where the rapid economic development since 1978 created another force of destruction, independent from modernist hostility towards tradition: The bulldozing of old infrastructure and living spaces to construct modern urban infrastructure and modern urban dwellings. In many Chinese cities, ritual spaces have disappeared and functional spaces reign, although their functional appearances may often hide modernist ritual meanings. Therefore, the case of Shenzhen is of particular interest, as we can observe an interaction between ritual spaces and urban development and notice the phenomenon of the sustainability of ritual spaces under the conditions of high-speed urbanization.

2 Ritual space and ritual places in Shenzhen

Shenzhen is mostly presented as a place without history. This reflects the modernist philosophy of Chinese reforms shaped by the intellectual revolutions of the 20th century: The city is mostly imagined as a place at which an almost blank slate has been filled with most advanced structures and systems of modernity, such as high-rise buildings, modern transport systems, and public parks.[13] This picture reflects the modernist rejection and amnesia regarding the history of the original settlement, which is in turn rooted in the denigration of rural society as backward and 'feudal', driven by superstitious beliefs and unwilling to improve itself. This attitude has been recently enshrined in the national programme of renovating the countryside, which projects methods of urban planning on the reconstruction and often wholesale rebuilding of villages.[14]

For understanding the situation in Shenzhen, it is important to lend more historical depth to this diagnosis, which reveals that it has ritual roots, too, as a modernist ritual that ties up with elite Imperial culture. In the 19th century, the region was still a frontier society which was disrupted by popular unrest and internecine struggles between the so-called 'original' ('bendi', 'pun-ti') population and Hakka, which added to the woes of the Opium wars and of the Taiping rebellion.[15] The Imperial institutions and society were concentrated at certain coastal places, especially Nantou, a garrison town in the county of Xin'an (Figure 3.2). Throughout the region, autonomous development of townships held sway, especially with the establishment of new local markets. One of these markets was Shenzhen ('Sham Chun'), which assumed a leading role in the regional marketing system

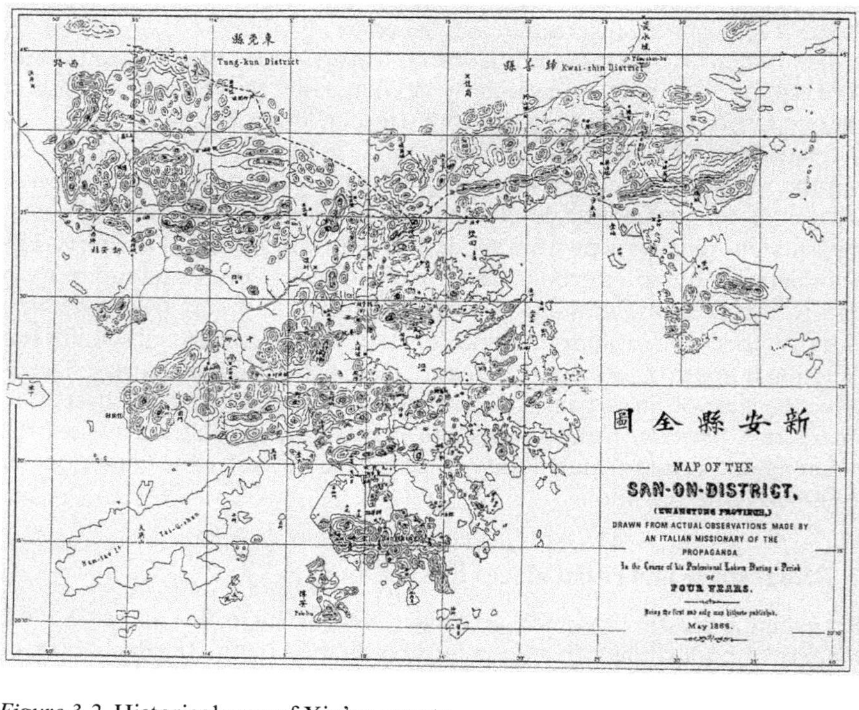

Figure 3.2 Historical map of Xin'an county.

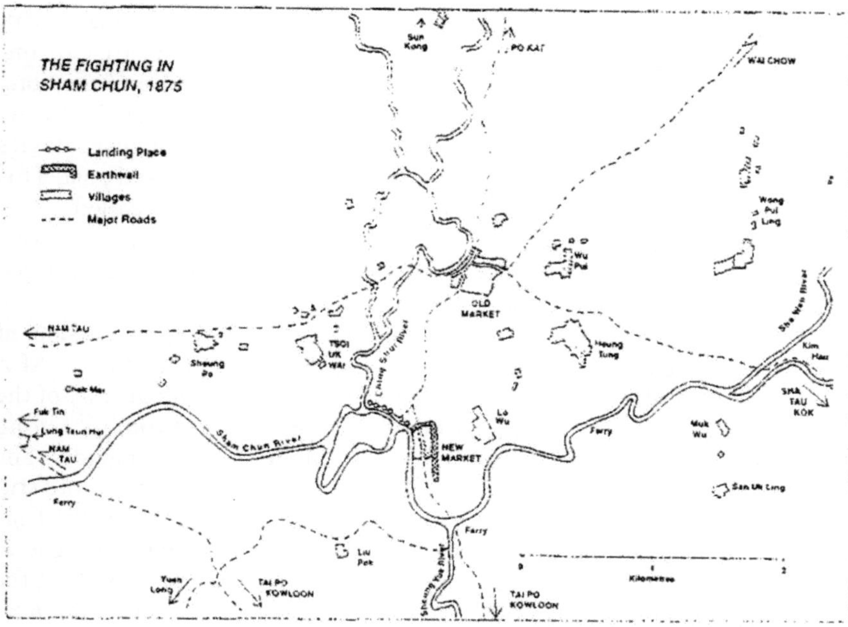

Figure 3.3 Shenzhen area 19th century.
Source: Hase (1990).

(Figure 3.3). The modernist refusal to recognize local culture bears much family resemblance with the description of local society by the Imperial and urban elites of Qing Dynasty in China who lived in the walled cities of Nantou and Dapeng. However, today Shenzhen authorities have begun to explicitly recognize this origin of Shenzhen xu 深圳墟, for example, with extensive instalments and murals at Luohu district and in the exhibition of the central Shenzhen museum. That compares with the 1980s and 1990s when even local intellectuals downplayed the historical role of the place as insignificant for Chinese culture.[16]

When Hong Kong gradually developed as a regional economic centre and was eventually expanded to include the New Territories, Shenzhen further strengthened its role as a trade intermediary. Certain lineages had emerged as powerful groups in the Hakka wars, such as the Zhang, who now controlled trade with Hong Kong, for example, via monopolizing bridge access. In the entire region, villages had literally fortified their relative positions, with strong Hakka communities at many places. This spatial distribution is still salient in Shenzhen today, for example, with Longgang as a district with many Hakka villages.

In other words, with the decline of Imperial power, the Pearl River Delta had emerged as a complex local society with much subcultural variety and certain distance from the Imperial centre and its mainstream culture. At the same time, however, local elites also established their legitimacy with reference to Imperial history. The background is the long history of immigration. A pivotal event was the disruption and final demise of the Song Dynasty by the Mongols, which drove many elite families to the South. As a result, many villages in the Shenzhen area have very extended genealogies which sometimes connect them with elite families of the Imperial past. This is even true for apparently peripheral groups such as the so-called 'guest people' Hakka: Many Hakka claim to have inherited the traditions of Song high culture and elite status, thereby explaining, for example, their alleged penchant for learning and education.[17]

It is important to understand how this historical background shaped the territorial evolution of Shenzhen after 1978. When the Shenzhen SEZ was established, the decision was based on the historical geography of the region, centring on the old transit point to Hong Kong at today's Luohu district. There was no long-term perspective where that would lead.[18] The first master plan of 1986 only presented a partial plan for the SEZ and still envisaged the surrounding Bao'an county as remaining rural for the near future. This reflected the socio-economic conditions that had emerged in the Maoist era: The 'fishing village' image was true, in the sense that the Maoist policies had destroyed local markets and had reduced the economic basis close to subsistence agriculture, with the consequence that Bao'an county had been depopulating at increasing speed because of emigration, exploiting the advantage of proximity to Hong Kong.[19] But that does not imply that the historical conditions before 1949 did not matter anymore. One reason is that the *hukou* system enforced on the countryside during the Great Leap Forward factually froze the spatial distribution of people or specifically kinship groups in the region in the pattern of the 'cellular economy'.[20] This also preserved collectively embodied memories and oral histories of the villages. Another very important accompanying factor is that the fixation of the spatial pattern implied that the socialist institutions often just superficially transformed the original relationship between kinship groups and land. Ownership of land by production brigades often factually meant that the local kinship group held the land property rights collectively. Accordingly, once the People's Communes were abolished and the original villages were re-established, this also restored the original relationship between village, land, and kinship group, albeit with a very different power structure and pattern of internal stratification.[21]

This fact became very important when Shenzhen municipality was expanded by merging the SEZ with Bao'an county while retaining border controls in the first years, thus creating the distinction between 'inner' and 'outer' city ('first line' and 'second line'), which is still visible today.[22] For our topic, this is highly significant because it defined the setting for a peculiar path of urban development which could be called 'modular': That means, Shenzhen did not grow out from a centre, but developed in various spatial modules, often centred on certain large-scale projects, but right from the beginning also involving the spontaneous processes at the village level.

In fact, immediately after opening the gates between Hong Kong and Shenzhen SEZ, villages assumed a significant role in driving urban development. Two major types of activity were prominent. First, villages could offer their territory as locations for export-processing industries in the first period, especially from Hong Kong and Taiwan. Second, villages started to build apartments for inflowing migrant workers that were employed by those companies. This triggered additional demand for complementary services (shops, restaurants etc.). All this mostly needed to be located on territory that was owned collectively by the villages.

Now, a very important fact needs to be taken into account: The market dynamics that was unleashed after 1978 simply overwhelmed the provincial and local authorities. The emerging new city neither had the administrative capacities nor the fiscal means to mastermind a comprehensive infrastructural design for the new megacity nor implement such a plan, despite political rhetoric.[23] This further leveraged the role of the villages as investors in the emerging urban infrastructure, very soon adding the entrepreneurial energies of real estate entrepreneurs and a wide range of commercial actors, including powerful state-owned companies. Indeed, this was another model that emerged right from the beginning of Shenzhen development, with the crucial role of China Merchants in developing Shekou partly independent from the administration of the SEZ, though being part of its territory.[24] However, these real estate investors often had to cooperate with the owners of the land – the villagers. Sometimes it also happened that the original state-owned agents in creating the first industrial estates, including even military companies, retreated and left an administrative vacuum because most decisions and measures were originally taken by them and not by the municipal administration. In other words, an important aspect of urban development in Shenzhen is institution building from both bottom-up and top-down, resulting in the hybrid structure of urban governance that we study in Chapter 7.[25]

As a result, against the picture of the ultra-modern megacity driven by modernist urbanism, we posit the picture of Shenzhen as an urban place partially, but significantly shaped by the grassroots-level structure of villages: These units mostly correspond to 'natural villages' in current administrative jargon ('ziran cun' 自然村). Of course, this does not mean that the villages were leading actors, but they were crucial participants in the interaction with other economic and political actors; and the villages often did not directly take actions, but indirectly shaped the processes in embodying local constraints and offering opportunities for others. In Figure 3.4,

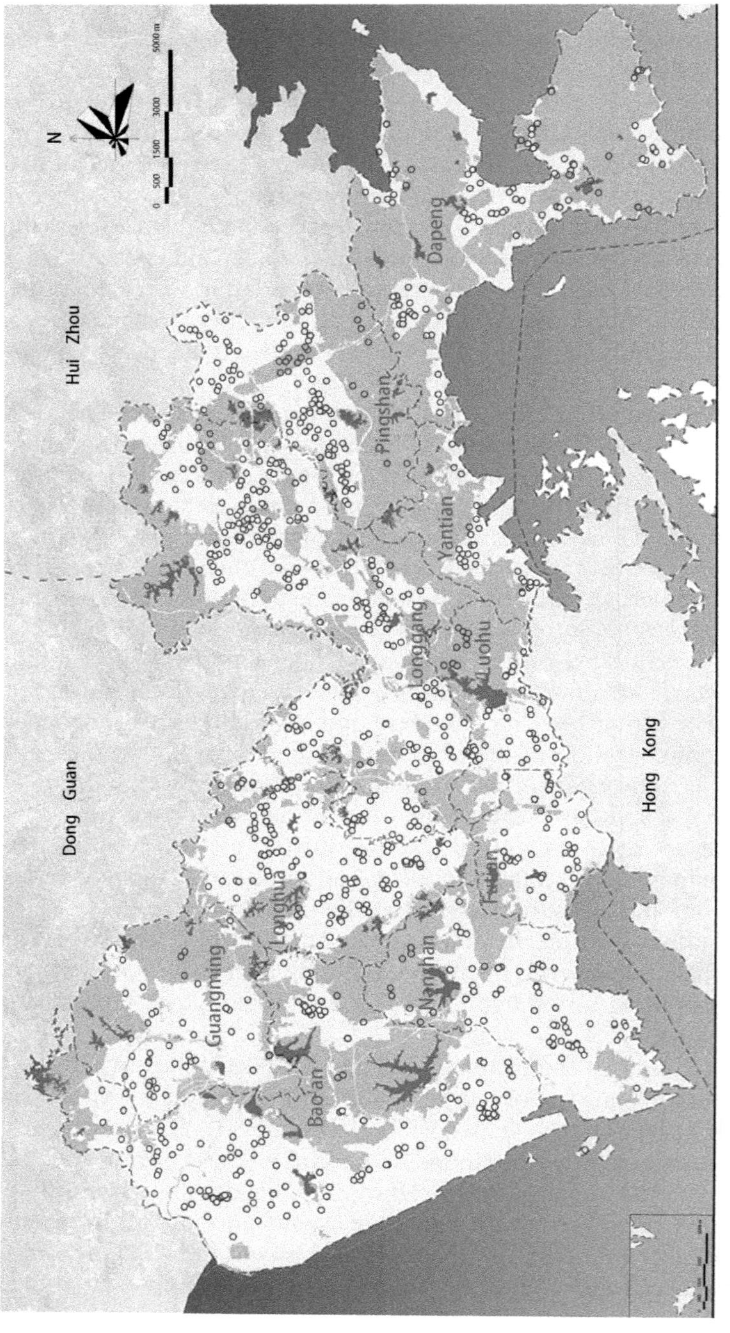

Figure 3.4 Distribution of natural villages in Shenzhen (black circles). Map created by Li Ling, Harbin Institute of Technology, Shenzhen campus.

we show the distribution of 'natural villages' in the Shenzhen territory, which directly reflects the historical situation, because these villages were not changed substantially during collectivization, mostly just being transformed into production brigades. Many of these villages have a long history, even over centuries, and often keep intact historical sites and artefacts relating to this history.

As we analyse in some more detail in Chapter 7, many natural villages are no longer visible in the administrative structure of municipality, even if they may be visible in physical manifestations. However, there are also many cases where natural villages are now identical with urban communities 'shequ' 社区: Figure 3.5 shows the distribution of natural villages compared to *shequ*. The cases where villages are now *shequ* are those where village communities could assert themselves as independent units of urban self-government. This organizational form manifests the concept of self-administration in the urban context and tends to cover areas which have a shared history, destiny, structural commonalities, or other aspects that create a certain socio-cultural cohesion. Therefore, *shequ* are not identical with street committees ('jiedao banshichu' 街道办事处), which are the lowest level government units subordinate to district 'qu' 区. The distinction matters in the current context. Obviously, a natural village is an ideal candidate for becoming a *shequ* after urbanization and formal transformation into urban territory. Indeed, this is mostly the case in Bao'an district: The vast majority of former 'natural villages' is now a *shequ*, thus directly reflecting the rural socio-political structure in the urban administration. Accordingly, these places often maintain the wording 'cunmin weiyuanhui' 村民委员会 instead of the proper 'jumin weiyuanhui' 居民委员会 (in Chapter 7, we see that this distinction is not just formal).

In comparison, in Futian district, the relationship between *shequ* and natural villages is much more complicated, as in some cases several former villages are now a *shequ* and in other cases the one-to-one relationship is maintained (such as in our case of Xiasha) (Figure 3.6).[26] In Republican times, Futian belonged to Bao'an county which was called Xin'An in Imperial times, and was part of Shatou township (沙头乡). In 1958, People's Communes were created and Futian underwent a series of administrative changes, which continued after reforms were launched. In 1980, Futian People's Commune became part of the SEZ together with six other communes, one of them named 'Shenzhen' which later became the name of the city, referring to the historical designation of the larger area. In 1985, the final administrative structure was settled, with the establishment of five Street Committees (*jiedao banshichu*): Futian, Nanyuan, Shatou, Yuanling, and Meilin. At that time, this still included 14 'village committees' (*cunweihui*) apart from 25 'residents committees' (*juweihui*) and 45 natural villages (*ziran cun*), thus reflecting the rural nature of the original territory. In 2004, these distinctions became obsolete administratively, because all territory was

Figure 3.5 Natural villages and *shequ* (white circles). Map created by Li Ling, Harbin Institute of Technology, Shenzhen campus.

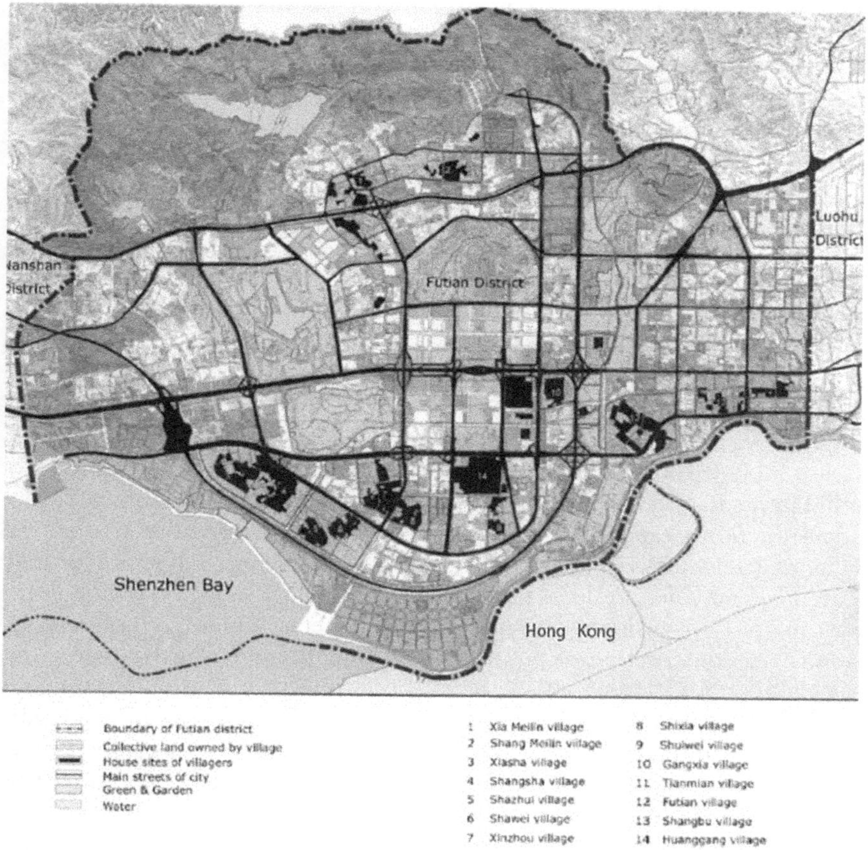

Figure 3.6 Map of Futian district 2005.
Source: Hang (2006).

transformed into urban territory and all farmers obtained urban *hukou*. However, the designations of 'village' and even 'village committee' survive until today.

The villages of Shenzhen have obtained a pivotal role in the urbanization process because they became home of so-called 'urban villages' ('chengzhong cun' 城中村). The term 'urban villages' is not synonymous with 'natural village', because it refers to the distinct phenomenon of emerging urban settlements which are not devoted to agriculture anymore, but where most of the land is now covered with urban infrastructure, residential, commercial, and industrial. Especially, the term refers to places where immigrants live, becoming by far the majority of residents at the place, though without *hukou* registration. Although the denotation of 'urban village' is not an administrative term, it is used in the context of urban planning, often also as 'old villages' '('jiu cun' 旧村). Once the area is redeveloped, it may no longer count as urban village, but that does not necessarily imply that the area is no longer associated with the former natural village. One can only determine this relationship when considering single cases in detail.

Modernism is deeply engrained in the way how Shenzhen development is mostly seen by economic and political elites, both domestic and abroad. Far into the first millennium, the urban villages were often depicted as decrepit and unruly places that were home to many undesirable social phenomena, such as prostitution.[27] This picture reflects modernist prejudice and certainly distorts the simple fact that roughly 50 per cent of Shenzhen population live in urban villages. But then the amazing observation counts that official population data just hide this part of the population, still lingering around 13 million, although even the municipal leaders give the number of about 22 million and even more.[28]

This amounts to a tension which we diagnose as the ritual tension between modernism and local culture: The blanking out of 50 per cent of inhabitants in official statistics is a ritual act of its own which has performative functions, especially if simultaneously the institution of the natural villages is reinstated in the shape of *shequ* where urban villages are located: The *shequ* may manifest the natural village in many ways, even though the vast majority of residents are not native villagers. A highly visible expression is the construction of public squares (for pictures of various squares, see endnote[29]). Often, in village renovation projects, a new ancestral hall is in front of a public square, sometimes with huge size. Squares have a highly symbolic meaning in China, as they reflect public authority as embedded in larger patterns of social and natural forces, traditionally explored by *feng shui* techniques. Constructing a square has an ambiguous meaning: One the one hand, this manifests the assertion of village identity and legitimacy as an autonomous socio-political actor. On the other hand, following the standard design of squares aligns the village with the comprehensive hierarchy of power, with Tiananmen Square as the pivot. This is a paradigmatic manifestation of a ritual space.[30]

The reconstitution of the territorial unity of land, village, and kinship group implies that, based on the previous discussion, it is straightforward to map the ritual spaces of Shenzhen. The first and simple criterion is to approach the villages on the original territory as ritual spaces and to check whether these ritual spaces are still reflected in the urban infrastructure of today. A very simple, though powerful, instrument is to identify the location of ancestral halls in Shenzhen and to project this on the location of urban villages. We posit a hypothesis here: If natural villages were strong enough to pursue their economic interests in Shenzhen urbanization, they would have been able to develop an urban village. One major indicator of the strength of a village is the continuing existence of an ancestral hall, because halls reflect the identity of the local kinship group. Hence, if the distribution of urban villages and ancestral halls is congruent, we can conclude that village communities play a significant role in urban development. In many other cases, villages may still exist formally, but villagers have left to make place for new urban developments and may even not maintain their ancestral hall properly. This does not necessarily imply that they also eschew ritual: as we shall see, villagers can often draw on ritual resources in the wider web of lineage and clan relations (see next section on Gangxia urban village).

There is no official list of all the ancestral halls in Shenzhen. Official lists only count those halls that are recognized as historical buildings.[31] In Maoist China, and in the first years of reforms, halls were often used for other purposes, such as storehouses. Newly built halls are not historical, and so may not be recognized officially, too. Maps do not identify all halls. Some villages have no ancestral hall, yet keep their identity as a village, indicated by other artefacts, such as the previously mentioned *torii*. In Futian, we observe this variance. There are villages like Xiasha, which we analyse in the next section, with a lavish ancestral hall and temple, and others, such as Futian village, which do not have a hall, yet maintain their identity in other ways, including the previously mentioned 'cultural square'. The specific reason here is that the Huang at Futian village, who are the dominant lineage, have close relationship to Hong Kong and affiliated themselves with a hall in Hong Kong already in historical times. Another reason that we can observe frequently is that villages may share a hall: In Futian district, the Zhuang at Shuiwei and Huanggang share the hall at Huanggang.

Figure 3.7 shows the location of ancestral halls in 2019 as far as we could identify them. It is straightforward to see that the entire space of Shenzhen is covered by ancestral halls, taking the hilly areas in consideration, where originally no villages where located and which today are often designated as natural resorts and protected areas. Halls are especially concentrated in Bao'an and Longgang, that is, in the areas that were originally designed to continue to be focused on agricultural production. However, even in the core areas of the SEZ, such as Futian CBD, we notice a substantial number of halls.

Figure 3.8 shows a map taken from the urban development plan of the mid-2000s, with the locations of the ancestral halls inserted. There is an almost complete congruence between those locations and the location of urban villages. Figure 3.9 shows the distribution of residential areas assigned to urban villages in the most recent redevelopment plan, with ancestral halls added. Although the area of urban villages has shrunk, at the same time most ancestral halls still associate with urban villages.

As a result of this discussion, we can conclude that the entire area of Shenzhen is covered by spaces that have the potential to be ritual spaces. There are few exceptions, which however are of special interest for our argument: Shekou, for example, which, as mentioned, was created by heavy intervention by the central government and China Merchants. However, at the same

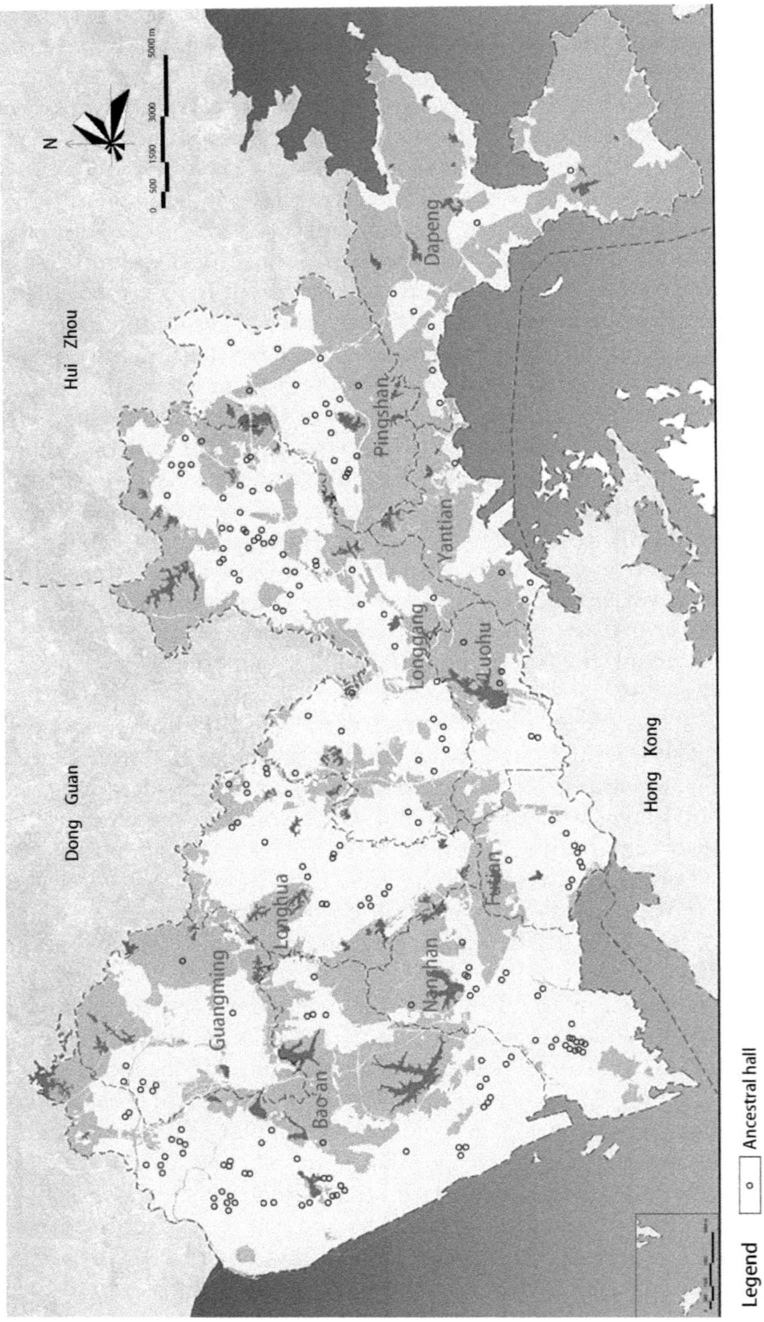

Figure 3.7 Location of ancestral halls in Shenzhen. Map created by Li Ling, Harbin Institute of Technology, Shenzhen campus.

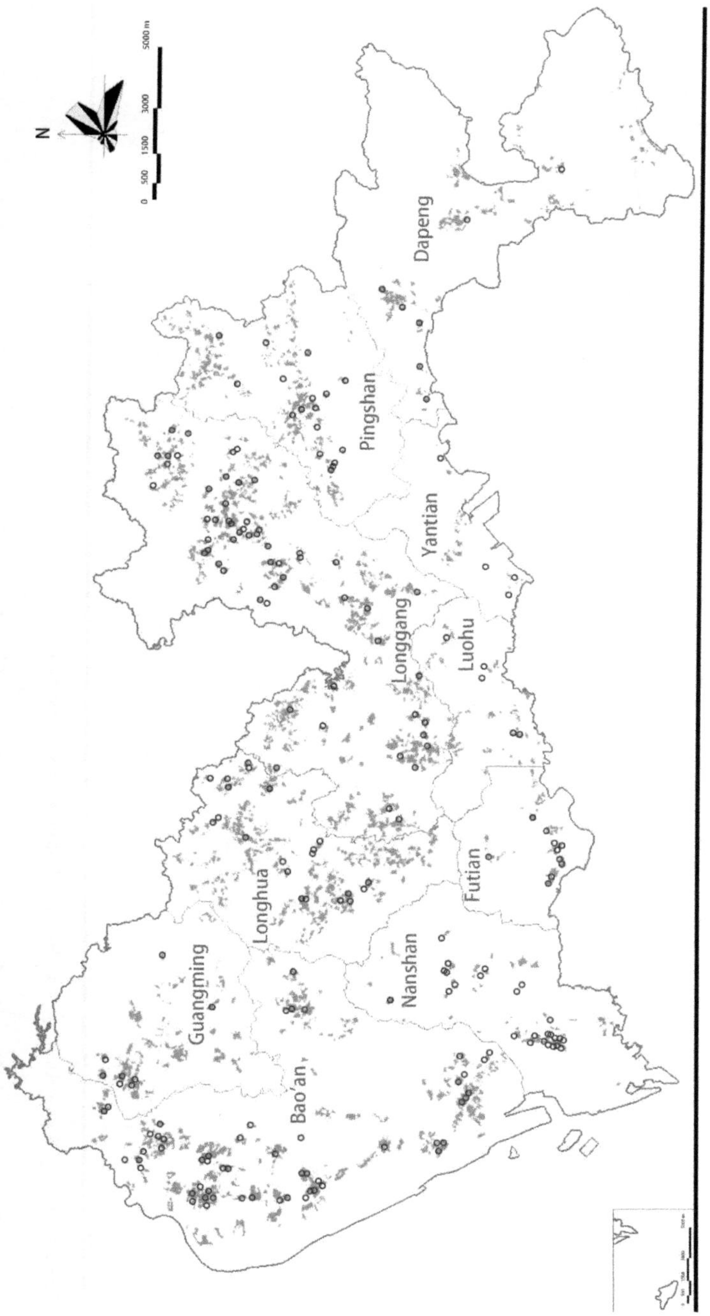

Figure 3.8 Ancestral halls and urban villages in the mid-2000s.
Source: Urban Planning & Design Institute of Shenzhen, map modified by Li Ling, Harbin Institute of Technology, Shenzhen campus.

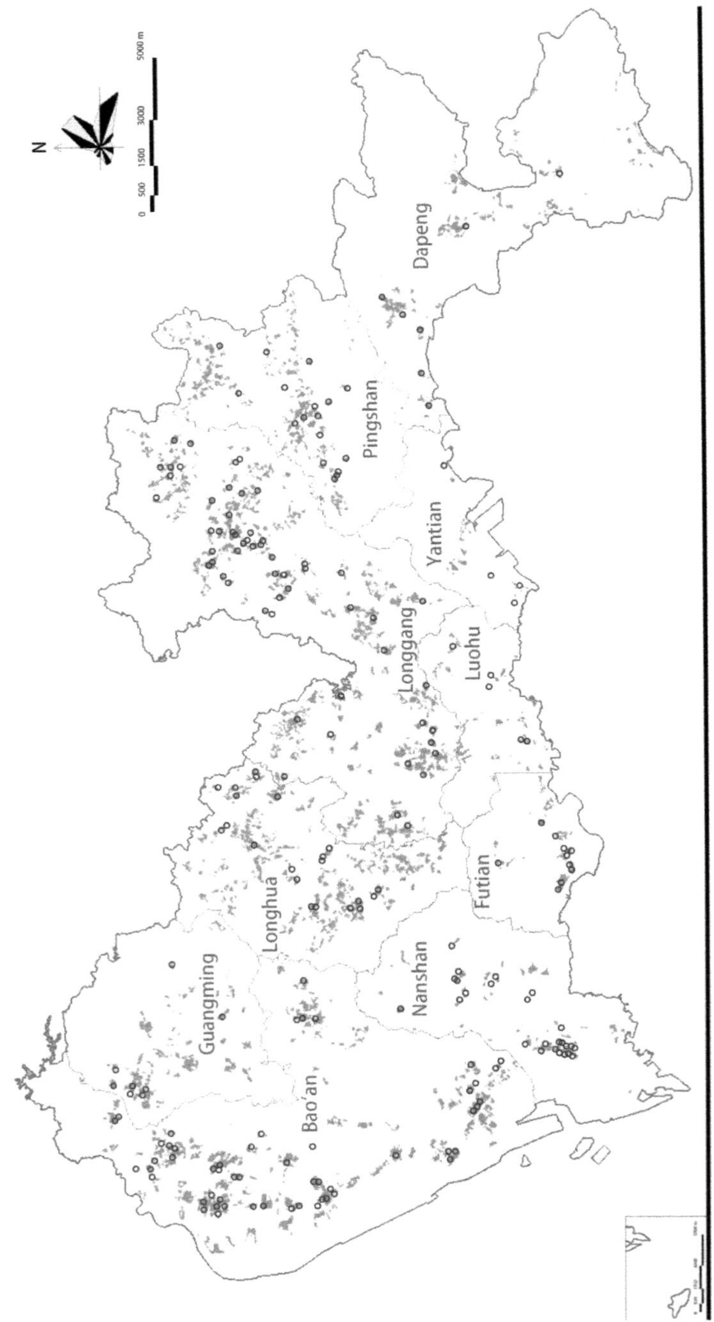

Figure 3.9 Ancestral halls and urban villages, designated residential areas.
Source: Shenzhen shi guihua he guotu ziyuan weiyuanhui (2018), map created by Li Ling, Harbin Institute of Technology, Shenzhen campus.

time, these were regions where historically the presence of Imperial power was strong, for the simple reason that it was focused on the coastal areas for military purposes. In this sense, the tension between ritual space and official space is itself not simply a conflict between tradition and modernity, but between hegemonic culture and local culture. Different parts of Shenzhen territory reflect different historical trajectories which reach back to Imperial China and continue to drive development today.

Ritual spaces can only be observed in action. This we will do in the next section.

3 Villages as places of doing ritual spaces

Based on the analysis of the distribution of ancestral halls, we surmise that the halls indicate the existence of ritual spaces. However, this can only be proven by moving to the level of detailed analysis of cases. There are three other possibilities. One is the case where no ancestral hall exists, but the place is connected to the ritual space of another location where we find a hall. In the case we present below – the Wen clan – there is no ancestral hall at Gangxia urban village, Futian district, but the Wen who live there identify themselves with halls at other places. Second, sometimes ritual locations are not identified as ancestral halls, but as memorial halls, such as the Wen Tianxiang hall at Songgang, Bao'an district. This is a situation that one can observe all over China, especially in the case if the memorial place is linked to a tomb of a historical personality that is a high ancestor of a certain lineage and surname group. Yet, these locations, as in the Songgang case, can also be involved in ritual activities, since at Songgang the tomb of Wen Yingling is located, a Wen Tianxiang descendant. Third, there is an ancestral hall, but it is no longer embedded in a broader ritual space: An example is the Zheng hall at Dachong, a place which has been entirely transformed into an upscale urban area. As a consequence, we need to check for particular halls whether they tie up with a ritual space or not. As sketched in Section 1, the traditional village is a continuous and compact ritual space defined by certain artefacts and marked by regular ritual activities that involve different levels, from the household to the village collective.

One of our core cases in this book is the Wen 文 (Cantonese: Man) clan in Shenzhen, which has also a branch in the Hong Kong New Territories. As we will discuss in much detail in the next chapter, we distinguish between the Wen clan, which defines itself as the larger group of Wen who trace themselves back to Wen Tianxiang, a Song loyalist and national hero also in contemporary China, and the Wen lineages at different locations which do not directly descend from Wen Tianxiang, but from his close agnatic relatives. We treat the 'clan' as the larger ritual unit and the lineage as the extended kinship group that centres on a specific location, the village. The ritual unit is mainly manifest in shared ritual practices devoted to the ancestor; the lineage is mainly embodied in certain collective actions and corporate entities as well as closer personal relationships in everyday life, though mainly among subgroups of relatives. The lineage connects with the clan via holding corresponding rituals and joining clan activities as a corporate group.

The Wen clan is one of the pivotal cases in creating the general conception of lineages in Chinese studies which had been shaped by field research in the New Territories of Hong Kong in the 1950s and 1960s, starting out from Maurice Freedman's seminal work. The Man (Wen) were studied by one researcher who became a leading authority in Chinese anthropology, James Watson, concentrating on historical developments after investigating the recent emigration patterns and transnational networks of Wen, later including observations on their interaction with Shenzhen Wen lineages.[32] The Wen have branches at different locations in Shenzhen (Bao'an and Futian district) and in Hong Kong; another three Wen villages are located in neighbouring Dongguan (see Figure 3.10).

In this section, we concentrate on the Wen at Fenghuang in Bao'an district. In 1985, the local per capita income of Fenghuang villagers was only 614 Yuan per annum, thus qualifying as a very poor and destitute place. Within just 20 years, per capita income rose to more than 20.000 Yuan per annum. The first factory invested by Hong Kong entrepreneurs was founded in 1984 on the premises of the Wen ancestral hall, since no other buildings were available for that purpose. In 1987, the village established the 'Fenghuang Economic Development Corporation' ('Fenghuang jingji fazhan gongsi' 凤凰经济发展公司); over the years, with the growing size and complexity of the economic activities, supervisory bodies were created under the auspices of the village council, which in 2004 resulted in

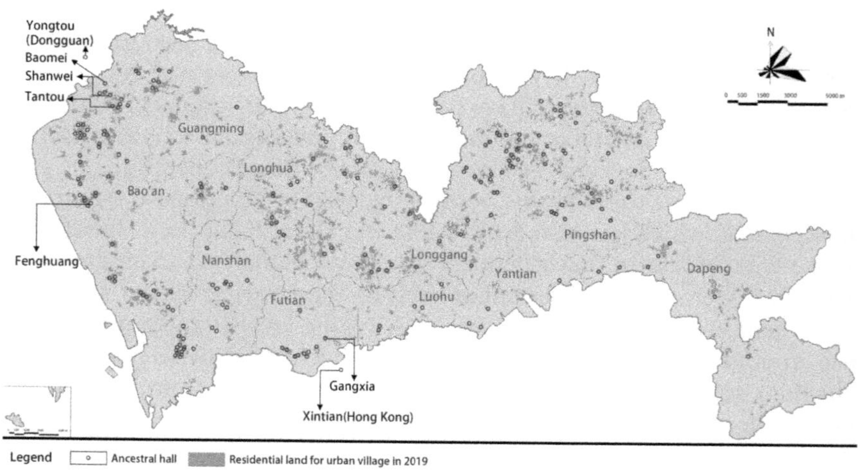

Figure 3.10 Location of seven Wen lineages at Shenzhen.

the establishment of a comprehensive organization, the 'Shenzhen Municipality Fenghuang Shareholding Cooperative Company' ('Shenzhen shi Fenghuang gufen hezuo gongsi' 深圳市凤凰股份合作公司). This coincided with the fundamental transition of incorporating Bao'an district into the administrative structure of Shenzhen municipality, thus turning all villagers into urban citizens with urban *hukou* and transforming rural collective land into urban state-owned land.

Today, Fenghuang has a population of about 150,000 inhabitants (*changzhu renkou*), of whom 2,187 have local residence status (*hukou*) almost equally divided into male and female; of these, 1,695 are shareholders, which was fixed in 2004 ('sheng bu jia, si bu jian' 生不加，死不减). There are about 1,200 entrepreneurs from Hong Kong and Taiwan living in Fenghuang; the rest of the population are migrant workers mostly employed in the 221 factories located in four designated industrial zones. The area is about 9.8 square kilometres, of which more than 50 per cent are environmentally protected, which provides the opportunity for developing Fenghuang as a tourist and leisure site. Hence, the conditions differ fundamentally from other Wen villages, such as Gangxia: until today, Gangxia almost ideal-typically fits the stereotype of 'urban village': On just 0.9 square kilometres in central Futian district, about 10,000 migrants live in cramped high-rise buildings owned by about 3,000 Wen with original *hukou*, many of whom have moved to luxury apartments in the immediate neighbourhood, literally 'overlooking' their original village, in which the private houses of the villagers have been superseded by huge blocks housing migrant workers (for pictures of Gangxia, see endnote[33]).

The ritual space of Fenghuang village is shown in Figure 3.11. It is spanned by two landmarks (for pictures of Fenghuang, see endnote[34]). One is the ancestral hall with the public square, the other is the holiday park with a temple complex. Another important landmark is the pagoda which is close to the Wen Tianxiang memorial hall at the entry to the village. The temple complex has been created in a coordinated effort to develop Fenghuang into a local centre of leisure and services, against the backdrop of the proximity to the Shenzhen international airport and the new construction of a giant convention centre (for pictures, see endnote[35]). However, what appears as a business venture is at the same time a constitutive element of the ritual space.

The temple complex is centred on a huge temple devoted to Guanyin. However, this was a decision taken to make it attractive to the general populace: In the eyes of the villagers, the real focus of the temple is the altar devoted to the local deities, which includes deified Wen Tianxiang, and which is located within the main temple building in a smaller room left to the main hall with the Guanyin statue. The temple complex is built on the premises of the old village temple devoted to Wen Yingling, the direct ancestor of the Fenghuang branch of the Wen. It includes various other sacred sites, such as an Earth God temple, sacred trees, or an artificial pond with numerous turtles, and a site with trees and stones where people can place wish cards on the trees (which they do in vast numbers, filling the place with red 'leafs'). There

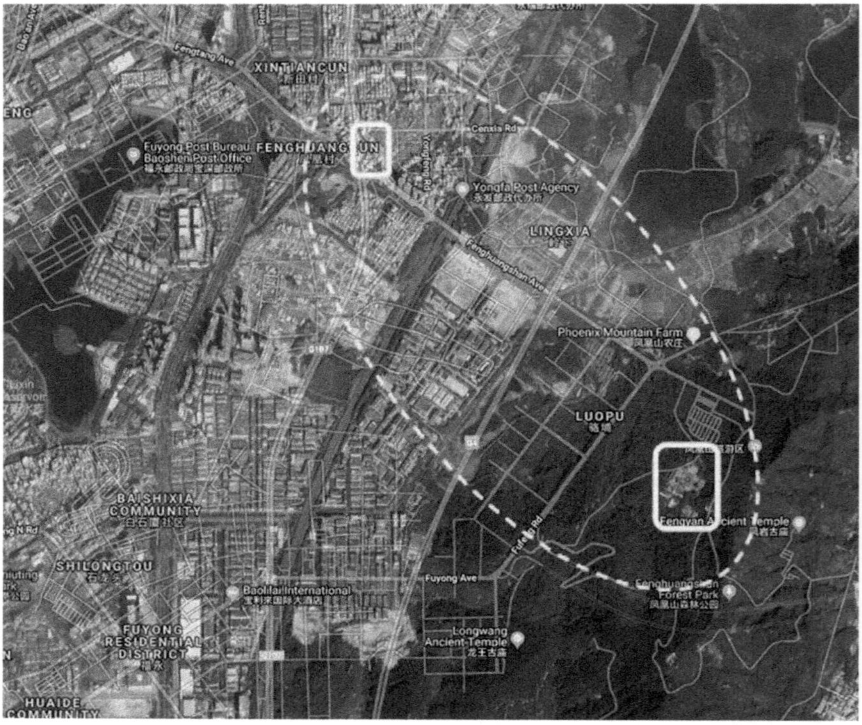

Figure 3.11 The ritual space of Fenghuang village (Google Earth satellite picture). Markers added by authors.

are many instalments that enable individual ritual practices and sacrifices, such as offering fruit or burning 'ghost money'. The entire complex is built around a vast square that includes the turtle pond and is oriented towards the direction of the village and its ancestral hall following *feng shui* rules.

The temple is located on a hill, and the way up requires physical effort, especially on hot days. Cars can drive up to a vegetarian restaurant, but access is tightly constrained, and parking lots anyway limited. Thus, most people must take the pain and climb the steep stairs. Nevertheless, the place is bustling with people, many of them in their 20s, and most of them conducting serious ritual activities. One attraction is fortune telling, which is prohibited at the state-owned temples. Remarkably, although the place has been only created very recently, the central Buddhist temple is officially recognized as a religious site, with a sitting Buddhist monk and the Guanyin statue 'activated' by proper rites ('kai guang' 开光). In other words, this is sacred territory, and hence a part of the sacred ritual space of the village.

For the village, the site is a place of pride and of serious religious devotion. The lineage head is said to walk up the stairs almost every day at night and to offer incense. Apart from individual ritual activities, the site is involved in village feasts which directly reveal the unity of the ritual space. For example, Lion's dance parades move from temple to ancestral hall, thus manifesting the interrelatedness of the ritual places in the ritual space.

The ancestral hall is located at the centre of the village in front of a public square, which also hosts some administrative buildings, all following the design of the newly reconstructed 'old village'. This is a copy of the former village that invokes the style of a historic site and is designed as a tourist and leisure location, with former inhabitants moved to the nearby apartment blocks. The ancestral hall is only accessible to the public in the entry hall, but not the altar room. The public square is the venue of important ritual activities of ancestor worship through the lunar year, including the 'pencai' 盆菜 ('common pot') feast at New Year when the dividends of the shareholding cooperative are distributed. We look at *pencai* in much detail in Chapter 5; suffice to notice here that this is a special collective dining ritual that celebrates lineage solidarity.

As mentioned, another important artefact is the pagoda at the entry to the village which is devoted to the Daoist God Wen Chang and is an historical site of Qing dynasty origin officially recognized at the municipal level. In *feng shui* context, the pagoda appears like a pen, and it is said that the surroundings look like a scholar's desk with paraphernalia for writing. This highlights the credentials of the Wen ancestor, Wen Tianxiang, who is also celebrated as a poet of national fame. His most famous poem, the 'poem on duty', is copied on a mural in front of the Wen Tianxiang memorial close to the pagoda. The memorial is a museum that tells the life of Wen Tianxiang and is designated as an official educational site of the CCP, receiving almost daily tour groups. The scholarly background of Wen history is also reflected in the establishment of an 'academy' located at the central public square.

This brief description reveals a paradigmatic case of the ritual economy manifest and unfolding in a ritual space. The ritual space is embodied in the territory of the village and marked by central artefacts as well as by various ritual activities, both individual and collective. Meanwhile, the temple complex almost exactly reproduces the economic role of temple buildings in the Imperial past, and as also practiced in many other places all over China: The temple is designed as a tourist attraction and as a display of the public status of the village, which itself is a manifestation of economic success and prowess.[36]

In addition, it is important to notice the connection to other Wen ritual sites. However, we must heed attention to the tension and balance of cooperation and competition between lineage branches, which ultimately is rooted in the fundamental pattern of competition between brothers in the traditional family.[37] Fenghuang originally included what is today a separate community, Baishixia. But the construction of a highway caused tension over the allocation of economic opportunities, and so the sub-branches split. The Wen at Baishixia continue to worship their ancestors at the Fenghuang hall, but express the discord in orienting their other religious activities towards an own temple in the hills neighbouring the Fenghuang holiday park, the Longwang (Dragon King) temple, whereas the Fenghuang temple is named Fengyan (Phoenix aery). However, the Wen lineages cooperate in many forms in terms of ritual organization. Right after opening up, the Hong Kong Xintian Wen donated for the restoration of the memorial hall in Songgang village, another location of a Wen branch in Bao'an district. In contrast, during urban development, the Gangxia ancestral hall was demolished, so the Gangxia Wen started to conduct rituals together with the Xintian Wen. The 'high ancestor' Wen Tianxiang unifies all these activities. Wen's native town is Ji'an in Jiangxi province, hence far away. Yet, the place is of primordial importance for ancestor worship in current Wen clan practice. For example, at Songgang's hall, it is mandatory that Hong Kong and Shenzhen Wen gather there and hold worshipping ceremonies, facing towards the direction of Ji'an. All the seven branches of Wen jointly organize trips to Ji'an to conduct ancestral rites together.[38]

The joint activities have gained in significance because of the recent efforts to find a new site for the Wen clan cemetery. The issue of cemetery is complex in contemporary China, because land formerly devoted to cemeteries is now extremely valuable and at the same time, the Communist Party pushed rationalization for decades, partly motivated by land scarcity, too. In Shenzhen, space for cemeteries is extremely limited, and permissions for creating new cemeteries or expand existing ones are not extended. Cemeteries may be moved to other places, and anyway, cremation is today the mandatory practice. Therefore, ancestor worship is often refocused on cemeteries and tombs with special significance, such as those of original ancestors.[39] Most importantly, the Wen clan pursues the project of establishing a joint ancestral hall and cemetery in Hainan, where they identified another Wen branch. This is centred on the grave of Wen Tianrui, Wen Tianxiang's brother. This is partly motivated by the Xintian Wen, because they directly trace themselves back to him; but the entire clan cooperates in the endeavour. The ritual activities combine with exploring business ventures in Hainan. The Wen clan branches cooperate in organizing pilgrimages to the Hainan tomb as convoys of cars involving hundreds of participants (the so called 'jizu chedui' 祭祖车队, 'worshipping ancestors convoy').

The Wen case can be approached as typical for the 'second line' regions in Shenzhen, especially the Hakka areas in Longgang. There was much leeway for autonomous action on part of the villagers, and relatively rich land resources available to spare for ritual spaces. Yet, it is most significant that ritual spaces also survive under conditions of extremely tight land supply. Our case for this is Xiasha. Xiasha is located at the centre of the CBD Futian district of the original SEZ, close to the municipal government. It is the village of the Huang lineage, one branch of the Huang clan. We will study the Huang lineage in Chapter 6 in some detail; suffice to state now that there are other local Huang lineages which do not relate directly to the Xiasha lineage, though sharing the same surname, such as Kengzi village in Longgang district, a Hakka village. Neighbouring Shangsha, however, is closely related, and a memorial stone at the border between the two villages celebrates their perennial cooperation. Yet, the two villages took a very different route of development in the first period after launching the SEZ: Whereas Shangsha created a technology park, Xiasha first emerged as the proverbial messy and unregulated home of red light activities and a 'second wife' home for Hong Kong people. But a new leader, Huang Yingchao, launched a U-turn in developing Xiasha as a site for leisure and tourism, using the shareholding cooperative as an investment vehicle.

The ritual space of Xiasha village is highly visible, though not, as in Fenghuang, spanning the entire territory in its physical manifestations (rich pictorial material is available, see endnote[40]). The core is a medium-sized square, on which both a large ancestral hall and a Houwang temple are located (Figure 3.12). The temple is open to the public and was supported by various big sponsors, such as real estate companies and Huang Yingchao who had emerged as an illustrious entrepreneur in recent years and public figure as a member of the Political Consultative Congress.

The square is labelled as 'cultural square', a designation that is shared by other squares, as mentioned. It shows various artefacts with religious and mythical references, such as the Eight Immortals crossing the sea on the small artificial pond, or a large Bodhisattva, but also a statue commemorating the farming life of the past. The headquarters of the shareholding cooperative is located at the square and hosts the Xiasha museum. Both the museum and a large mural at the ancestral hall tell the story of the mythical genealogy of the Huang, which ultimately leads back to the Yellow Emperor. The ancestor which has more historical authenticity is the Tang dynasty official Huang Qiaoshan, to which all so-called 'Jiangxia' Huang trace

Figure 3.12 The ritual space of Xiasha.
Source: Google Earth satellite picture.

back their origin, a place near Wuhan where their ancestors migrated before moving further on to Shenzhen area (see chapter 6 for more detail). In addition, the square displays important Huang personalities, such as the first Huang *jinshi* degree holder in Imperial times, with a huge bronze statue at the entrance to the square.

The Xiasha Huang are remarkable because their leader has adopted a strong strategy of developing the location as a heritage site, including intangible heritage, and combining this with international connections. The Huang ancestral rites are displayed at a video instalment at the Shenzhen museum, led by Huang Yingchao. This is a special occasion, namely the rites held at the World Huang Surname convention. We discuss this convention in Chapter 6. The Huang differ from the Fenghuang Wen in actively pursuing a strategy of internationalizing their ritual activities, with the internet as one medium. This is enabled by a much more inclusive use of the surname Huang, which includes even deliberate ambiguities regarding the subethnic identification: There are conflicting views on whether the Xiasha Huang are *guangfu* or Hakka. Via the internet, the Huang connect many local ritual activities in a digital ritual space, such as in numerous reports about mutual visits of Huang groups and pilgrimages to sacred places, thus also establishing the transregional and even transnational ritual unity of Huang.

This internationalization effort proved to be very successful, with the Xiasha Huang leader eventually even obtaining the position of the President of the World Huang Association. This is a modern metamorphosis of the ritual economy that combines internationalization with the development of local tourism. It needs emphasis that Chinese with surname 'Huang' number about 60 million worldwide, which is alone a huge market for any project that piggybacks on clan and surname rituals. Hence, the Xiasha Huang leaders pursue a very active strategy in building local cultural heritage, including the invention of new forms of traditional rituals. The Huang 'hereditization' strategy includes launching a version of the 'common pot' *pencai* as an intangible cultural heritage. We look at this phenomenon in some detail in Chapter 5.

In sum, both cases illustrate how the ritual artefacts create a spatial structure which is activated in many ritual actions that, in turn, create the ritual space. This space is then sustained by ritual actions that invest into the maintenance of ritual artefacts. As a result, urban development is deeply shaped by ritual spaces.

4 The role of ritual spaces in urban development

When comparing the cases of Fengguang and Xiasha with other cases, the role of cultural frames becomes even more salient. One very important case is Baishizhou, the biggest urban village with a population density roughly double the Shenzhen average.[41] Baishizhou was originally an area that included five villages and covered what is today Overseas Chinese Town and

Baishizhou. During Maoist times, the two areas were combined into a big state farm, thus defining a fundamental difference to the other cases. In addition, on the high time of collectivization, new brigades were created that hosted workers from Sichuan province that worked in the construction of a water reservoir for Hong Kong, today resulting in villages with much less depth in terms of shared histories of villagers. Indeed, the only ancestral hall still existent is that of Zeng family, in a poor shape and not active. There are a few 'holy trees' with small altars, but no official temple.

After the creation of the SEZ, the two areas also divided socially, meaning that what is now the OTC continues to be controlled by a state-owned company. This company rushed ahead with transforming the entire area into a site of theme parks and leisure facilities, following top-down methods of comprehensive urban planning. Neighbouring Baishizhou was left to the five villages under collective control. However, this meant that there was no unified representation of collective interests. In particular, the villagers did not establish a shareholding cooperative in the first stage. Yet, the transformation into a densely populated urban village proceeded with high speed, beginning with the construction of the so-called 'handshake buildings' on the private plots of the villagers. Baishizhou was ideally located between Luohu and Shekou and offered cheap housing to workers in the surrounding industrial parks, increasingly also becoming first home for young professionals who in the early stage of their career could not yet afford more standard housing. That means Baishizou became a vibrant urban place for low-income and lower-middle-income people at the centre of Shenzhen.

The villagers eventually created a shareholding cooperative, as they realized that they were latecomers to the development and that there would be a need for integrating development of private plots and collective land. Yet, for that reason Baishizhou did not develop the same kind of ritual economy features that we can see in Fenghuang and Xiasha. For example, the Cultural Plaza in Baishizhou is an ordinary public space without ritual artefacts. In other words, Baishizhou is not a ritual space.

This mattered a lot in the 2010s when plans for redeveloping Baishizhou were continuously projected. Whereas at that time Fenghuang and Xiasha launched comprehensive activities in strengthening physical manifestations of their identity as a village, relationships between villagers as owners and the location became increasingly tenuous, for example, because buildings were sublet to other investors. Yet, in spite of early plans, the demolition of Baishizhou proceeded only gradually, only gaining speed in recent years and appears to approach consummation in the early 2020s. The resistance against demolition mainly comes from the tenants, including many small business owners, and the public against the backdrop of growing concerns about gentrification.[42]

Hence, the Baishizhou case is a litmus test showing the relevance of ritual spaces: Ritual spaces are performative phenomena, and they can fail to come into existence, even though the wider cultural reference frame may be similar. The question is what the default case is. We argue that this is the ritual space, salient in the wide variety of ritual spaces and places across Shenzhen territory, and more or less congruent with the territory of urban villages (including redeveloped areas), as shown in the maps. By implication, of course, this means that the 'other half' of Shenzhen is not part of a ritual space. Yet, this would be a premature conclusion.

One reason is that the ritual space may include artefactual constructs with wider spatial impact, and that real estate projects operate partly independent from the regional distribution of land ownership rights because of the separation between land ownership and ownership of buildings. However, this impact is difficult to ascertain empirically and in a systematic way. We just present a few preliminary observations.

To begin with, as in the case of cultural squares, there is a direct impact of artefacts on the spatial environment, as when very valuable land is devoted to large squares. There are contrasting cases, such as the previously mentioned Zheng ancestral hall in Dachong which is surrounded by office buildings and a huge shopping plaza, and lineage members no longer living there. Yet, the place is vibrant with ritual activity at important periods of the lunar year, even filling the few spaces available with *pencai* tables. But there is another aspect of ritual directly affecting construction.

This becomes evident if one considers the historical conditions of lineages in pre-Communist China: Lineages were directly competing over control of land, and landed assets were the most important determinant of relative power, as typically profits from other activities were reinvested in territorial expansion. Wealthy lineages controlled substantial assets in the form of lineage estates: a major part of the income earned from renting out the land was invested into collective activities, such as building lavish ancestral halls that signalled the status and achievements of the family. This also applies for the current situation: Lineages compete over prestige by means of real estate projects that are realized together with big developers. The Huang at Xiasha invested in a huge shopping mall with apartment block, the K.K. mall, together with Kingkey real estate. Typically, lineages compete against other lineages in terms of such projects, which, as in the case of Dachong, can even imply that the lineage no longer lives at the place, yet claims the prestige of the urban architecture surrounding their ancestral hall. In other words, there is a modern metamorphosis of lineage competition over land, in terms of the height of buildings which multiplies the area of the ritual space of the lineage, including buildings outside the original territory. There are cases of shareholding cooperatives which morphed into real estate companies active in many other places, such as the Pan lineage of Huaide in Bao'an, neighbouring Fenghuang, which is one of the richest *shequ* in Shenzhen, as far as the prosperity of the resident native population is concerned.

There are other aspects of ritual that involve immigrant families who invested acquired wealth in real estate. This is certainly true for the biggest groups of private real estate investors, the Chaoshan entrepreneurs. The ritual aspect comes into play when considering the organization of the family and the intergenerational transfer of wealth. One implication of traditional rules of inheritance is that property is divided equally among sons. In old China, this meant that families aimed at controlling various types of land so that during division of assets each new family would be entitled to a diversified composition of land to sustain it. Observers report that real estate family businesses in Shenzhen may pursue similar concerns, that is, when considering the type and size of investment, also avoiding complications during later division among children. In particular, Chaoshan real estate family businesses tend to follow traditional rules in dividing the family fortune among sons. That means ritual aspects may affect a wider range of construction projects in Shenzhen. It is difficult to assess the quantitative relevance of such observations.[43]

One indirect indicator is the strong role of families in Shenzhen real estate business, apart from the big developers. Of special interest in the context of Chapter 6 is the role of real estate investors with surname Huang, which also attracted the attention of the Chinese media. A list provided by a Shenzhen newspaper in 2016 puts this into full limelight (Table 3.1).[44] This list includes 16 Chaoshan Huang. In this group, four are brothers, Huang Shizai, Huang Maoru, Huang Maozhan, and Huang Zhenhua. There are also other cases, with the most important one Lvjing group listed in Hong Kong, which was founded by a Huang immigrant from Maoming, who is also actively sponsoring ritual activities at his native place.[45] Lvjing corporation is active in connecting with local lineages in Shenzhen in developing real estate projects. We may surmise that these families tend towards more traditional behaviours which influence their decisions about investment.

Table 3.1 Top managers in Shenzhen real estate business with surname Huang, 2016

Name	*Position*	*Representative works*
Huang Chulong	Xinghe real estate CEO	Coco Park, Xinghe World
Huang Maoru	Maoye Mall CEO	Maoye Mall
Huang Wei	New world real estate CEO	Season Garden
Huang Shizai	Great China CEO	Center Project
Huang Maozhan	Guodu Group CEO	Guodu Golf
Huang Zhenhua	Sino Group CEO	Sino Square
Huang Maoxiong	Jijian investment CEO	Jijian Garden
Huang Xiangmo	Yuhu Investment	Baoan Project
Huang Chubiao	Donghai Group	Donghai Airway
Huang Junkang	Laimeng Group	Leimeng real estate
Huang Hui	Sanxiang Group	Main real estate in Shanghai
Huang Yaowen	Guang xingyuan	Baoan Project
Huang Guangmiao	Zhouzhou Group	Zhouzhou real estate
Huang Zhenda	Liantai Group	Liantai real estate
Huang Shaoqin	Dongfang real estate	Dongfang tea house
Huang Rongcheng	Rongling industry	Construction
Huang Erchun	Jingang industry	Jigang Technic Park
Huang Yuhong	Mingzhu real estate	Mingzhu Hotel

A pertinent observation is the data on vacant space in commercial buildings, which refers to both office and residential buildings on the market. In the past decade, there was a consistently high stock of vacant space, averaging about three million square metres. At the same time, the prices on the secondary market tripled, from below 20,000 Yuan per square metre to almost 60,000 Yuan. Building activity, after a high time in the 2000s, was more or less stable, oscillating around four million square metres completed every year, only falling below three million in 2017.[46] These observations suggest that investors do not strongly react to short-term market data on vacancies but adopt a long-term perspective. One explanation could be that families aim at accumulating stocks of real estate that can be held by the next generation after family division. Interestingly, such an argument may also apply for the buyers of residential housing. Specifically, the average investor in residential property often accumulates wealth in the context of family formation and marriage; such motivation would also shape family business concerns in the real estate industry, as argued previously.[47]

There is another aspect that indeed affects the entire Shenzhen territory – *feng shui*. We need not go into details here, because evidence is difficult to collect. *Feng shui* is an ancient Chinese practice that comes along in many variants and schools which are represented by *feng shui* masters. In the PRC, *feng shui* is officially designated as 'superstition' and was ruthlessly suppressed during the Cultural Revolution. However, it survived among Chinese communities abroad and, in particular Hong Kong. In Mainland China, *feng shui* experienced a rapid and strong revival after 1978. In our context, it is important to emphasize that *feng shui* is widely practiced in subethnic groups, especially the Chaoshan.

Basically, and sufficient in the current context, *feng shui* is a technique to identify the propitious flows of cosmic force *qi* in the natural and artificial environment. In the first place, this means to analyse the natural environment of a place, such as mountains and rivers. Next, based on this analysis, humans can adapt their artefacts, especially buildings, to these conditions. Buildings can obstruct the flow of *qi*, or they can even further capture and concentrate the flows (such as in the case of the Fenghuang pagoda mentioned previously). Therefore, *feng shui* is an essential ritual practice in architectural design. The traditional village is a place that is deeply shaped by *feng shui* practices. However, it is important to notice that this does not mean that the entire artificial structure has grown by comprehensive *feng shui* planning, because *feng shui* is a layered and interlocking system of practices on different levels. This is because *feng shui* is also a means of competition between families: Constructing a house that captures *qi* may block access to another pre-existing building. Hence, *feng shui* can be even used as a deliberate means of competition, implying that the resulting allocation of artefacts does not necessarily represent an optimal or harmonic state.

In traditional belief, especially in Guangdong province, the flow of *qi* directly influences the flow of wealth. That implies that certain territories may be perceived as especially conducive to economic prosperity. According to *feng shui* analysis, the entire territory of Shenzhen locates in an auspicious way relative to Hong Kong, with *qi* channelled by dragon-shaped mountains and other natural patterns that embed the two places. Accordingly, *feng shui* analysis suggests that today there is a flow of wealth back from Hong Kong to Shenzhen.[48]

In our context, what is more relevant is the role of *feng shui* in urban development. Although one cannot present numbers, as *feng shui* is still a hidden practice, we can safely assume that most buildings constructed by Chaoshan people follow *feng shui* principles, for example. In this sense, the role of *feng shui* would be pervasive in Shenzhen. According to some reports, there are more specific phenomena that relate to the relationship between wealth and *qi*. This is salient in the popular view that there are 'rich people's areas' ('fu ren qu'富人区), which is reflected in very high real estate prices which naturally filter out the richest buyers. *Feng shui* may be involved in explaining where these areas are located. One example is the Donghai Park near Xiangmi Lake in Futian, which was early targeted as a high-end location for resorts and apartment blocks. Clearly, the beauty of the place may suffice to explain the attraction, but during the early development by Baishida corporation *feng shui* was very prominent in designing the architecture. It is straightforward to interpret this as reinforcing the attraction of the place. Rising real estate prices filter out the rich as buyers, which create new networking opportunities and closed social circles on golf courts, clubs, and restaurants. Eventually, the good *feng shui* of the place becomes a self-fulfilling prophecy.

We do not want to overstate the role of *feng shui*, but together with the strong impetus of lineage and family competition it seems justified to argue that ritual spaces extend beyond the borders of urban villages in many ways.

5 Conclusion

This chapter has presented empirical evidence that the urban infrastructure and layout of urban design of Shenzhen is influenced by ritual spaces which are created by actions of many individuals and groups. We will discuss the role of government in Chapter 7. In the current context, our argument is mainly based on the observation that in the past decades, the phenomenon of urban villages has manifested large domains of autonomous societal action which drove urban development partly autonomous from municipal government master plans. There are two worlds in Shenzhen, the modernist world and the ritual world, and urban development emerges from the interaction between the two.

These phenomena can be straightforwardly interpreted in terms of Collins' ritual theory. Ritual spaces are typically demarcated by artefacts that play a pivotal role in collective activities that involve emotional entrainment and effervescence emerging in situations of bodily co-presence. In principle, this involves two different groups, the original villagers and the far larger immigrant population. Therefore, Collins' mechanisms of ritual unfold differently in both cases. This is salient in case of the Fenghuang temple: The much smaller altar devoted to the local deities is what manifests lineage solidarity, and the central Buddha is more inclusive vis-à-vis the wider population. This inclusiveness is a hallmark of many ritual spaces in Shenzhen: The Xiasha public square was deliberately designed as expressing the diversity of the urban village, manifest in various religious artefacts. The Houwang temple is open to everybody, whereas the ancestral hall is closed to the public. The place becomes an exclusive Huang ritual space only on certain occasions: However, its totality is also a ritual expression of the status of the local lineage: Shopping mall and ancestral hall are both ritual objects.

In Collins' view, ritual drives markets, not the other way around, in the sense that ritual embeddedness is essential for enabling and sustaining economic action. This makes it difficult to reach clear-cut empirical assessments as long as markets flourish, since one can always argue that ritual is merely instrumental in markets. One simple litmus test is whether actors incur costs that directly relate to sustaining ritual. These are simple indicators, such as investing in public spaces in extremely valuable areas: Shangsha follows Xiasha in creating a 'cultural square', while renovating the local ancestral hall and temple, real estate investors may accept vacancies and so forth.

In Collins' framework, the ritual dynamics involves the building up and sustenance of certain distributions of emotional energy. In the ritual spaces of Shenzhen, this involves two major phenomena. One is the role of family and kinship in motivating economic actions, and the other is the role of leaders who engage in projects that combine business and urban development. Both factors can be observed in many ways, but mostly work in the background, for sure, such as the effort in creating family fortunes and eventually feeling satisfaction in achieving the goals displayed in various symbols of status. An important visible form of effervescence is the revival of many traditional festivals, which always have two dimensions, the ritual and the fun of experiencing 'renao' 热闹, with the latter being a most inclusive social action. This is an important pillar of ritual economy today, merging ritual for some with fun for everyone.

In the subsequent chapters, we will look at the role of family and kinship first, and next to the role of entrepreneurial leaders, that is, collective and individual agents of ritual action.

Notes

1 We cannot enter the adequate theoretical explorations here, which are the topic of the discipline of cultural geography and involve many, often conflicting views in the social sciences. We notice however that one of the seminal contributions establishing the field was by a Chinese author, Tuan Yi-Fu (1977), with his duality of space and place.
2 Hang (2006: 205f).
3 Kuah-Pearce (2011) presents a network analysis of Singaporean Chinese 'searching their roots' in China.

4 For example, see McNeal (2011).
5 See Chau's (2006) extensive study of the 'Black Dragon temple' in Sha'anxi.
6 We refrain from exploring the theoretical dimensions here. Chau (2013) shows how Actor-Network Theory can help to understand the distributed agency and autonomous causal forces of artefacts in networks of artefacts and people.
7 The plural nature of even the traditional single-lineage village is emphasized by Chun (2000).
8 Lagerwey (2011).
9 The paramount importance of *feng shui* for traditional Chinese life was mostly emphasized in the older literature but is no longer prominent today; see, for example, Freedman (1967).
10 Mao and Gu (2019).
11 On the role of idiosyncratic religious rituals in manifesting village identity, see DuBois (2005).
12 Chau (2014) highlights the household-centred nature of popular religion in China as opposed to the community-centred organization of Christianity. Yue (2014) shows in detail how household and the public domain interact.
13 This picture is not only emerging in journalistic accounts, but also in in-depth scholarly work, such as Tao Qing (2007), as the perception prevailing among immigrants who may not connect to native villagers. In a place such as the electronics market Huaqiangbei studied by Tao, local history is almost forgotten or has never been remembered.
14 Bray (2013).
15 For a fascinating contemporary account, see Hase (1990).
16 Wang (2016); O'Donnell (2019).
17 On the general background of Hakka, see Constable (1996). We discuss this in more detail in Chapter 7.
18 Huang (2017).
19 Wang (2016: 56).
20 Locus classicus for understanding this phenomenon is Shue (1988).
21 We will analyse this in more detail in Chapter 4. The continuity of kinship-based land allocation under the guise of Maoist institutions was seminally analysed by Potter and Potter (1990). The inherent tensions were documented in many village studies, some in the Pearl River Delta, such as Chan et al. (2009).
22 Ma and Blackwell (2017).
23 This factor is much emphasized in Po (2012).
24 O'Donnell (2017).
25 This institutional vacuum is vividly described by Tao Qing (2007). In his case, however, the original villagers left their land, because it was not deemed so productive anyway, and gave way to military SOEs who prepared the first sites for welcoming foreign investors.
26 https://baike.baidu.com/item/%E7%A6%8F%E7%94%B0%E5%8C%BA#4, accessed November 2, 2019.
27 This is vividly described in Wang (2016).
28 According to the Shenzhen Statistical Yearbook 2018: 3, the permanent population ('changzhu renkou' 常住人口) is 12,528,300, of which only 4,347,200 have a Shenzhen hukou. However, the true population is sometimes even estimated about 25 million; see http://finance.sina.com.cn/stock/jhzx/2019-01-13/doc-ihqhqcis5857700.shtml (accessed September 27, 2019). The reason is that official statistics also knows the category of 'liudong renkou' 流动人口, which includes workers who do not have the right to stay permanently at Shenzhen, yet may live there for many years. This is a grey area, because this category also includes visitors who stay longer than a month, but at the same time including all visitors, expanding the number of people even more who factually create demands on urban infrastructure, transport, and accommodation.

29 https://wapbaike.baidu.com/item/%E6%B0%B4%E5%9B%B4%E6%9D%91/2646702?ms=1&rid=9917881990917371198 (Shuiwei); http://ilonghua.sznews.com/content/2017-03/08/content_15618020_13.htm (report on reconstruction of Shangsha square); http://blog.sina.com.cn/s/blog_bc9f8f830102x6ae.html (Fenghuang): all accessed January 22, 2020.
30 Oakes (2019).
31 http://wtl.sz.gov.cn/xxgk/tjsj/zxtjxx/200909/t20090910_1192315.htm, accessed December 16, 2019. This list recognizes 294 ancestral halls as 'cultural relics'. We have complemented the list by researching Baidu and Google maps, and using materials such as http://hk.crntt.com/crn-webapp/cbspub/secDetail.jsp?bookid=21703&secid=21728, accessed December 16, 2019, resulting in a list of 310 halls. We are grateful to our research assistant Li Ling and other master students at HIT Shenzhen for collecting and checking the information. In drafting our map, we noticed that often halls may be very close to each other, so that they merge in the dots at the current scale of resolution.
32 Watson (1975, 1985, 2004).
33 https://shenzhennoted.com/2015/06/06/gangxia-walking-the-remaining-village/, accessed January 18, 2020.
34 http://blog.sina.com.cn/s/blog_bc9f8f830102x6ae.html, accessed January 22, 2020.
35 https://www.meet99.com/jingdian-shenzhenfenghuangshan-70418.html, accessed January 22, 2020.
36 Compare Chau (2006).
37 Rubie Watson (1985).
38 https://m.sohu.com/a/209699730_275216/?pvid=000115_3w_a, accessed January 21, 2020.
39 Compare the case reported by Trémon (2014, 2015a).
40 https://shenzhennoted.com/2017/05/04/xiasha-k-k-one/, accessed January 18, 2020.
41 On Baishizhou, there is an excellent Shenzhen university master thesis supervised by Mary Ann O'Donnell, Wan (2017). Wang (2016) has also rich information on Baishizhou.
42 The Baishizhou saga is continuously narrated and pictorially documented by Mary Ann O'Donnell on her blogsite 'Shenzhen Noted' https://shenzhennoted.com/.
43 Wan (2017).
44 http://news.szhome.com/233392.html, accessed April 12, 2018.
45 http://www.mymm.cc/forum.php?mod=viewthread&tid=12244, accessed March 7, 2019.
46 Shenzhen Statistical Yearbook 2018, pp. 231, 235.
47 In a stimulating paper, Steffen (2017) argues that in Zhengzhou, Henan province, real estate business is deeply shaped by cultural constructs in which buyers do not react to data about vacancies, but take lost opportunities in failing to build long-term stocks as a reference, even refraining from renting out vacant property. Long-term stocks embody future opportunities for growing wealth when conditions change. Glaeser et al. (2017) confirm with statistical and econometric methods that Chinese investors tend to be oriented long term, and mention family motivations in buying residential property. This shows that real estate is a form of savings, motivated by family interests, especially for marriage and next-generation family formation, as seminally analysed in Wei and Zhang (2011).
48 https://m.baidu.com/ala/c/www.360doc.cn/mip/823025195.html; https://m.sohu.com/a/282406017_603579, both accessed November 19, 2019.

4 Lineages and shareholding cooperatives

1 The problem of the Chinese lineage

In this chapter, we look at the core institution of the traditional ritual economy – the lineage – and how it relates to institutional structures in the modern Shenzhen economy. The central institution is the cooperative shareholding company 'gufen hezuo gongsi' 股份合作公司, henceforth 'shareholding cooperative'. The shareholding cooperative is the institution that designs, enacts, and maintains ritual spaces, as analysed in the previous chapter. In many districts of Shenzhen, the *shequ* is often congruent with the shareholding cooperative, in the sense that the shareholding cooperative is a para-governmental institution that assumes important functions for the *shequ* in providing for urban infrastructure and a wide range of services, such as organizing public festivals and other activities, which sometimes have a ritual meaning. We will look at this role in more detail in Chapter 7. In this chapter, we concentrate on the core issue: Can we interpret the shareholding cooperative as a modern transformation of the ritual economy of lineages? In answering this question, we focus on shareholding cooperatives in which the relationship between shareholding cooperative and lineage is active and dominant. As we discuss in Chapter 7, this does not apply for all shareholding cooperatives in Shenzhen.[1]

However, we cannot take the notion of lineage for granted. There is a double challenge. One is obvious. If many observers diagnose a revival of lineages in China today, they certainly do not refer to the full meaning of the traditional concept. This is because the traditional lineage was part and parcel of the Imperial political system and was undergirded by a ruling Confucian orthodoxy. Hence, modern lineages appear to be much weaker in institutional terms than traditional lineages.[2] In addition, the revival seems mainly a rural phenomenon, hence possibly a transient phenomenon withering away with economic development and modernization. And finally, lineages are weak or even non-existent in many regions of China, especially in North China. Taken together, even if we diagnose a revival today, we may expect that this is only a temporary and regionally circumscribed phenomenon.

However, the Shenzhen case is of interest as we observe a growing integration of lineages in public spaces, urban environment, and public life concomitant with a growing political recognition of their role in society. As a result of rapid urbanization, we see the re-emergence of urban lineages.[3] Early commentators expected that their exploding wealth would undermine their cohesion and cultural identity, but we observe many cases where this goes along with growing self-confidence and cultural assertiveness, as in the Huang hereditization strategies which are manifest in the ritual space of Xiasha. That being said, the regional peculiarity of the phenomenon is beyond dispute, although this should not be misperceived as a merely local trend. Even if we highlight the regional variety in lineage distribution, areas of strong and resilient lineage traditions includes various provinces such as Fujian or Jiangxi, and therefore encompasses hundreds of millions of Chinese. In that context, the interaction between lineage revival and urbanization in Shenzhen may be an exemplary illustration of larger trends during the urbanization of rural areas awaiting further research.[4]

The other challenge in approaching lineages relates to what we conceive as traditional lineage. In recent decades, the concept has been subject to many debates, both with reference to historical conditions and its modern manifestations. In relation to our case, we notice that modern research on lineages has been shaped by field research in the Hong Kong New Territories.[5] As we have seen, cases like the Wen directly connect lineage branches across the border; hence the Hong Kong case was often approached as being a 'pure' manifestation of tradition, which is not disrupted by political interference and violent suppression as in Mainland China. However, in this respect, anthropological research has recently raised serious doubts in pointing out that colonial rule was much more intrusive than it seemed.[6] For a long time, the working hypothesis was that British rule respected the cultural autonomy of the Chinese in Hong Kong, even to the degree of recognizing many aspects of Qing Law in Hong Kong legal practice. But that overlooked the fact that the colonial system implemented various far-reaching changes of the institutional context in which lineages operated. The first, with radical and lasting impact, was the abolition of the permanent tenancy system in clarifying land ownership at the beginning of the 20th century.[7] The permanent tenancy system had allowed for the coexistence of land ownership by lineage estates and quasi-ownership by tenants who paid rent but otherwise enjoyed long-term possession of land, even across generations. The British intervention disentangled these complex systems, often with layers of subtenants, and thereby induced a major reshuffling of power among lineages, which also changed their nature, especially in relation to social stratification. Indeed, as James Watson has shown in his path-breaking historical and anthropological research on lineages in Hong Kong, these developments shaped the fate of one of the lineages that we study in this chapter, and which were also studied by Watson, the Wen (Cantonese 'Man'), driving many of them to emigration.[8]

Another major intervention was the political alliance between the lineages of the New Territories and the colonial government that emerged after the Communist riots in the late 1960s when lineages helped to restore order. This strengthened the legal protection of lineage rights such as lineage trusts and tombs, and added new forms, such as the 'ding hu' policy which gave lineage members the special right to construct three-storey houses in the New Territories, which is a substantial privilege vis-à-vis other Hong Kong citizens, who often complain about this discrimination.[9]

In other words, one cannot say that the Hong Kong lineages represent a 'pristine' state of the Chinese lineage, because they experienced similar environmental impacts as in other cases. This adds to the historical ambiguities that surround the notion of the lineage. This is particularly true for the economic aspects. The reason is that most historical records of lineages were written by Confucian scholars, and hence the lineage was interpreted in terms of Confucian orthodoxy. Family and kinship had obtained a central political significance in Neo-Confucian scholarship, promoting ancestral rights and lineage organization as a means of civilizing and pacifying society.[10] Originally, the construction of ancestral halls and the conduct of large ancestral rites was a privilege of the Imperial family, gradually extended to elite families of the bureaucracy. Therefore, the collapse of the Song dynasty was a highly significant event in cultural evolution, because many elite families migrated to the South, lost their economic basis, and became commoners. At the same time, when Mongol rule ended in China, the new Ming emperors faced the challenge to rule frontier societies such as in the Pearl River Delta, where Han Chinese had intermingled with natives and where waves of newcomers had entered the territory and started to compete over scarce land resources. Large-scale migration events continued to shape the history of the South-eastern region, such as triggered by the Ming policy to depopulate the coastal line for military security reasons, and then the reopening of these areas under the Qing.

Against this backdrop, the Imperial administration had an ambivalent attitude towards lineages. Lineages often caused local conflicts as they battled over land, and they were difficult to control, as they could form alliances that would become countervailing powers in the Imperial system. However, lineages were a centrepiece in disseminating Confucian ideology among the ordinary population and, given the difficulties in setting up alternative systems of local control such as the *baojia* system, lineages had been co-opted in enforcing Imperial role in the frontier societies. In sum, the second aspect prevailed, and the Imperial administration spent great effort in standardizing lineages practices, such as by influencing lineage rules as applied in customary law via adjudication by the magistrate.[11] One factor that contributed to this symbiosis between lineage and empire was the Imperial examination system: Local lineages were attracted to invest into bureaucratic careers of their male progeny, and for those who succeeded, including an official in the genealogy, it was a boon for boosting local reputation, accumulating social capital and political connections and assuming local leadership roles.

However, this 'Confucianization' of lineages also means that the historical record partly distorts social reality that has been gradually recovered in research about social history.[12] One central topic is the economic functions of lineage organizations, which comes to the fore, for example, when studying local gazetteers or archives of court proceedings. Originally, the central economic role was landholding, so that in some definitions of the term corporate land ownership appears as a necessary feature. Lineages established lineage estates which operated as corporate landlords and were managed by elite members. The driver of this organization was lineage competition, because corporate landholdings were essential to produce certain collective goods, such as funding lineage schools and supporting candidates for the Imperial examinations. However, the economic activities of lineages extended beyond this core activity. One other channel linking lineage with territory was the control of local markets.[13] Lineages often established markets as corporate entities, which meant that they provided the space and rented it to traders, but also assumed control in terms of other activities, such as controlling the measures, managing transport bottlenecks such a bridges or adjudication of disputes. Local lineages could also effectively act as tax farmers, concluding an agreement with the magistrate about collectively paying the tax and collecting it from the individual taxpayers.[14] In other words, the hierarchical structure of the marketing system was partly reflected in the power structure of lineages. Indeed, establishing and developing local markets were a major alternative means of competing against other lineages beyond mere control of land, which drove the expansion and deepening of the marketing system. Beyond this, larger lineages could also use the organizational blueprint of lineage estate to set up other corporate entities that operated in other commercial fields. Therefore, merchant families might also assume the organizational form of a lineage.[15] These roles were much under-represented in the Confucian accounts of lineages.

To sum up, when assessing the current role of lineages in Shenzhen, it is necessary to achieve an adequate historical contextualization. The revival of lineages can build on deep and specific historical roots that are implicit in the imaginaries and rituals today. For example, the Wen were one of the most powerful lineages in Xin'an county before 1949, directly competing with the Tang over hegemony in the area.[16] Their claims on supremacy were also grounded in their reference to a most prestigious 'high ancestor', and this deep genealogy also offered the symbolic means to create more complex alliances between different local Wen lineages. The Wen revival today builds on this history. As a consequence, for understanding endogenously evolving economic institutions such as the shareholding cooperative, it is important to include these historical and anthropological dimensions,[17] even more so because history is increasingly invoked by the lineages themselves. There is a considerable number of surnames in Shenzhen, especially in the largest *guangfu* segment of original settlers, which today are traced back to migration history via genealogies over hundreds of years, often beyond Song dynasty. At the same time, there are also many historical monuments which witness this deep history, such as tombs and ancestral halls, even if sometimes claims of age may appear dubious. Names such as Zhang, Huang, Chen, He, Wen, or Yuan are frequent all over China, but, as we discuss in Chapter 6, they are also associated with accounts of chain migration which resulted in certain early settlements in the Pearl River Delta, for which more precise genealogies can be constructed and which relate with villages in which today groups with the same surname reside, constituting lineages in the stricter sense.[18]

2 Conceptual frameworks: Family, kinship, descent

One of the challenges in dealing with the revival of lineages is conceptual. Our concepts create the lens through which we approach reality. The study of extended kinship in China has languished for decades because the general presumption was that political interventions destroyed their social and economic basis. The first blow against lineage power was the collectivization of corporate landholdings, which was bolstered by the aggressive policy against rich landlords who were often lineage leaders. The second blow arrived with the radicalization of the cultural critique of lineages, with Red Guards destroying genealogies and ancestral halls turned workshops. And the third blow was the one-child policy, thus constraining the size of families and limiting the expansive scope of family division.

Yet, at a closer look these blows appear less serious, and this also opens fresh perspectives on conceptual issues. Most fundamental is the issue of land ownership. As we mentioned previously, in Hong Kong, British rule abolished an important institutional means which supported corporate landholdings, the permanent tenancy system. Now, if we look at collectivization and the current system of land ownership in China, we can reach the surprising and apparently paradoxical conclusion that the socialist system factually universalized corporate landholding by lineages. This is conceptually important, as this shows that there is a complex bidirectional causality between kinship and institutional environment.[19]

In the early accounts of collectivization based on interviews of refugees to Hong Kong, researchers already made the observation that the system of Peoples' Communes, after the decentralization following the Great Leap Forward, cemented the pattern of lineage-based land ownership because the underlying residential structure of villages was not changed and even frozen by means of almost suppressing any form of migration via the household registration and internal passport system (*hukou*).[20] That simply means, extended kinship groups living together in a certain area and the distribution of surnames across villages, including single-surname villages, were stabilized and turned into collective holders of land according to the constitution. This became very important when the People's Communes were dismantled after 1978: The system of contracting out land to farmers bears much functional similarity to the relationship between tenants and lineage estates in old China.[21] Indeed, with the extension, tenancy contracts in the current system moved towards the model of the traditional permanent tenancy system.[22] This is especially true for the functional similarity to the legal distinction between 'bone' and 'skin' in traditional customary law, that is, the rights of the owner (who recognizes that in paying the land tax) and of the tenant, which might obtain quasi-permanent nature, though with important limitations such as in selling the land (different from subletting).[23]

The implicit use of cultural templates in the socialist institutional design was salient in the first stage of collectivization, when a share system was employed to allocate land that was subject to expropriation from lineage estates, such as orchards. Whereas such economic assets were often in the hands of lineage branches or even fewer elite members, they were now simply redistributed by expanding the scope of shareholders. In other words, we can interpret the system of collective ownership as an institutional surface phenomenon, which factually referred to overturning the power structure within lineages and equalizing the relative status of members but did not change the basic structure of ownership as possession and control by kinship groups. In fact, the system of household registration even reinforced lineage ownership of land because the collective rights were exclusive to the residential community, which, in case of single-surname villages, is coextensive with the lineage, and the rights could not be alienated to others by individual acts. Thus, we can conclude that the socialist system did not really abolish the lineage as a social structure in the economy. To a certain extent, collectivization was even less intrusive than the British abolishment of the permanent tenancy system and the underlying duality of ownership rights.

Regarding the second blow against lineages, the conclusion may be less clear; yet, feminist scholars have early diagnosed that socialist morality and certain institutional practices amounted to a democratization of patriarchy, but not to its withering.[24] Indeed, a conspicuous feature of the socialist system was to treat the household as a unit, for example, in allocating work points and tasks with males as leaders. Socialist sexual morality bore much resemblance with most austere lineage rules, and the suppression of markets reduced domains of freedom of casual meetings among the sexes anyway. Marriage customs certainly became very simple and frugal, but families mostly retained their roles in arranging them.[25]

A similarly ambivalent nature of socialist transformations even affects the assessment of the third blow to the lineage system – the one-child policy. In Guangdong province, the one-child policy was often undermined by deviant actions, especially by more affluent families (in our interviews, we met entrepreneurs in their late 40s with five children). There were different ways, such as bribing officials, simply paying the fees for transgressions, or giving birth to children in Hong Kong. In the former rural areas or among Chaoshan immigrants, it is easy to meet families of larger size. One driver of deviance is that the one-child policy fired back in terms of hardening central beliefs in the patriarchal system, especially the preference for sons. If the first child is a daughter, families continued to try for a son. This hardening of traditional beliefs is most obvious in the fact that Guangdong province emerged as the province with the most distorted sex ratio between males and females in China. One-child policy also undermined gender inequality in other ways, especially in assigning the duty of birth control mainly to the women.[26]

To summarize, the socialist transformation, apparently radical in terms of transforming traditional kinship, in many respects may have even had the opposite impact. Therefore, in order to assess the role of extended kinship in Shenzhen today, it is necessary to clarify concepts.[27] We start with the relationship between the family and the lineage. The root term for 'family' is 'jia' 家, which in certain contexts is extended to 'jiazu' 家族, as in 'family business', 'jiazu qiye' 家族企业. This alone creates a productive ambiguity, as *jiazu* is often translated as 'lineage'. The reason is the word 'zu', which refers to descent. Clearly, depending on the genealogical depth considered, the *jia* easily emerges as a lineage. This idea has been systematically developed by the eminent sociologist Fei Xiaotong, who tried to clarify the distinction between family in the West and in China. Fei argued that Western societies pay much emphasis on groups formed by categories (the company, the soccer club, the nation), whereas the Chinese emphasize social relations and fluid network structures, which he designated as 'circles', 'quanzi' 圈子. Hence, the Western family is a category with clear membership criteria and boundaries, whereas the Chinese family is a system of circles which can flexibly adapt to circumstances. Accordingly, the *jiazu* is a simple extension of the family by expanding the scope of active kinship relations. In fact, for Fei this is the 'family at large'.[28]

Interestingly, this offers a first important insight for discussing the modernization of the family, which is often seen as the emergence of the 'Western' elementary family in China. In fact, the traditional family was always centred on the elementary marital unit, with marriage often implicating family division even before the passing of the father and hence the event of inheritance.[29] Even joint families were rare, because the Chinese family system generated internal forces of competition among brothers, thus pushing family division. In other words, the traditional Chinese family is structurally very similar to the 'modern' Western family in pre-women lib times. This is very important for judging current conditions: Even at times of lineage revival, the families firmly remain centred on the conjugal bond, and family business is typically led by elementary and stem families. The strong impact of family division on Chinese family business has always been emphasized in explaining limitations to growth of family firms.[30]

The term *jiazu* comes along with other terms that are often even preferred in relating to the lineage. A most widespread term is 'zongzu' 宗族. The difference between the two terms becomes obvious when we include another most generic term, 'qin' 亲.[31] *Qin* refers to relatives with which one is close in everyday life and implies stronger emotional engagement and attachment. One occurrence of the term is in 'qinqi' 亲戚, which means 'relatives', but often more specifically affinal relatives, including both mother's relatives and wife's relatives. *Qin* defines an important difference between *jiazu* and *zongzu*: *Jiazu* relates to an active kin relationship in daily interaction, which can be mostly taken for granted in a single-lineage village; and *zongzu* relates to a ritual unit in which membership is defined by the rules that determine membership and access to rituals, such as inclusion in genealogy or participation in ancestral rites. Here, Fei Xiaotong's reasoning come into full play: The *jiazu* is an open and flexible system, which can even include affinal relatives or give strong position to women even as household heads ('jiazhang' 家长), whereas the *zongzu* is an exclusive patrilineal group centred on rituals, which, for example, does not recognize any rights and role of in-married women and their relatives. In other words, the *jiazu* is the lineage with in-married women, the *zongzu* without. That matters substantially, because the elementary family is conceived as the conjugal unit.[32]

The proper recognition of this essential difference is difficult in English, because there is some confusion about the use of 'clan' versus 'lineage', which are often treated as synonyms in the non-specialist literature. Clan is often the translation of *zongzu*. But this is misleading in a very significant way.[33] Basically, the Chinese system of extended kinship is a nested structure, with a local lineage as the core which corresponds to *jiazu*.[34] The *jiazu*, in terms of the ritual unit, is mostly coextensive with the *zongzu*, excluding members who are *qin* but excluded from the genealogy, especially all in-marrying women. But lineages can combine into 'higher order' lineages, such as the Wen in our Shenzhen case, and subdivide into branches ('fang' 房). That has implications for ritual practices. For example, a prosperous *fang* may set up its own site of ancestor worship, or the higher-order lineage congregates at a special place, perhaps a site hosted by the most powerful local lineage in several villages. This is where lineage-internal competition over ritual dominance comes into play. The transition from lineage to clan is fluid: Typically, the clan would be an even larger federation of local lineages, historically mostly headquartered in cities, and with a strong political position, probably including degree holders.[35] For all these groups, the term *zongzu* can apply, since the basis for their identity is its manifestation in shared collective rituals and focal artefacts. In Imperial China, clans could also be created as artificial kinship groups, with no previously recognized consanguineal relation between the member lineages, which included the fabrication of a clan genealogy,

This transition to artificial kinship is possible because once one considers the clan another ambiguity comes into play, which is the surname.

In fact, locally, lineages would often be referred to as 'names', such as in 'jiaxing' 家姓. There is another Chinese term which is translated as 'clan' and invoked by Fei Xiaotong, 'shizu' 氏族, which refers to family name 'shi' 氏. That means, sharing a surname has two different dimensions. One is the surname as such, the other is linking the shared surname to a history of migration. That is the reason why the term 'clan' can be even used in referring to the very large group of people with the same surname. But factually, only the subgroup with shared descent matters. Yet, even then, if we consider deep migration history, this can include millions of people. There is an important consequence: Surname can bridge distinctions, which in the present relate to subethnic differentiation. For example, the surname Huang in Shenzhen can be found among Guangfu, Chaoshan, and Hakka, hence with very different dialects and customs. But all of them may refer back to the same 'high ancestor'.[36]

Therefore, considering Shenzhen, the role of migration as related to descent is of paramount importance. Descent is mostly directly related to a history of migration over many centuries. The further the origin lies in the past, the more diluted or simply dubious may be any claims on consanguinity in biological sense. Therefore, we need to approach kinship as a purely cultural category.[37] This establishes the central role of ritual: Villagers who are organized in families and *jiazu* of related people, via consanguinity and marriage, can activate the symbolic capital of descent to form more complex alliances and networks in which ritual activities and artefacts are prominent as anchors.

If we want to render this analysis in more practical terms for empirical analysis, the distinction introduced by Zheng Zhenman is most helpful.[38] Zheng distinguishes between three manifestations of lineages. The first is the 'inheritance lineage' which emerges from the conjugal unit undergoing division. In the perennial competition of families over control of resources and status, family division is a corrosive force. Inheritance lineages emerge when a family decides to keep a certain amount of assets separate from the division, with the eldest son as a steward. This is sustainable because it is made sacrosanct via the connection to ritual obligations. Therefore, the inheritance lineage takes the form of a *zongzu*.

The second form emerges when an inheritance lineage becomes locally powerful and assumes a position to exert control over a territory, typically the village, but also larger spaces, as in the local marketing system. Whereas the inheritance lineage directly builds on consanguinity, the 'control-subordination lineage' mainly builds on shared ritual to establish collective identity and cohesion. The third type of lineage is the 'contractual lineage', which is based on shared interest. In the contractual lineage, the concept of 'share' ('gufen' 股份) looms large: Members who share ritual identities agree to join efforts in a project, such as establishing a local market, and obtain rights in terms of shares which are mostly the right to vote and the right to receive dividends.

It is important to notice that these three forms are ideal-typical distinctions. If we consider a specific case, all dimensions may be relevant, but possibly with various overlapping circles. For example, a powerful control-subordination lineage may consist of different branches which are inheritance lineages, but not the former. One reason for this is that rich branches may wish to protect their assets from dilution in the wider kinship group. However, rich branches may connect with lineages of same surname at other places and create a contractual lineage, apparently just moving to historically deeper layers of share descent.

If we pull all these considerations together, we can state that Chinese extended kinship is mainly based on cultural descent, as epitomized in ritual practices. At the same time, the local community as co-residential group of relatives matters, which differs significantly from cultural descent as the latter has been more thoroughly shaped by Neo-Confucian norms of ritual. This duality explains much of the wide variety of actual kinship practices in China and the adaptability to local context. This is most evident in the rise of shareholding cooperatives.

3 Shareholding cooperatives: Background and the Fenghuang case

As described previously, the hidden preservation of lineage institutions via collective organization of rural society became immediately visible when reforms were launched. Collective property rights corresponded to the traditional subsoil rights, and the surface rights to the contractual relation between households and the village. In the Pearl River Delta, however, this construct was rapidly substituted by more sophisticated arrangements that often directly reflect lineage structures. In this section, we look at one case in much detail, Fenghuang village, and draw comparisons to other cases: We already studied its ritual space in the previous chapter. On the one hand, these arrangements were and are enabled by the distinction between rural land rights that are owned by the collective and which can be inherited, and on the other hand urban land use rights that are limited to a 70-year period (for residential land), which, however, implies that even when the former are transformed into the latter, a three-generation perspective would still govern the incentives and interests of rights holders.[39] In other words, even after nationalization of rights, customary interpretations of ownership continue to hold.

The setting for these complex interactions between formal property institutions and informal lineage structures is the so-called 'cooperative shareholding system'.[40] This is an institutional form that is only applicable in the former rural areas, though being an urban entity today; it is not formally regulated in the national Company Law, but only on the provincial level via administrative regulations; some of the more detailed regulations are even issued on the district level. Already in 1994, the Shenzhen government promulgated detailed regulations for the SEZ, ten years before the model became applicable for the entire territory, including the second-line districts. In August 2019, these regulations were comprehensively reinstated with many edits and changes, though not transforming the essentials as defined 25 years ago. This clearly demonstrates the resilience of the model and its political support in the future.[41] These regulations define the shareholding cooperatives as organizations of the collective economy, either on the level of the administrative village (*xingzheng cun*) or the natural village (*ziran cun*), and clearly identify the group of shareholders as the 'native villagers' ('yuancunmin' 原村民). There are two different ways to establish a shareholding cooperative, which can be combined by either using existing collective capital and transforming this into shares or injecting new capital. The latter would allow for individuals to become independent shareholders: For example, there are shareholding cooperatives in which the top managers are also individual minority shareholders.[42] Hence, there are three types of shares: the 'cooperative shares', 'hezuo gu' 合作股, which are owned by individual villagers as members of the cooperative and village community and which allocate dividends on the basis of households; the 'collective shares', 'jiti gu' 集体股, which allocate dividends to the collective (hence mostly equivalent to retained profits); and the 'invested shares', 'muji gu' 募集股, which result from individual contributions of villagers and workers of the company. The latter regulation explicitly refers to executives and other professional staff, thus opening the possibility for shareholding cooperatives to hire non-villagers as professionals and give them stakes in the company and voice in the shareholder assembly: In the new version of 2019, this category has been substantially broadened and now includes any kind of investor as determined by the company statutes.[43] The collective shares and the invested shares both cannot amount to more than 30 per cent of total shares each. Specific allocations must be determined by the company statutory rules which need to be approved by the village assembly (*cunmin weiyuanhui*). In principle, the invested shares allow for the injection of new capital, and these shares can be mortgaged and traded, different from the other two types.

The shareholding cooperatives have a governance structure that is basically like the regulations that apply in the Company Law for listed companies, that is, distinguishing between the shareholder assembly, the board of directors and the supervisory board. In addition, however, there is a special board that is responsible for the collective capital. The profits of shareholding cooperatives are distributed to shareholders as dividends, unless there is an accumulated loss to be covered, and are transferred to two other funds, the common accumulation fund 'gong ji jin' 公积金, which is retained profits for investment and increase of equity, and a common welfare fund 'gong yi jin' 公益金, which is devoted to the employees. The dividends paid for the collective shares partly accrue to a special type of capital under this rubric, namely the cooperative shareholders welfare fund 'hezuogu gudong fuli jijin' 合作股股东福利基金; this means, part of the dividends can be used to the benefit of the individual households, depending on the decision of the shareholder assembly. As for the collective shares, the amended regulations of 2019 fixed the previous practice that dividends were also used for community investments beyond the narrow business scope of the company, thus clearly manifesting its parafiscal status.

In a nutshell, the original shareholding cooperatives and their precursors such as the 'village development corporations' were real estate companies, in the sense that the collectively held land rights were transferred to them, but later morphing into holding companies with broad business interests. This was possible because during collectivization, the lowest formal administrative level in the rural areas was often identical with the People's Communes. When the Communes were abolished in the changing of the constitution in 1982, this left the issue of land ownership in a legal limbo, because the meaning of 'collective' was often interpreted as referring to the village level ('cun' 村), but also allowed for other assignments.[44] So, villagers could opt for transferring the property rights to the company, which, in the Fenghuang case, included even replicating the original structure of production teams by distinguishing between the two original levels of production brigade and production team. In many cases, shareholding cooperatives are direct institutional descendants of 'natural villages' and the upper-level administrative unit was projected on a 'associative' cooperative. As we explore in Chapter 7, shareholding cooperatives are often taking the place of a para-governmental unit that fulfils basic administrative tasks in the *shequ*, which is the case in Fenghuang, too.[45] However, the regulatory framework also allows for other forms, which would loosen the relationship between village and company via the stronger role of individual investors, such that the company would almost assume functional similarity with a private enterprise that includes collectively held equity.[46]

This had far-reaching consequences for the relationship with Shenzhen government, because the municipality could no longer claim the land for urban development by simply changing the administrative structure from rural to urban, meaning transforming a *xiang* into a *jiedaobanshichu* 街道办事处 (street committee) and a *cun* into a *shequ* (community), which is today the administrative status of former Wen villages (see previous chapter). Regarding property rights, that is, nationalization, and transforming collective land into state-owned land would have entailed compensation mainly paid to the collectives; in many parts of China, this was cause for local unrest and serious conflicts if compensation was seen as unfair.[47] Paying appropriate compensation was beyond the fiscal means of Shenzhen municipal government, given the sheer number of villages and area affected, so it had to start negotiations with the villagers about the terms of the transformation.

The result was in Fenghuang, as in many other cases, where the government left much of the former collective land under the control of the village to enable profitable uses in accord with the demands of urban development:

That means the shareholding cooperative controls the new urban land use rights on behalf of the municipal government and leases these rights out to tenants according to the stipulations of the law on urban land. Native villagers can also lease the land, but only by paying a smaller 'management fee', because formally they are still seen as the owners of the land; they can then sublease the land to other users. This constellation was undergirded by the concomitant national drive to strengthen village democracy: Fenghuang established a new village committee in 1991, and held the first direct elections on the level of 20 villager groups (*cunmin xiaozu*) whose representatives become members of the village council. Even after transforming the village into a *shequ*, the villagers use the term 'village council' (*cunmin weiyuanhui*) instead of the proper 'residents committee' (*jumin weiyuanhui*). The villager groups were formed on the basis of the production teams of the People's communes. This is important for the transformation of land use rights, since in the early stage of reforms, the rural 'Production Responsibility System' (in which land use rights were contracted out to farm households) was managed by the production teams. However, as we discuss in Chapter 7, there is serious legal tension between the shareholding cooperative and residents committees: Whereas all residents with Shenzhen *hukou* at Fenghuang can vote for the residents committee or can become members, only native villagers have the right to be shareholders at the shareholding cooperative.

Certainly, one cannot claim that these developments are representative for China as a whole, or even for South China. This applies both for the phenomenon of urban villages in general and for the specific outcome of negotiations between municipal governments and villagers.[48] In many cases, villagers, often from sheer ignorance, could not strike a good bargain in their negotiations with the government. However, in the case of the Wen lineage, power and size have clearly mattered in determining the outcome. In that context, it is also important to recognize a further differentiation of property rights that drove the emergence of urban villages: One is the collectively owned rights and the other is the individually held rights on the private houses owned by the families ('zhaiji di'宅基地).[49] The initial trigger of emerging urban villages was often that individual villagers started to rent their houses to migrants and expanded via adding additional storeys, as in Gangxia. This was the model most prevalent in the original SEZ.[50] Eventually, however, this rush into real estate required coordination on the village level, also involving the agricultural land which is collectively owned. In the Fenghuang case, this kind of individual activity was supported by the collective when in 1992 and 1993, 600 allotments of former crop land were rented out to farmers for private investment projects, applying rules based in family size and rents to be paid to the collective (locals recall this step as establishing two roles for them, farmers and businessmen). Again, the previous division into production teams shaped this allocation, based on the physical proximity of private house plots and collective agricultural land held by the teams.

This construct paved the way for the emergence of a new informal property rights regime in housing, since especially in the 'second-line' districts, villages started to invest in high-quality housing estates that combined the different types of land in one comprehensive development project, typically in cooperation with developers. In these complexes, apartments are sold to private buyers, which, however, is illegal according to Chinese law, given the underlying property rights structure. These so-called 'small property rights housings', 'xiaochanquan fang' 小产权房, were traded on a market where the rights were semi-formalized by lawyers acting as mediators, but not enforceable via courts.[51] Via this construct, the shareholding cooperatives, independent from municipal government initiatives for redeveloping urban villages, embarked on creating upscale transformations independently, thus creating new forms of community governance that increasingly involves developers, with some shareholding cooperatives themselves establishing real estate companies (see the Huaide case considered later in this chapter).

It is interesting to compare Shenzhen developments and earlier changes in Hong Kong.[52] In the Hong Kong case, collectively held lineage property was sold to developers and the proceeds were allocated to individuals and to lineage estates, which consequently owned large cash deposits held on bank accounts or invested in safe assets with interest divided annually among lineage members: That means landless lineage trusts emerged. In Shenzhen, the proceeds from transferring land rights to the municipal government were also allocated among individuals and the collectives, that is, the shareholding cooperatives. Different from Hong Kong, the shareholding cooperatives securitize collective land ownership and the villagers obtain rights to dividends. If land use rights are finally sold to developers, the proceeds are divided among individual members and the company, often with the latter keeping the larger share, so that the shareholding cooperative can engage in other business, including real estate in cooperation with the developer on the original land. Yet, a share of land is kept under collective control for public investment, including for ritual purposes: As seen in Chapter 3, a conspicuous example is the construction of public squares on which not only the ancestral hall and a temple would be located, but also other public buildings, such as open-air theatres or administrative offices. At Fenghuang, the ongoing renewal of the 'old village' as a tourist site includes a square of this type.

As mentioned, the Fenghuang shareholding cooperative property rights structure has become entrenched in directly reflecting the original structure of the village, because after the village-wide cooperative was established in 2004, another 20 subsidiaries were created, numbered 1–20.[53] These subsidiaries correspond to the earlier division of the village into production teams, as the previously mentioned 'villager groups', 'cunmin xiao zu' 村民小组. That means there is a two-layered structure with two different types of shares, the *hezuo gu* and the collective shares *jiti gu*. On the level of the subsidiaries, the former amount to roughly 80 per cent of capital. The cooperative shares are owned by individuals and enjoy a degree of fungibility, that is, they can be inherited and traded, although only within the village. The collective shares are not fungible. The subsidiaries have a similar range of business like the parent company, reaching from private equity and real estate to domestic trade.

A typical phenomenon in transitional corporate arrangements during the 1980s and 1990s was that, following the basic idea that investments should create claims on shares, a part of profits was not distributed and turned into additional fixed capital: If the collective invests, the corresponding shares belong to the company. Accordingly, the corporate governance structure of the cooperative shareholding company differs from the stipulations of the national Company Law in putting a special 'Committee for the Management of Collective Capital' (CMCC; 'jiti zichan guanli weiyuanhui' 集体资产管理委员会) below the General Assembly on equal footing with the Supervisory Board and above the Board of Directors.[54] These 'collective shares' play a pivotal role in the governance structure of the shareholding cooperative at Fenghuang, because they reflect the balance between the political and the economic functions of the corporation as well as the balance between villagers' interests and local government. According to the local regulations of Bao'an district government, the chairperson of the CMCC should be the party secretary of the village, who in Fenghuang is also the lineage head.[55] The general regulations of Shenzhen municipality on the role of CMCC stipulate that the CMCC has voting rights in the General Assembly according to the proportion of the collective shares, and that one task of the CMCC is to propose, launch, and monitor activities of the shareholding cooperatives that involve the construction of local infrastructure and other public goods, such as public welfare. These roles have been further formalized in the addenda and edits of the general regulations promulgated in August 2019 (see previous discussion), which assign an autonomous status to the CMCC and its rights to send representatives to the meetings of the regular bodies of corporate governance, in particular the board of directors. The CMCC also directly connects to the supervisory body in the district administration.

Historically, the allocation of shares between the villagers and the 'parent cooperative' was settled at 51 and 49 per cent, respectively; this still applies for the parent cooperative. But since 2017, a new regulation was promulgated that applies now for the subsidiaries: the number of collective shares is limited to a range of between 15 and 20 per cent of total shares in principle. Apparently, this is a safeguard measure so that the interests of the villagers cannot be simply overruled on the group level; after all, an increase of collective shares would automatically imply that fewer dividends could be distributed among the villagers. Dividend distribution has been a contentious issue since the inauguration of the cooperative shareholding model, with many villagers complaining about unfair and unequal allocation.

In other words, the CMCC is the institutional bridge between the original village as an administrative unit and the local government mediated by the Communist Party, thus reflecting the factual status of shareholding cooperatives as para-governmental entities (we discuss this in more detail in Chapter 7). This is manifest in the appearance of the headquarter: To the public, the building in Fenghuang is modest and looks like any other kind of office building, with a large office space on the first floor open to the public. But the floor where the management is located looks like a government office, with all kinds of government paraphernalia, such as national flags, CCP announcements, and public messages by President Xi Jinping. Indeed, after 2004, the cooperatives became institutional mediators between the district government and the original villagers-turned wealthy landlords and more specifically, parafiscal agents in building local infrastructure following a protracted and never-ending bargaining process over the conditions of urban development.[56]

Today, the Fenghuang shareholding cooperative operates as a holding company that has stakes in dozens of other companies that partly were established by the Cooperative in forming partnerships with other investors, or where the cooperative joined an existing company.[57] This includes industrial enterprises in Fenghuang, such as plastics products or garment factories, but also enterprises involved in larger-scale projects that combine business and local infrastructure development, especially in the context of tourism and leisure, and engagements in companies outside Fenghuang. In addition, the shareholding cooperative holds 100 per cent shares in several companies that are directly involved in local development, especially real estate. Thus, the shareholding cooperative is, in fact, the lead unit in a complex system of crossholdings in the local economy and beyond.

Beyond this type of direct business engagements via crossholdings, the shareholding cooperative also operates like a 'business angel', mainly via three channels:

- The first is giving interest-free loans to start-ups, which is mostly in the context of supporting problem households that need social assistance and are incentivized to launch their own business.
- The second is to develop new premises for factories and offer infrastructure at low cost.
- The third is consultancy regarding the whole range of business issues, reaching from legal advice in labour disputes to business intelligence.

If we look at the organization of shareholding cooperatives, the inherent role of lineage structures is salient in many ways. In Fenghuang, one simple fact is the almost complete dominance of Wen lineage members in both the board of the company and the Residents' Committee in Fenghuang village, with one leading Wen holding the double position of managing director and chairman of the Committee; at the same time, he is also the lineage head ('zongzhang' 宗长). In the top management of the shareholding cooperative, of the 13 leading positions only one is held by a non-Wen. The same applies for the 20 subsidiaries, which often involve closer relatives in the leadership structure, as in the original production teams (the chairpersons of the subsidiaries are also the chairpersons of the residents' groups aka villager groups). There are few non-Wen shareholders, mainly representing minority surnames in the original village or external 'talents' that moved to the place early in the 1980s and were co-opted by the lineage, mostly via marriage relations.

It is essential to distinguish the two analytical levels of the formal structure and the individuals that figure as shareholders. The fact springs to the eye that the cooperative shares are very different from stocks of public companies. One reason is that the number of shares has been frozen, even in the sense that shares owned by dead people continue to be registered as such: This is possible because in the original constellation, households were the basic unit. All shareholding cooperatives need to deal with the problem of demographic change and family life cycle, which were already virulent when the cooperatives were set up, such as with respect to the question who counts as original owner (e.g. there were requirements of minimum length of residence in the village, so that returning emigrants cannot make claims on shares). That means, the shares are not individualized in a strict legal sense, but reflect a hierarchy of levels in the village: The parent shareholding cooperative is on the village level, the 20 subsidiaries on the villager group level, each level with collective shares, too, and finally the member shares on the level of the family.

A litmus test for identifying the relationship between lineage and shareholding cooperative is the treatment of women, which in the public regulations emphasize gender equality in the rights allocation.[58] The shares can be inherited, but only via the male line, thus within the lineage, although given the relatively short time since the establishment of the companies, inheritance is still a rare occurrence and even stalled. Apparently, this reflects a tendency to regard the shares as property of the lineage and families as constituent units, formally allocated per capita during the first act of share creation. Of course, this creates tensions with the legal stipulations of gender equality in Chinese family law; so, there have been arrangements that women can hold shares, but they are not allowed to inherit them outside the lineage. This only applies for Wen women, and not for non-Wen women married to Wen males. The crucial reference is the lineage genealogy ('jia pu' 家谱), in which women are not included, and the lists of family property to be inherited. Whereas items such as furniture can be inherited along both lines, the shares, representing land, cannot. Daughters marrying out and assuming the *hukou* of their husband would lose the right of inheritance. Women may obtain a dowry when marrying out or, what one interviewee called a 'face saving' measure, obtain a minor asset (such as a small house) as a gift, but they do not inherit the rights to family owned real estate. The genealogy also determines the voting rights in the shareholder assembly which would be per household, which is represented by the male head. By these means, the formal structure of the shareholding cooperative accommodates lineage rules. This is clearly demonstrated at rituals that are organized and funded by the shareholding cooperative. At Fenghuang, regular rites are held on the conventional festive occasions, such as Chongyang holiday. Important rites are collectively held by the Wen clan at the Wen Tianxiang memorial site at Songgang. At these rites, gender distinctions are highly visible, as women are not allowed to enter the memorial during the rites.

However, this does not diminish the role of the conjugal unit, as discussed previously. We can also view the shareholding cooperative structure from the perspective of the individual household: Households hold shares in different entities that may also include shares in other companies, which may have been launched by the cooperatives, and eventually also shares in regular corporations. A typical Wen family operates like a 'mini-holding', with both husband and wife acting in business: For example, apart from the shares in the parent cooperative that the family holds, they would be shareholders in factories established on the premises created by the villager group, they would own housing or even factories rented out, and would have invested into other business, such as a trading company.

Among the villagers, one group stands out – the group of entrepreneurial leaders. Indeed, when comparing the fate of various shareholding cooperatives, the role of leaders becomes very prominent, because their ideas and values often determine the direction taken, such as quasi-privatization or even strengthening the collective economy.[59] However, from the viewpoint of the lineage structure, this very distinction becomes blurred, because if the 'collective' is perceived like a *jia* in terms of *jiazu*, then family leadership appears almost natural.[60] Apart from being shareholders, the leaders assume the roles of directors and members of the various business entities, and often act as individuals who are also engaged even in companies at other places, thus creating wider-reaching business networks. Overlapping directorates are an important second channel by which the business empire controlled via the lead cooperative is held together. Again, the fact is essential that those individuals are members of the Wen lineage almost exclusively.

To summarize this section, in the case of Fenghuang, the shareholding cooperative apparently reflects social structures that underlie the organization of the village as a single-lineage village. It must be emphasized that this is not evident from the formal institutional set-up of the shareholding cooperative, but becomes evident when we want to explain certain features of the regulations on shares, the factual patterns of leadership, or certain practices. This implies that in practice, shareholding cooperatives would operate as hybrids that manifest both traditional and modern features. For example, on the one hand, women hold shares as long as they hold the village *hukou*, which recognizes women's rights in modern Chinese law. At the same time, the principle of one share, one vote does not apply effectively, since voting is per household, by the representative to the General Assembly. Of course, this allows women to take the position of the leader of the household, which is also possible in traditional practice ('jiazhang' 家长). But mostly, this means that patriarchal lineage rules still apply. The ambivalence between formal organization and lineage reality is sometimes hidden in adopting a neutral organizational language. For example, the shareholding cooperative at Xiasha has various departments designated as 'propaganda department', 'organization department', and so on, but factually the departments are in charge of different central activities related to the lineage, such as the ancestral hall and the cultural square.

4 Collective interests, ritual, and lineage

Based on the observations in the previous section, we argue that the complex structure of the shareholding cooperative mirrors the structure of the Wen lineage in substantial respects. In more explicit terms, the shareholding cooperative apparently is a functional equivalent to the lineage trusts, which were widespread in South China in Imperial times and still play a formal role in the Hong Kong New Territories, especially with reference to the complex internal subdivision. The basic principle of these traditional trusts is that lineages and lineage members jointly invest in various compositions of trust members into joint business endeavours, which often also includes the pursuit of shared goals in terms of public interest, such as when funding a school or providing the means for certain festive events. This combination of public and private interest is also a defining feature of many of the modern shareholding cooperatives. However, one important difference is that via the CMCC, the Communist Party and indirectly the local government has a direct stake and voice in these companies, which represents and strengthens the role of public interest, at least in theory.

The ultimate evidence of the implicit ritual status of the shareholding cooperative is its role in organizing and funding ritual activities and pursuing collective interests. As Christine Trémon argues in her case of a Hakka village, if a shareholding cooperative bears the costs of ritual investments, it shows that they follow the principles of a moral economy of kinship, and do not just maximize profits and search for efficient and effective solutions.[61] However, in the framework of the ritual economy, these two aspects might be very difficult to disentangle. We have already considered the huge temple complex established by the Fenghuang shareholding cooperative. Although this is clearly a central ritual artefact in the community, it also pursues business goals, apparently with success. Similarly, activities that aim at finding solutions for the cemetery issue may happily come along with business ventures, such as in the Wen Hainan project mentioned previously. In other words, often it is possible to advance a purely instrumental interpretation of the ritual aspects. Yet, rituals also manifest features that cannot be explained by reference to instrumental motivations, such as the gender aspect.

As in most other shareholding cooperatives, access to certain public services funded by the cooperative can be limited to the villagers, which is often an indirect, though desired, result of complementary institutions, especially the household registration system.[62] For example, access to local public schools is often limited to registration at the community in which the school is located. Until most recently, this required owning an apartment, which was mostly excluding all migrant workers. As a result, for example, at the well-endowed Gangxia public school mostly Wen children were enrolled, although it is directly bordering the urban village; only since 2013 did the rules change allowing for households renting homes in the community to send children to the school. This kind of differential access can be also implied in paying directly for retirement and health insurance via the cooperative, thus easing the financial burdens only for Wen lineage members.

Hence, we can say that shareholding cooperatives clearly serve the interests of the lineage in those cases where these are strong. Another example is that Wen lineage members have privileged claims on jobs in village-directed companies. In Fenghuang, this even applies for the foreign-invested companies: When the village rented out factory premises in the early stages of development, the leasing contract included the obligation to put one Wen lineage member into the formal position of a 'factory director' ('changzhang' 厂长) and one as a secretary. This provides regular income and work for Wen lineage members aside from their substantial income generated by their shares, and enables them to supervise the activities of foreign investors. Another collective activity is business networking: That means, for example, small businesses in the neighbourhood of a village project are reserved for Wen family members: for example, if you buy an ice cream at a shop near the mountain temple at Fenghuang village, the shop would be owned by a Wen and the ice cream would be produced by a subsidiary of the shareholding cooperative. This also applies for other small-scale businesses: At the temple, the dustmen are mostly Wen, who collect incense sticks from the burners once devotees had left and take them back to Wen factories where they are reprocessed for re-sales. Of course, this is small fry compared to the business networks created by the local elites, including the chairman and party secretary of the cooperative. As mentioned previously, they typically engage in networks of directorships in various companies and act as investors with their private wealth. In this context, affinal relations are of significance, a pattern that could also be observed in historical times for elite lineages.

One way to disentangle the complex relationship between interest and ritual is to interpret the Fenghuang case along the lines of the tripartite view on lineages championed by Zheng Zhenman. We can say that, first, we find the inheritance lineage, which corresponds to the original surname group in the village. Here, we observe a clear tension between the existing legal regulations on property and inheritance and lineage practices, which might eventually threaten the sustainability of this lineage, especially if alienation of shares would become possible via the in-marrying wives and out-marrying daughters' lines. In this regard, the household registration system becomes of paramount importance, because formally the claims on shares are not based on lineage membership, but on *hukou*. For example, as women have a Fenghuang *hukou*, they have rights to shares, and when a woman marries out, she might try to keep her *hukou* and thereby keep the share. But at the same time, the construct of collective capital keeps the shareholding cooperative intact as a unit affiliated with the local lineage, again via the *hukou* system. Since collective shares are not fungible even within the village, they protect the shareholding cooperative against the risk of dissolution.

Next, one can safely characterize the shareholding cooperative as a core institution of a control-subordination lineage. Yet, its scope does not extend beyond Fenghuang. As we will discuss in Chapter 7, the shareholding cooperative is a parafiscal institution, implying a symbiotic relationship between lineage power and government which is ambiguous in terms of its status at this type of lineage. The core question is the role of the party, which leads to consider the role of lineage elites. One problem in assessing the status of shareholding cooperative is to understand the internal processes of social differentiation. Different from the egalitarian imposition of socialist institutions on the villages, shareholding cooperatives are often led by a small group of powerful leaders who turn into wealthy businessmen, as mentioned previously. They are often co-opted by the CCP via membership, assuming the position of party secretary or assignments to political bodies of the municipality. This results in ambiguous roles, as the leaders may eventually pursue interests which do not fall in line with the majority of villagers' interests. In other words, 'control and subordination' may apply mainly within the lineage. A case in point is Xiasha, where villagers even staged a protest against their high-profile leader in 2016, claiming that the shareholding cooperative does not distribute a fair share of dividends, and that profits are partly channelled into uses that involve private business of leaders. Even a court case was filed, but later apparently withdrawn. Rumours spread that the leader even had close connections to Hong Kong triads.[63]

This leads us to consider the third dimension, the contractual lineage. We will discuss this in more detail in Chapter 6; suffice to state here that one channel by which business interests may extend beyond the local community, even possibly to their detriment, is the connections that can be created via shared surname, thereby teaming up with 'relatives' in other places, even other countries, to pursue business deals. The Xiasha Huang are very different from the Fenghuang Wen in this respect: The latter do not engage in much business with other Wen branches as they declare, whereas the former actively pursue cross-regional connections and position Shenzhen as a central place where wider Huang business networks may be crafted. Although we do not have firm evidence, this clearly may drive a wedge between the larger Huang circles, the 'contractual lineage', and the local lineage.

If we compare shareholding cooperatives across various urban villages, there is indeed considerable variety, which may partly concur with subethnic identities, especially Hakka. Hakka communities in the region had a strongly collectivist culture, hardened by centuries-long effort to secure land in Guangdong and the so-called 'Hakka wars' in the 19th century. This culture was physically embodied in the circular walled compounds of Hakka villages, typically single surname in this region, centring on the ancestral hall. Until today, Hakka claim to be especially prone to scholarly pursuits and striving for office, even when considering businesspeople. In some cases, this attitude is reflected in the strong public spirit of managing shareholding cooperative. A famous early example is Nanling, a showcase of rapid development in Longgang district even before the unification of inner and outer areas.[64] Whereas the archetypical urban villages in the SEZ struggled to overcome blind alleys such as morphing into red-light districts, Nanling analysed its weakness, a remote location for foreign-invested enterprises, and decided to pursue a vigorous policy of building infrastructure, and most significantly, launched a so-called 'New Population Policy' which aimed at attracting migrants with skills needed for industrial development. They even decided to open top management positions in the shareholding cooperative to outsiders. However, even this step cannot be interpreted as a deviation from lineage traditions, since in Imperial China lineage businesses often employed non-family members in management, and even adopted non-kin for that purpose. In this sense, offering *hukou* to talented migrants is functionally equivalent to adoption.

Hence, internal stratification of lineages may not jeopardize the collective nature of shareholding cooperative. There are examples where this nature is most visible, as in one of the richest urban villages, Huaide, of Pan lineage next to Fenghuang. Huaide shareholding cooperative is one of the most developed shareholding cooperatives in Shenzhen: In 2009, it span off a 100 per cent subsidiary, Huaide Real Estate, which mainly concentrates developing large areas of Fuyong district, in the neighbourhood of the international airport and the conventions centre, and also is engaged in large-scale area development projects such as the Daqianhai project in Nanshan (nicknamed the 'New Manhattan'). Its main operations, however, concentrate on developing a low-carbon integrated urban community at Huaide. Evidently, in separating this company from the shareholding cooperative, two entities were distinguished, one exclusively focusing on business operations, and the other, the owner, being the original shareholding cooperative merging business and collective interests.

A case in point is the public announcement board placed outside the community centre, just opposite of the local training site for Lions' Dance and martial arts. The board offers rich information about the financial situation of the shareholding cooperative, including daily copies of transactions of the bank account and loans extended to outsiders (including Fenghuang Wen). There are strict regulations on the use and calculations of profits and distribution of dividends, especially in case of losses. Decisions must be subject to the scrutiny and the consent of the shareholder association. The corporate charter of the shareholding cooperative includes caps on the individual accumulation of cooperative shares. Although fungibility applies within the village, within one year, individuals are not allowed to transfer a volume of more than 5 per cent of the total value of cooperative shares; if they accumulate more than 2 per cent of all shares, they are obliged to hand over the surplus shares to the collective to be transformed into collective shares. That means the regulations clearly impose a certain degree of distributional equality among the lineage members. In fact, the regulations clearly stipulate that the 'cooperative shares' are derivatives of the 'collective shares', which amounts to 40.03 per cent of shares. The Huaide regulations also manifest other similarities with what was said about Fenghuang, such as assigning the voting rights to the households, not to the individual shareholders.

When we visited Huaide in 2018, a major renovation project was being prepared, during which villagers would move into new apartments for free. The allocation process is transparent and follows egalitarian principles, and the villagers receive subsidies for furnishing the rooms. Huaide is an urban village which looks like the prosperous villages in the New Territories, with many three-storey buildings and tightly regulated access to cars and parking. The central place has a beautiful pond and public garden. The similarity with villages in the New Territories reflects that many Pan went there already before 1949 and returned after reforms started. The village community agreed to impose similar regulations on buildings as in Hong Kong, akin to the 'dinghu' policy. This was deliberately done to constrain the demonstration of wealth and status by competitively building lavish houses, and to avoid the commercial exploitation of private houses for building apartments blocks for migrant workers. The original Pan village residential area is clearly separated by turnpikes from the area which is further developed, originally the collectively owned agricultural land.[65]

The Pan expressively emphasizes their lineage identity as defined in the lineage rules (*jiafeng*) and traditions. There are regular activities and meetings that discuss and decide issues related to ritual questions, such as the genealogy. The Pan recently created a surname association to deepen their relations with other Pan branches worldwide. The collective nature of the lineage is manifest in the 1998 adoption of rules for self-government, which, as mentioned previously, give all Pan rights to participate in decisions and monitor shareholding cooperative operations.

In sum, many shareholding cooperatives actively pursue collective interests of the village community aka lineage, and they explicitly refer to shared descent as a means to creating the necessary cohesion and shared identity. Indeed, as Trémon argues, the high ancestor becomes a strong symbol of that cohesion, especially if this person, as typically the case, assumes almost mythical status with moral excellence, such as Wen Tianxiang, who, as often happens with historical personalities, has morphed into a god worshipped at the temple, as we have seen.[66] Cultural descent can become almost literal, as in the case of Huanggang and Shuiwei villages, both locations of Zhuang lineage. The Zhuang certainly move beyond genealogical truth when claiming philosopher Zhuang Zi as their high ancestor, yet this reference sends strong signals about civilizational aspirations. As we will discuss in Chapter 7, these aspirations of local lineages are supported by the Communist Party, both locally and on the national level. Many shareholding cooperatives have emerged as a para-governmental entity that assumes important administrative tasks in Shenzhen municipality, while their organizational culture is based on lineage traditions.

5 Conclusion

One problem in assessing the relationship between shareholding cooperative and lineages in Shenzhen is the pivotal role of land. This is also true for the New Territories: Some observers argue that the British land policy and the privileges given to the New Territories have been a major factor in stabilizing local lineages. This is especially true for the sustainability of global networks of lineages, because even younger members living abroad may still be motivated to claim rights on valuable land in Hong Kong. In this view, interest may be stronger than ritual in explaining the continuity of lineages.[67]

Yet, in Collins' framework, this is not a contradiction. In the Shenzhen case, what drives lineage revival is the hybrid nature of the property rights system and the identity politics of a rapidly urbanizing former rural area. It is important, as we have seen, to avoid treating lineages as collective actor sui generis. From the perspective of individuals, the primordial unit remains the family and the household, which is active in many business pursuits, including their role as shareholders in the shareholding cooperative. Yet, when it comes to negotiations about profitable uses of land rights, the collective power of the village in its negotiations with the municipal government is essential also for the individuals: The lineage becomes an important part of individual social capital. For stabilizing and expressing this social capital, ritual actions are efficacious means, thus confirming to all members that they can trust in the original community. In addition, the lineage community is also a factor in maintaining certain values and beliefs that stay at the centre of the Chinese family and its undergirding value system and its driving aspirations.[68]

This does not mean that there are no conflicts and tensions. In fact, rural collectivization until 1978 was accompanied by severe and often hidden struggles between different branches of the original lineages, hidden beyond the surface of socialist institutions.[69] This rivalry is continuing until today: As we mentioned in the previous chapter, a Wen branch moved to neighbouring Baishixia because of serious tension over land allocation when a new highway was built. The Fenghuang Wen also keep a distance to Wen associations, because there was a quarrel about ritual activities in the past when the Fenghuang Wen felt to be discriminated against. Against this backdrop, we need to interpret the lineage revival in another way: Reforms relieved much pressure on individuals in organizing the relationship between private and public interest. That means the revival of lineages should not be conceived as a strengthening of collective organization, but as the emergence of an effective balance between individual and collective, thus enabling individual action potential via building social capital. In this view, individual interest is a major motivation in the revival of lineages, but that does not mean that ritual is merely instrumental. Where ritual really works, it creates the necessary level of trust and commitment that allows for a combination of collective and individual interests also to the benefit of the latter. This is exactly what is stated in Collins' approach to ritual and markets.

There are many and diverse forms how this is negotiated and finally instantiated in specific actions and forms of expressing ritual commitments. In the Huaide case, the separation between the shareholding cooperative and the real estate company means that the latter operates free from all ritual concerns. Ritual concerns centre on the internal scene of the village, even separated from the rest of the territory by turnpikes. In Huaide, as noticed by many observers, the 'spirit' of the Pan lineage is embodied in the unique architectural layout and design of the village, embodying egalitarian ideas and public interest. In contrast, the Fenghuang shareholding cooperative created a massive temple complex that combines ritual and business, yet again signalling the shared identity of the village and its capacity to act collectively. It would be misleading to confront these two cases; they are just alternative creative ways to find a synthesis between various functional and ritual demands and concerns.

Collins' approach also helps to clarify the relationship between kinship and ritual. If we conceive of kinship as a specific emotional attitude towards others with whom individuals share an identity that is based on relatedness, the Chinese case shows how ritual is mobilized to create such attitudes, ultimately rooted in particular emotional stances that are deemed defining features of being 'kin'. That means we would not start out from given kinship relations, but approach these as cultural constructs by ritual action. In other words, what kinship means in the Chinese concept is not fixed, and there would be no static 'tradition' that undergoes 'revival' today. It is true for both past and present that ritual was not a medium of fixing kinship relation, but a medium of adaptive and creative responses to local contexts, leveraging individual and collective action potential via producing kinship relations. At the same time, however, in the Chinese case, this was also embedded into a larger political and ideological context in Imperial Confucianism. Again, this does not simply mean that the political and cultural centre shaped kinship, but that it also offered symbolic means for its creative construction while contributing to the maintenance of social and political order at large. Apparently, this also applies for our Shenzhen case, despite radical revolutionary transformations in the 20th century. This is what we will scrutinize in Chapter 7.

Notes

1 Compare Wang (2016).
2 Kawagusa (2016). The phenomenon has also attracted the attention of Chinese researchers; see Dai and Zhang (2014).
3 On their historical role, see Baker (1977).
4 Compare Wong (2015) and Wang (2016) who argue that the phenomenon of lineage-based shareholding cooperatives as business ventures is unique to the Pearl River Delta, perhaps even for Shenzhen. Japanese anthropologists have contributed substantial research on lineage revival cross China. The edited volume Segawa and Kawagusa (2016) includes fieldwork in provinces beyond South-eastern China. Kipnis (2017) ponders the survival of rural kinship conceptions in an urban setting in Shandong. The work that comes closest to ours is Trémon (2014, 2015a, 2015b) who studied a Hakka lineage in Shenzhen and arrives at conclusions quite similar to ours. Many other contributions, most notably Wang (2016), notice the role of lineages, but do not flesh out more anthropological detail. Regarding property rights, most scholars just refer to 'informal institutions' without focusing on their specific nature; see, for example, Lai, Chan et al. 2017; Lai, Wang et al. 2017.
5 Influential contributions were Freedman (1967) and Baker (1979). For an exemplary critical assessment, see Stafford (2000).
6 Chun (2000); Cheung (2016).
7 Nissim (2016); Watson (1985).
8 Watson (1975).
9 Nissim (2016: 127ff).
10 Ebrey (1991); Faure (2007).
11 Faure (2007) is the authoritative monograph on this.
12 A seminal synthesis is Gates (1996).
13 Siu (1989).
14 Mann (1987); Duara (1988).
15 Zelin (2004, 2009).
16 Freedman (1967: 83ff); Watson (1985).
17 A landmark contribution in this approach is Zhou (2014).
18 For an extensive survey in Shenzhen *guangfu* surname groups and clans, see http://bbs.tianya.cn/post-free-5960713-1.shtml, accessed November 21, 2019.
19 This is also noticed by Watson (2004).
20 Parish and Whyte (1987: 304f); Stacey (1983).
21 Potter and Potter (1990: 261ff, 334).
22 This is implied by the analysis of Prosterman (2013), although he does not explore the historical similarities.
23 On this distinction in customary law, see Kroker (1959) and Chen and Myers (1976). On similar terminology in China today, see Tan (2010: 171, 234).
24 Stacey (1983).
25 Madsen (1984).
26 Greenhalgh and Winckler (2005); Greenhalgh (2012); Eberstadt (2011).
27 On the historical etymology, see Ebrey and Watson (1986).
28 Fei (1947). A similar view on *jia* also prevails in Western literature; for example, Gates (1996).
29 Cohen (1970). On continuities in rural China, see Cohen (1992).
30 Wong (1985).
31 For an illuminating discussion, see Chun (2000).
32 Gui (2014) distinguishes between 'horizontal' and 'vertical' lineage, referring to a similar distinction between conviviality and ritual desent.
33 This was already emphasized by Freedman (1967).

34 It must be noticed that the term is almost a technical term. Local people rarely use it; instead, they would mostly refer to themselves as people of surname X, or as descendants of ancestor X etc. *Zongzu* is the term that is used to refer to this type of group in general, thus focusing on the ritual aspect.
35 Baker (1977).
36 On 'high ancestors' see Cohen (2017). On the relationship between surname and subethnic distinctions, see Inazawa (2016).
37 We cannot go into the details of the anthropological debate about kinship, which after Schneider (1984) almost resulted in a complete deconstruction and a sort of conceptual nihilism. The state of the debate is succinctly summarized in Sahlins (2013), which builds on seminal contributions such as Carsten (2004). The modern view on kinship appears to recognize its independence from any biological concept of consanguinity, but does not result in postmodern arbitrariness, because once kinship has emerged in its specific cultural forms, it goes along with distinct emotional states, practices, and commitments which clearly distinguish kin relations from other relations.
38 Zheng (2001).
39 Bach (2017). Economists therefore often argue that state-owned land leases amount to a private property regimen; see, for example, Clarke (2014).
40 Po (2008); Trappel (2011).
41 https://baike.baidu.com/item/深圳经济特区股份合作公司条例/16824926; http://www.szrd.gov.cn/szrd_zyfb/szrd_zyfb_cwhgb/201909/t20190906_18200655.htm (both accessed November 22, 2019).
42 As an example, see https://xin.baidu.com/company_detail_30967564392082?fl=1&castk=LTE%3D, accessed November 2, 2019.
43 For example, Nanling village, Longgang district, a Hakka community, early adopted as so-called 'new immigration policy' acknowledging the dearth of qualified personnel in the village, and even gave *hukou* to professionals employed in its cooperative, see Liu (2002).
44 Ho (2001, 2013).
45 The merging of business organization and village administration has been noticed already in the seminal work by Hu (2007) and is a phenomenon that can be found in many Chinese villages.
46 Kan (2019) has a detailed comparison between two cases that represent the two basic variants.
47 World Bank (2014: 206f). For a famous example in Guangdong, see He and Xue (2014).
48 Wang (2016: 141ff); Tang (2015); Wong (2015).
49 Lai, Chan and Choy (2017).
50 Chung and Unger (2013).
51 Lai, Zheng et al. (2017).
52 Chan (2001).
53 Information on the shareholding structure and the leadership of the shareholding cooperative can be obtained via the database Tianyancha 天眼查(see https://baike.baidu.com/item/%E5%A4%A9%E7%9C%BC%E6%9F%A5).
54 https://baike.baidu.com/item/深圳经济特区股份合作公司条例/16824926
55 Shenzhen shi Bao'an qu (2018).
56 Po (2012).
57 See Tianyancha database (endnote 53).
58 Zhou (2014) is a rich monograph on another case study, a shareholding cooperative in Guangzhou, which shows many similarities to the situation in Fenghuang.
59 Wang (2016: 96).

60 Kan (2019) reports for her case that the more privatized shareholding cooperative is characterized by the villagers as 'family-style management' 'jiazu shi guanli' 家族式管理.
61 Trémon (2014a).
62 For a comparable case in Yantian analysed in much detail, see Saich and Hu (2012).
63 http://beiliu.gxorg.com/20170915/83.html, accessed March 6, 2019.
64 Liu (2002).
65 http://ibaoan.sznews.com/content/2019-07/17/content_22262981.htm, accessed September 3, 2019.
66 Trémon (2014).
67 Watson (2004).
68 On this complex question, see Sangren (2013).
69 The classic is Madsen (1984) and Chan et al. (2009) who studied a village in Shenzhen, presumably (it is kept anonymous).

5 Ritual as means, medium, and mode of entrepreneurship

1 Shenzhen: Culture in a global city

For many years, Shenzhen has been characterized as a Chinese melting pot geared towards high speed innovation and globalization. At the same time, however, concerns were soon raised about the cultural identity of the place. Earlier, the local media launched debates about what it means to be a 'Shenzhener'.[1] This reflects the status of the city as an immigrant society, with Chinese from all provinces and from all social strata moving there in search of economic opportunity. As we have seen, however, this status of a 'multi-subcultural' place also shaped pre-1949 history. Therefore, many local intellectuals and local leaders contribute to the discussion on Shenzhen identity against the background of Hong Kong as a neighbouring place of similar melting pot characteristics.[2] The question of what constitutes 'Shenzhen culture' is taken seriously by local CCP leaders: For example, Wang Jingsheng, the head of the Shenzhen CCP propaganda department, has been a prolific writer and editor of books and pamphlets about cultural issues in Shenzhen.[3] Even within the domain of CCP propaganda, this seems a somewhat ambiguous issue, however. Two important museums send a different message about the specific relationship between CCP ideology and Shenzhen. Whereas the flagship Shenzhen museum clearly highlights the role of central leaders in promoting Shenzhen development, the new reform museum at Shekou extolls the leading role of Yuan Geng not only in the early history of the SEZ, but also in shaping Shenzhen spirit in the longer run: A former spy and local Hakka.

One view is epitomized in the so-called 'ten principles of Shenzhen' formulated by Wang Jingsheng, of which the first is the famous quote from Yuan Geng, leader of the initial launch of the SEZ, 'time is money, efficiency is life', which invokes a kind of capitalist business culture without any reference to Chinese tradition. Instead, a new tradition is emphasized, which is the tradition of reform and opening, led by the CCP.[4] This includes all kinds of roles that Shenzhen has taken in spearheading reforms, operating as a laboratory of testing measures such as liberalizing the labour market. The role of migrant workers is only highlighted in a very generic way, coming close to the 'model worker' image in traditional socialist propaganda, without, for example, telling the history of urban villages. Similarly, there are efforts to develop a model of 'Shenzhen businessman' image, such as by the consultant and author Lao Heng: He cites Vanke founder Wang Shi who uses the term 'contractual spirit' ('qiyue jingshen' 契约精神) to describe the emerging business culture in Shenzhen and thinks that this matches with the needs and challenges of a 'society of strangers' ('mosheng ren shehui' 陌生人社会).[5] Interestingly, this effort seems to stand in the tradition of distinguishing different types of regional business cultures in China, such as in the reform era Wenzhou, but also in a longer historical perspective, distinguishing between regions such as Jiangsu and Guangdong in terms of business norms and practices: Accordingly, Lao Heng speaks of 'shen shang' 深商 as a newly emerging type.[6]

In this chapter, we approach these discussions from a different angle, because they sometimes point to the phenomenon that we will explore: Businesspeople are concerned about their cultural identity, and they may launch efforts in constructing and expressing it. In recent times, this works together with the diagnosis of Shenzhen leadership that the previously sketched image of Shenzhen may need to be grounded in broader and deeper cultural contexts. One manifestation of this is the growing interest in the pre-1949 history and the many investments into recovering this history in artefacts, exhibitions, and cultural events. For example, Shenzhen museum today may still not cover urban villages after 1978, but has many installations about the history of local communities such as Hakka. There are many initiatives that involve also the broader public such as guided tours that aim at reconstructing local history and which eventually also trigger activism of protecting cultural heritage. For example, a local publisher recently published a volume on Guangming town 光明镇, part of Guangming xinqu 光明新区 bordering Dongguang, which is mostly praised for being a model area of modern urban development. At the same time, the traditional village still exists, with many historical sites, including several ancestral halls of various local lineages, as the place historically was a multi-surname settlement. Some of the buildings are centuries old, and the local population includes rare surnames such as Mai 麦 (Cant. Mak), reflecting the deep history of migration.[7]

The intensifying efforts of positioning Shenzhen as a place with cultural significance must be seen against the backdrop of the general strategy to develop Shenzhen as a 'global city'. The diagnosis is that the old modernist strategy has many flaws. The still fragile status of Shenzhen as a global city is evident in the recent A.T. Kearney 'Global Cities Report' where Shenzhen is lingering in the middle field. The report distinguishes between two different indices, one is current performance and one is future outlook.[8]

In the first index, Shenzhen fell back from the position 65 in 2012 to 79 in 2018, and compares with cities such a Bangalore, Ho Chi Minh, or Caracas. Hong Kong has been consistently on position 5; Shanghai is on position 19 and could improve 2 positions. This clearly reveals that Shenzhen development is stalled, in spite of huge efforts at urban renewal. The picture becomes even bleaker when we consider the second index on 'outlook': Shenzhen lost two positions (from 50 to 52) between 2016 and 2018. This compares with rapid progress of other cities: For example, Ho Chi Minh city advanced 14 positions or Nagoya 13 positions. The 2018 issue of the report focuses on China and the fact that six Chinese cities have been newly included in the index: Changsha, Foshan, Ningbo, Tangshan, Wuxi, and Yantai. For example, Wuxi entered on position 130 of the performance index, but on position 57 in the outlook index. Among Chinese cities already included in the index, Xi'an could improve 19 positions in the outlook index and is now on position 66. Obviously, there is a strong urban dynamic in China, but Shenzhen is losing steam in comparison with others.

The A.T. Kearney index follows established wisdom about what determines the status of a global city. A core determinant of performance is business activity, especially regarding services that create business connectivity, as we have already seen. This is mostly finance and producer services. The other major components are information networks, cultural activity, and political engagement. In the outlook index, the components emphasize innovation and entrepreneurship, well-being, economic growth, and governance. Surprisingly, in related research, Shenzhen appears to be somewhat inward-looking: A telling indicator is the list of city pairs in the world economy that are tightly connected via communication and service links published by the 'Globalization and World Cities Research Network': Among the set of tightly interacting cities, Shenzhen only appears once, and the partner is Beijing.[9] In comparison, Hong Kong is one of the most connected cities in the world, linking up with all other major global cities. Surprisingly though, Shenzhen is not included, which reflects the fact that these data are based on information of multinational corporations.

The concept of a 'global city' suggests the idea that there is a limited number of urban places in the world that transcend the role of cities in a national context.[10] Global cities are central nodes in the global economy with specific characteristics, such as a high share of business services and finance in local GDP, or the presence of a global economic elite recruited internationally, which in turn generates the demand for high-quality and often high-end consumer culture, reaching from luxury goods and fashion to influential creative industries and cultural centres, such as the world leading opera houses. This seems to point towards a certain uniformity in the appearance of global cities, and indeed, high-end shopping malls may feature the same luxury goods and companies across the globe. But research has also shown that global cities build on strong path-dependencies even in seemingly uniform sectors such as finance: History matters. Global cities often rely on distinct comparative advantages that are also related to their cultural roots.

In addition, culture matters in shaping the experience of living in a global city and is also a major attraction for short-term visitors. However, culture also requires a certain level of liberal political environment and governance structures: For example, although Istanbul holds a strong position at 26 in the A.T. Kearney performance index and could improve 11 positions since 2012, it suffered a blow in the outlook index despite huge infrastructural efforts, and lost 16 positions, now on position 96. This clearly reflects the political climate and governance conditions in Turkey today.

In emphasizing the role of business elites, the picture of global cities in the public distorts another fact about global cities in recent years: Global cities also have a large share of low-income population, often belonging to the group of immigrants. They mostly work in the services sector, from cleaning to taxi driving and household services, with a high share of women. This is a major factor in creating risks for social stability, as the gap between low- and high-income groups is often much larger in global cities than in the national average of the countries where they locate. Yet, at the same time, the diversity of cultures contributes to the positive experiences of global cities in terms of openness, lifestyles, and inspiration. Therefore, in the past decades, successful global cities have also developed proactive approaches to governing cultural diversity, often under the heading of 'diversity management' and inclusive social welfare policies.

To sum up, recent assessments of the status of Shenzhen as a global city have highlighted that its modernist image fails to mobilize the cultural resources that are indispensable for achieving this status. This has motivated much action on the part of the municipal government in reinventing Shenzhen as a place with history. But at the same time, this has not only created space for grassroots-level entrepreneurship, but seems to go along with an independent effort of many entrepreneurs to express and explore their own cultural identity. Entrepreneurs are the drivers of economic dynamics in Shenzhen. They include various social groups and strata. On first sight, however, their role in the revival of cultural traditions may be judged as marginal. On the one hand, many of the villagers turned rentiers, enjoying the flow of rents generated by the collective land rights. On the other hand, most of the entrepreneurs in the lead industries are immigrants with a specific background, often highly educated people from other provinces, mostly graduates of universities located in metropolitan areas. This group is secularly minded, their families have few extensions into wider kin relations, and they mostly subscribe to a modernist and secular worldview.

It is difficult to ascertain how far this view can survive further scrutiny, because we have no demographic data in this dimension. The 'rentier' perspective on villagers is partly misleading, since many families have developed a range of entrepreneurial aspirations, at least as investors across various businesses, which includes the support of entrepreneurial activities of others, as we have seen in the previous chapter. Further, as we noticed earlier, there is a subgroup of business elites in the villages who indeed take initiative in projects that revive local traditions, and who increasingly also have higher educational levels.[11] But if we consider the size of the entire native village population, their numbers would not be representative for Shenzhen.

This argument overlooks the internal differentiation of the migrant population. Apart from the tech migrant, there is the huge group of Chaoshan immigrants, many of them working in the construction sector in the 1980s, and later emerging as a strong business community in Shenzhen. As we shall see, the Chaoshan entrepreneurs played a significant role in the development of the vast network of small-scale suppliers to the electronics industry, and specifically in the emergence of the *shanzhai* phenomenon, the unique business phenomenon of creative copying in Shenzhen. In demographic terms, this is a group of very substantial size, roughly about two million people. Chaoshan subculture manifests many phenomena that are relevant for understanding the ritual economy in Shenzhen, such as the role of popular religion. There are other groups that can be included in the analysis in a similar fashion, such as Hakka entrepreneurs from other places, especially within Guangdong province, such as the core Hakka region, Meixian county. In other words, if we consider immigrant entrepreneurs, there is considerable subcultural diversity far beyond the 'tech' type.

Even when considering the more advanced part of the economy, we cannot generally exclude it from the ritual economy. Although it is quite rare that tech companies might engage in traditional rituals, there is the important question of how far corporate culture may be ritualized, mostly in the sense of modernist rituals that may show no direct connection to traditional ritual.[12] In fact, the notion of entrepreneur may also include ritual innovation. This observation helps to narrow down the focus of this chapter. When we look at the relationship between entrepreneurs and ritual economy, we can approach this is in a more general way, or indeed concentrate on what might be dubbed 'ritual entrepreneurship'.[13] As a first approximation, we define ritual entrepreneurs as entrepreneurs who take entrepreneurial action in the ritual domain. In Collins' theoretical framework, these are actors that drive the causal interdependence between ritual and market. This includes all forms of ritual, reaching from investing in the construction of a new temple to conducting group weddings in the company as a manifestation of corporate culture. However, in this chapter, we concentrate on ritual entrepreneurship that directly relates to the local contexts, lineages, ritual spaces, and subethnic groups.

2 Introducing the concept of 'ritual entrepreneurship'

In our theoretical framework, ritual is a medium to create, express, and sustain culture. In contemporary China, entrepreneurs often pursue cultural endeavours in the broadest sense, such as setting up public libraries with free access in the urban areas or supporting the establishment of a new temple in the rural areas. Recently, the concept of 'cultural entrepreneurship' has been suggested in Chinese studies, in the context of research on similar phenomena in Republican China and in Chinese emigrant communities in Southeast Asia.[14] Christopher Rea argues that cultural entrepreneurship is a phenomenon specific to the Chinese setting in the first place, but also extends to other societies.[15] A similar concept, employing the same term, has also been independently introduced in research about former socialist countries in general, here referring to the more abstract idea that in times of rapid socio-economic and institutional change, cultural innovation driven by entrepreneurial action, often also by political entrepreneurs, is a common phenomenon.[16] Indeed, under the conditions in Republican China, after the collapse of the Empire and facing social upheavals in many ways, both approaches easily converge. For sure, the same applies for China today, and especially for a place like Shenzhen.

Accordingly, in this chapter, we employ a two-step specification of the term. We start out from the generic notion of cultural entrepreneurship, and then consider specifications for China. We claim that this specification includes one peculiar phenomenon, which is cultural entrepreneurship in terms of activating and promoting certain forms of ritual action. In other words, we do not treat cultural entrepreneurship but ritual entrepreneurship as possibly being specific to China.

The term 'cultural entrepreneurship' is also used in the context of the cultural industries, referring to any kind of business-oriented activity on the part of creative actors, such as artists marketing their creations or museums adopting business-like strategies for attracting visitors.[17] That means actors are first defined as operating in the creative sector and then as 'entrepreneurs'. We reverse this order: A 'cultural entrepreneur' is a businessperson who becomes active in the cultural domain in the broadest sense. This does not exclude artists in so far as they engage in economic activities, which has always been the case, such as the workshops of the Cranachs or Shakespeare's theatre. Yet, we normally assume that in these cases, the artistic motivation is the first driver of cultural entrepreneurship. However, in the Chinese case, this distinction may be difficult to maintain as the role may blur for certain types of activities. In Republican times, this was also salient. Chinese entrepreneurs often pursued broader cultural concerns of entrepreneurs, such as establishing a certain brand as part and parcel of larger efforts of changing cultural practices in China, or explicitly communicating the personality of the entrepreneur in cultural terms.[18]

Christopher Rea distinguishes between three types of entrepreneurs (cultural personality, tycoon, collectives) and establishes historical linkages to the merging of the roles of scholar and merchant in the Late Qing society.[19] The distinction between merchants and scholars in Imperial China was mainly a ritual differentiation, so that we can interpret the merging of roles as a ritual innovation. However, this allows for an important turn in the argument: The historical connection to the scholar-merchant synthesis establishes a bias towards elites, whereas cultural entrepreneurship is by no means an elitist concept, as we saw. Reflecting upon this, many other phenomena of cultural entrepreneurship in Imperial China spring to the mind, such as the activation of the symbolic capital of lineages for launching business activities beyond agriculture (i.e. land estates). What is common in these activities is the economic use of ritual, or the 'ritual economy'.

If we refer to culture in general, our theory deployed in Chapter 2 excludes those activities in the creative sector that remain idiosyncratic, in the sense of being expressions of individual cultural creativity without necessarily adding or changing the stock of cultural capital in a certain society. This is also implied by the definition: If an individual piece of art does not touch upon or does not affect aspects of the 'constructed identity of a community' via its reception in society, they do not fall under our notion of cultural entrepreneurship. This may also relate to the issue of 'high culture', as changes of popular culture, triggered by entrepreneurial action, may be more significant in affecting shared collective identities than products of 'high culture', which may only slowly, and often only after acts of authorization by cultural elites, become 'essential' for the identity of a community, being merely idiosyncratic acts of cultural creativity at the origin.

Thus, the concept of cultural entrepreneurship builds on the following elements:

- Cultural entrepreneurs deliberately aim at adding to the existing stock of cultural capital in society by pursuing their economic goals, such as creating products with a cultural dimension or investing into non-profit projects complementary to their business;
- They build on cultural capital to extend and strengthen the social capital (e.g. reputation and fame) that they mobilize in their entrepreneurial activity, thereby also reinforcing culturally mediated identities in their communities;
- And more specifically, they rely on the existing social imaginaries to express their individual identities, thereby also creating an impact on the society at large, if their pursuits meet broader resonance.

As argued, we suggest approaching cultural entrepreneurship as ritual entrepreneurship in the Chinese context. Indeed, Collins introduces the concept of a 'market' for ritual interactions, which ties up with the market for goods. In the Chinese context, this focuses our attention on cultural entrepreneurship in the domains of kinship, religion, and subethnic identities. Yet, in doing this, we do not suggest that all cultural entrepreneurship in China is ritual entrepreneurship. We only distinguish between the generic term of cultural entrepreneurship that applies across all societies, and for which we can identify many examples in the Chinese context too, especially in the context of modernization as process of globalizing Chinese culture, and those forms of cultural entrepreneurship which may be conceived as specifically Chinese and which therefore also bear certain continuities between past and present.

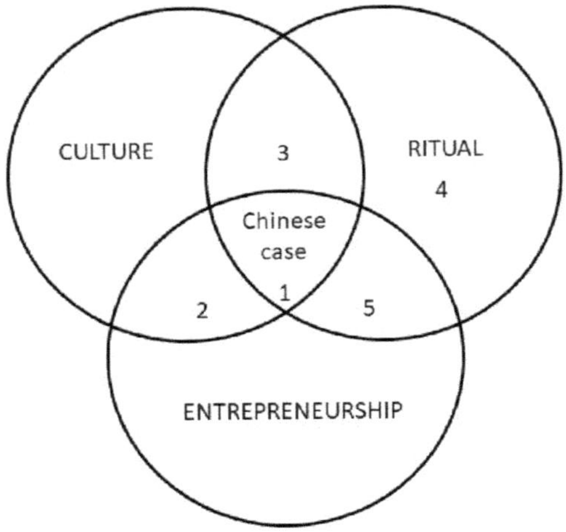

Figure 5.1 Dimensions of cultural entrepreneurship and the Chinese case of ritual entrepreneurship.

In Figure 5.1, we systematize our conceptual clarification in distinguishing three conceptual domains:

- The first is entrepreneurship in the economy, which mostly is not concerned with cultural issues, but with creating and operating markets of products and services (which includes cultural goods, so there is overlap with the cultural domain);
- The second is culture, which extends beyond the economy and encompasses all activities of sense-making that relate to creating shared identities of communities, including society at large, and which is partly created and reproduced by ritual activities;
- The third is ritual, which partly goes beyond culture and economy and includes all activities that create and maintain ritual interactions by individuals, groups, and society at large, and which are not tied to goals beyond ritual (such as creating efficient organizations).

The three domains overlap with each other as dyads and in the centre of the diagram involving all three together (see numbers in diagram): This is where we locate Chinese cultural entrepreneurs as ritual entrepreneurs (1). Apart from that, there is the production of cultural goods in the economy (2) (which is the previously mentioned alternative use of the concept of 'cultural entrepreneurship' in the creative industries), and economic activities are embedded into frameworks of meaning; culture is partly generated and reproduced by rituals (3), yet there are many rituals that may not affect culture (4), such as rituals of the military or individual rituals of friendship among individuals. Rituals can be part of the economy, such as rituals in management that are not included in the culture of the larger community (5). Thus, there are distinct areas of overlap that are specific to the societies in question, and the relative size of overlaps varies widely across societies (e.g. imagining modern Western societies as 'rational-bureaucratic' would possibly imply small overlap with rituals in intersection 5).

Of special interest in our context is the overlap between all the three domains. We argue that in China, the area of overlap (1) between culture, ritual, and economy is relatively large comparatively speaking (this is caught by the concept of 'ritual economy'). Yet, in China, the overlap between cultural and economy (1) may also be larger than in other countries. For example, today there is a lot of cultural entrepreneurship in the creative industries that does not involve rituals. However, this is a generic phenomenon without much specificity for single societies, especially against the background of globalization. Accordingly, our empirical focus is only on one part where China appears special, and this is cultural entrepreneurship as ritual entrepreneurship. Again, this does not mean that the phenomenon may not emerge in other societies: For example, the symbiosis between Evangelicalism and business in the US may be interpreted as a case in point.

In the following, we look at different aspects of ritual entrepreneurship. In the next section, we approach ritual as a medium of entrepreneurship, which as such may not even take culture as an object or means of entrepreneurial projects. Yet, entrepreneurs need to create and activate ritual as a medium in which the quintessential entrepreneurial resource can be created – trust and trustworthiness. In the next section, we analyse how this affects entrepreneurial action in the technology sector, where the *shanzhai* phenomenon is not only enabled by activating social capital of a distinct group in Shenzhen, the Chaoshan entrepreneurs, but is also a mode of cultural innovation. Finally, we look at one case where ritual becomes a means and object of entrepreneurial action, partly in the context of tourism and leisure projects, but also networking strategies of a local native group.

3 Entrepreneurs, networks, and ritual as a means of producing trust

One indirect way to quantify the potential role of ritual entrepreneurs is to look at the extent and scope of entrepreneurship in general, especially in small- and medium-sized non-state-owned enterprises and combine this with data on economic structure. It should be noticed however that the statistical data about the Shenzhen economy are lacking systematic integration, for example, when it comes to classifying ownership types across different parts of the statistics. This only allows for some cursory observations.

We can start with judging the overall size of the 'modernist' sector of the Shenzhen economy. There are data on the value added of 'emerging industries', which include IT, Internet, robotics, biotechnology, and so on: In 2017, this was 918,719,000,000 Yuan. The total for that year was 2,249,005,860,000, which means that the modernist sector is about 40 per cent of the Shenzhen economy, which is certainly substantial. We can assume that this is least affected by the phenomena of the ritual economy. The emerging industries number is of the same size as of 'industry' in the general sectoral decomposition (38,8). In this separate decomposition, IT and Software is 7.9 per cent. In comparison, real estate and construction together amount to 11.1 per cent. However, the industry sector includes companies of all sizes, which matters, as we will see below, when judging the extent how far ritual economy phenomena may be pertinent.[20]

One observation is that the real estate sector is a very substantial driver of economic growth in Shenzhen: In 2017, 41.5 per cent of investment in fixed assets was in real estate. Over the past 30 years, the share of real estate always was at least more than 20 per cent, mostly more than 30 per cent. In some more detail, investment in fixed assets was 260,240,120,000 in real estate in 2017, compared to 79,593,710,000 for manufacturing and 9,183,380,000 for information technology. As the previous chapters have amply demonstrated, real estate is a sector that is deeply enmeshed with the ritual economy, although this may not affect the majority of real estate projects, though a substantial part. One pointer is the prevalence of different types of enterprises. In terms of gross output, private enterprise achieves almost the volume of limited liability companies, of which roughly only one-sixth are exclusively government funded. Private enterprises make up for roughly more than 20 per cent of listed companies. This does not mean, however, that other types of companies do not include major roles for individual entrepreneurs, since typically this may involve entities such as investment funds.[21]

Another very broad perspective is to distinguish between different types of enterprises and their shares across various economic categories. To begin with, the total number of enterprises is 1,769,876, of which 1,710,105 are registered as 'private', thus involving entrepreneurs in a most general definition. In the industrial sector, only six companies are registered as 'state owned'. There are 4,104 private companies; however, limited liability companies (1,031) and publicly listed companies (361) are counted separately, which might involve hybrid ownership status, especially with the latter. Listed companies include various sizes: Only 62 are 'large' and 197 qualify as 'small'. In industry, in terms of size, 401 enterprises count as 'large', 1,605 as 'medium', and 5,937 as 'small' (SZTJNJ 2019: 80). Of them, 75 private enterprises count as 'large' and the vast majority, 3,449, as 'small'.[22]

The official employment statistics is also potentially relevant. The total number of employees is given as 9.43 million, which is of significance as this obviously includes employees independent from the household registration status. Roughly, these divide into the two groups equally of 'fully employed' individuals (4.47) and 'self-employed' (4.78). Considering the sectoral decomposition, only 176,812 individuals work in the IT and software industry, but 453,775 in the construction and real estate. Manufacturing has 2,290,486 employees, which, as we have seen, includes a very large number of small- and medium-sized economies.[23]

To sum up this impressionistic collection of data, apparently a large chunk of the Shenzhen economy is dominated by companies that involve private entrepreneurs that operate outside the scope of the high-tech sector. The high-tech sector is strong in terms of generating value added, but, as in the case of high-tech industry in other places, does not generate much employment. In addition, as discussed in the next section, when it comes to electronics and IT, manufacturing is divided roughly into two domains, one is the megafactories (such as Foxconn) that assemble the devices of international brands such as Apple, and the other is the network of SME that produce parts, operate ODM and OEM, or produce for the domestic market, especially lower-end segments. In simple terms, in assessing the role of the ritual economy, we need to distinguish between the sectoral composition as measured in terms of value added or share in exports, and the allocation of labour and company types across sectors. In fact, the Shenzhen economy has a very high share of small- and medium-scale companies, and hence a substantial number of entrepreneurs who might be connected to the ritual economy.

As we learned from our interviews, the typical private entrepreneur in the Shenzhen environment is a self-made man (gender is used intentionally here, because male entrepreneurs dominate by far) who relies on few supports outside the network of the business contacts that he himself crafted. He would rely on family relations, yet within a narrow circuit. This is the characteristic constellation of small- and medium-scale family business. Some entrepreneurs would include brothers in their business, others the brother-in law, depending on conditions in the family. But generally speaking, the single entrepreneur is the average case. However, it is important to notice the subcultural variation. Many Chaoshan entrepreneurs would not even include their wives in important business activities, whereas this can be observed much more frequently in the case of Hakka.

This diagnosis does not imply that we deal with an anomic individual struggling in a ruthless market. One important ingredient of entrepreneurial activity is the formation of social networks that support business, the much cited and much studied *guanxi*, which we already introduced in Chapter 2. Shenzhen business culture does not differ from common phenomena in the Chinese context, especially when considering local population and immigrant groups like the Chaoshan. What counts is that *guanxi* have been universally characterized as a core social ritual that involves strong moral commitments among network partners, and that the topic overlaps with the issue of associations that we scrutinize in the next chapter: Associations are platforms for the formation of *guanxi*. In general, *guanxi* formation requires the creation and utilization of platforms and arenas where people meet and exploit opportunities to create relationships. Creating these arenas requires action, and this can be an entrepreneurial act of its own (see next chapter). Often, this action involves rituals. The most elementary form of these rituals is inviting a group of carefully selected individuals for dinner. The host, who will pay for this, acts as a *guanxi* entrepreneur not only for himself, but also for others, thus producing a social 'club good', as the relations as such are open and have even the property of intensifying with use, but remain exclusive in so far as nobody can invite himself to such a dinner, that is, the host is in charge.

As was already argued in Chapter 2, the standard business dinner is a ritualistic event that governs social exchange among the participants.[24] It is important to recognize that the dinner as such is a form of gift exchange, since it is typically expensive and can include indirect gift giving, such as leaving a bottle of expensive spirits that is still almost full for a cherished guest. In other words, there is a moral economy of gift exchange that governs the circuits and rounds of business invitations in the larger network of relationships. Traditionally, this moral economy has been described as 'li shang wanglai' 礼尚往来, that is, the rules of proper behaviour in social intercourse.[25] It is of utmost importance to acknowledge the difference to corruption in the narrow sense: Corruption is an act in which one party gives a favour to another party and expects immediate payback, such as when bribing an official to get a license. There is no moral dimension here, as the two parties do not need to build a stronger relationship of trust. But nurturing trust is a core motivation of building *guanxi*. The ritualization of interactions is a major means to frame the relationship as trustworthy. Ritualization relates with important characteristics of *guanxi* that we have summarized in Chapter 2. An essential feature of *guanxi* is that favours are not immediately returned, which is exactly where ritual obligations count, as rituals anchor expectations of long-term reciprocity. There is a ritualistic component to creating emotions, as emphasized by Durkheim's analyses of effervescence: Ritualistic drinking and Karaoke stimulate emotional excitement, as do shared transitions into the illicit domain, such as enjoying female companions in Karaoke establishments.

In sum, *guanxi* formation is a case in point for ritual entrepreneurship in two specific senses: Entrepreneurs take action in creating arenas for network formation which is often shaped by rituals, and the network dynamics itself is governed by ritualized rules of social exchange. This argument can be further strengthened, when we consider the cultural roots of the mutual commitments in social relations. One aspect that is rarely dealt with in the literature on *guanxi* is the role of religion. There are several values that are invoked in constructing and maintaining *guanxi* that are themselves also emphasized in ritualistic contexts which are rarely directly present in the arenas of *guanxi* practice. Yet, they form a deep structure of beliefs in which those values are grounded. Two notions loom especially large, trust and reciprocity. When considering the conditions in Shenzhen, it is illuminating to focus on the subcultural setting to render this argument in concrete empirical terms.

Trust and loyalty are values that are especially prominent in Hakka customs and ritual practices. Hakka entrepreneurs typically claim that Hakka customs are explicit in committing entrepreneurs to become trustworthy and avoid any form of cheating in business relations. This must be seen against the backdrop of the strong role of Confucian precepts in Hakka cultural imaginaries. This is most evident in the explicit reference to scholarly values in describing Hakka business culture. As we discuss in Chapter 7, one implication of this is that there is a strong inclination of Hakka entrepreneurs and family business to search for public roles and supporting the transition of children to government and academia. This scholarly spirit is said to foster the corresponding Confucian values of integrity and trustworthiness. In this sense, there is a relatively weak religious backing of these values. Often, the values are enshrined in Hakka family traditions, even in explicit form, namely the 'family customs' *jia feng* (see Chapter 7), or in the rituals of Hakka associations (see Chapter 6).[26]

This is very different from many Chaoshan entrepreneurs, which is notoriously confirmed by interviewees from both groups.[27] Chaoshan entrepreneurs may even openly shun Confucian references and instead emphasize their local traditions of popular religion. Chaoshan environments typically show a very lively and intense religious atmosphere. One location where this aspect of Chaoshan culture is most salient for the visitor to Shenzhen is Hubei village in Luohu. The place is replete with small altars and instalments for incense at almost every corner of the narrow alleys criss-crossing the place; some smaller temples invite worship combined with furnaces to burn 'ghost money'.

Chaoshan popular religion manifests a bewildering variety of gods and deities, varying across localities. However, one universal component is Buddhism. In the Chaoshan variant, popular Buddhism is the context in which ideas about reciprocity are grounded.[28] There are two aspects here. One is that reciprocity grounds in ideas about moral commitment. That means, since popular beliefs expect reincarnation, individuals expect universal retribution, if only in later stages of that eternal process. As a result, ideas about social reciprocity directly refer to retribution in the transcendental realm. Clearly, this way of committing to trustworthiness is very different from Hakka reference to Confucian norms. Ritual activities become very significant in signalling trustworthiness: The entrepreneur who publicly expresses belief in Buddhism by donating to temples and worshipping reveals his convictions about retribution, and therefore creates expectations that his commitment to long-term reciprocity can be trusted. An example for this in our fieldwork is the Chaoshan real estate mogul who has a club-like establishment on the upper floors of one of his high-rise buildings which includes not only a bar, a pool, and a small golf court, but also a large Buddhist temple where he daily worships. The establishment serves to invite business partners and officials for socializing. Hence, in this specific case, the religious domain and the arena for *guanxi* formation are even spatially merged. Generally speaking, positioning religious paraphernalia in the office of an entrepreneur is quite usual and mostly includes the typical altars and objects related to the God of Wealth. But in many cases, this also includes religious items that connect with Buddhism and are authentic objects of daily worship.

In many ways, the rituals of popular religion, similar to our previous analysis of *feng shui*, invoke a dual to the ritual economy. In fact, as has been argued by several scholars, the relationship to the netherworld is governed by similar rules of reciprocity as the social world, epitomized in the continuous flow of gifts (incense, fruits, etc.) which create expectations about reciprocal support.[29] The transcendental cosmos is replete with flows of cosmic forces and agents who trigger them that are dual to the flow of wealth and the emergence of opportunity in the real world where entrepreneurs must cope with radical uncertainty every day. This creates the metaphysical background in which Chaoshan business culture is grounded, interpreted by many interviewees as opportunity seeking, highly flexible, and focusing on the flow of wealth or money. In this larger cosmological setting, money obtains almost a religious meaning, thus becoming ritually enhanced, as epitomized in the ubiquitous use of ghost money in popular practices in relating to the netherworld.[30]

Hence, rituals are essential in enabling specific business practices in Shenzhen, as far as important subcultural formations are concerned. Beyond this, there are many forms of entrepreneurship that more directly relate to the ritual economy in the traditional sense, specifically to the role of kinship. We will postpone the question of surname associations to the next chapter. At this place, we just consider how entrepreneurs may activate ritual in managing their business. An interesting case from the construction and real estate industry in our interviews is that of an incipient lineage – Sanke Holdings. Sanke refers to the three sons of the founder Li Keji, another Chaoshan immigrant who rose from rags to riches. The headquarters of the family business is deeply shaped by ritual and religious concerns. It is a row of three-storey buildings, which are connected via open doors that lead into large inner entrance halls in each building. In the middle of the row is a lavishly decorated ancestral hall, replete with exquisite carvings about Chinese history and mythology. The central altar shows the immediate ancestor of the immigrant, hence starts a new branch. The name of the firm, Sanke, refers to the three sons of the founder, who live on the premises together with the father, thus establishing the joint family pattern before 'dividing the family'. Their homes are located next to the hall. The row is completed with the headquarter offices at the end of the building, which are filled with religious paraphernalia and artefacts that refer to traditional myths and beliefs, especially Buddhism.

This case demonstrates the potential role of ritual in operating family business, especially also in the context of the relationship between generations in the family. The general situation is very difficult to assess, as this is affected by complex, multifarious, and fast social changes; to present another example, a female entrepreneur from Fujian, a province where lineage organization is also strong. The original family business is clearly shaped by traditional conceptions of extended kinship, as it emerged as a conglomerate in trading and later producing parts for the electronics industry. The conglomerate consisted of the companies of six brothers, the sister working in the financial management. Although these companies were legally independent, thus manifesting the autonomy of the six households, they were intimately connected via networks of mutual supply and investment which enabled the conglomerate to achieve economies of scale and price advantages. The strength of family tradition is manifest in the fact that the founding brothers live in a co-residential complex in their Fujian hometown.

However, in the successor generation these relationships tend to weaken, since the children in the six branches and companies begin to pursue their own business building on the acquired wealth, such as moving into real estate. However, there is one eldest son among the successor generation who assumes the role of a leader, trying to hold the family business network together. One interesting example is our female entrepreneur who married one of the second-generation descendants. Her husband proved to be not interested in business, but she, a gifted and motivated entrepreneur, faced gender discrimination in the larger family. Thus, she gradually moved out of the original business domain and established her own business in Shenzhen, merging creative industries approaches with merchandizing, such as developing new forms of individualized gifts with luxury products. Yet, she remains tightly connected to the family, frequently visiting the hometown of her husband's parents.

To summarize this section, there is a wide range of activities in which entrepreneurs activate ritual as a medium for pursuing their concerns. Two general functions of ritual loom large: One is the expression of cultural identity and the other is the creation of trust and trustworthiness. Trust is a central motive in Chinese business life and is embodied in the *guanxi* network of social relations. Ritual entrepreneurship is about the creation and stabilization of business networks by means of rituals.

Now the interesting question emerges on how far network relations created by rituals also affect the structure of the economy. In the traditional ritual economy, one essential reflection was the core role of the family in the economic structure, with family units dominating over all other kinds of larger-scale commercial operations or production units. Social networks stabilized by rituals were the complement of the dominant role of markets in coordinating decentralized economic activities of family based entrepreneurs.[31] The question is how far this pattern survives in the modern economy of Shenzhen. The paramount example is the *shanzhai* 山寨 phenomenon.

4 *Shanzhai* entrepreneurs: High-tech industries and the ritual economy

As we have detailed in the first section, one facet of 'Shenzhen identity' is being a leader in the four decades of reform and opening up and entrepreneurial spirit. However, this theme is not without internal tension, as entrepreneurial spirit is manifest in different forms, which partly relates to the variance between modernist conceptions of urbanity and local society. A case in point is the *shanzhai* phenomenon, which emerged in the 1990s and started to flourish in the 2000s, probably with roots in Hong Kong, where previously the term '*shanzhai*' was referred to the relocation of factories to the New Territories.[32] In the 2010s, *shanzhai* has been established as a key feature of certain core industries in the Shenzhen economy. In Western eyes, *shanzhai* is often conflated with counterfeiting, but after many legal battles have been fought, *shanzhai* could attain a certain degree of legitimacy (for a collection of pictures of products, see endnote[33]). In fact, *shanzhai* is today seen as one precursor of a new open innovation system, which at least partly builds on open-source software and even open-source hardware design, and which breaks down rigid barriers between companies in flexible and agile networks of cooperation and interactive learning.[34] In the debate of the business literature, this model has been closely connected to the concept of disruptive engineering in markets 'at the bottom of the pyramid', which means that mainstream industries may eventually fail in meeting the needs of low-income consumers who represent huge market potential in countries such as China and India.[35] The Shenzhen case is symptomatic for this, because the two segments are present at one place, with the huge low-income migrant population on the one hand, and the middle-income strata working in the formal and mainstream economy on the other. The *shanzhai* phenomenon first emerged in the context of imitative consumption and copy-cat production against this background of Shenzhen social structure, and then swiftly expanded its spatial reach in China, initially mainly via middlemen and eventually globally, now mainly via the internet such as trading platforms.[36]

As such, *Shanzhai*, meaning 'bandit castle', explicitly refers to grey and even illicit business activities, with openly subversive motivation. But the grown-up *shanzhai* way of business mainly operates in an area which does not transgress boundaries of legality. The typical *shanzhai* product adopts certain design characteristics of an original product, but modifies them in a substantial way so that it is easy to recognize that this is not the original: This distinguishes it from counterfeiting which would aspire to be as perfect a copy as possible, partly to cheat the customer, partly to enable her or him to show off expensive brands without the costs. The *shanzhai* product does not meet this condition and therefore can be considered as legitimate, in principle. In addition, a *shanzhai* product would have some important additional features or even innovative ones that improve its performance relative to the original, meeting certain needs of customers which are ignored by the standardized products of the original (e.g. adapting mobile phones to the environment of farmers by making them more resilient, or adding stronger loudspeakers).

Shanzhai created many troubles and tension in the official development strategy of Shenzhen, which focused on attracting mainstream producers: Alongside of becoming the prime location for producing iPhones, Shenzhen became the prime location for producing *shanzhai* iPhone clones, easily achieving volumes that are far bigger than the official sales in China. That was possible because in some of the lead industries of Shenzhen, modularization of technology had become the standard. That means, products would be modularized, with several components that require different degrees of sophistication in production. Producers could specialize on inventing new combinations of existing modules without having to develop the underlying technologies. In the mobile phone sector, the commoditization of the core chips was a crucial point of transition, which allowed large numbers of small-scale producers to enter the *shanzhai* business of making mobile phones (MediaTek chips were the essential input).[37] Another important organizational element was the independent design institutes which created the software on demand.

For many protagonists of *shanzhai*, it is both a subversive business practice and a cultural movement. In this sense, we can speak of ritual becoming a mode of entrepreneurial action: As ritual theorists always emphasize, much of modern consumer culture manifests phenomena of ritualization (think of the events announcing new rounds of Apple products), and *shanzhai* explicitly pursues a form of subversive ritualization. It partly defies international standards of intellectual property rights and copyright, and the agents are small businesses, highly agile, flexible, and creative, who exploit the potential of modern technologies in creating an explosion of creativity in varying shapes and functions of electronic devices and other consumer goods. In other words, *shanzhai* represents the always active world of deviance in traditional Chinese culture, epitomized in the famous *jianghu* stories, the world of freely roaming, but courageous and even noble bandits, and celebrating values of independence, liberty, and male prowess.[38] In Shenzhen, an important aspect of this is that *shanzhai* was mainly propelled by immigrant Chaoshan entrepreneurs, highlighting their traditions of flexibility, risk and opportunity seeking, and social life apart from hegemonic culture.

In the arts, this phenomenon is sometimes approached as a genuinely Chinese form of creativity, as people do not simply copy or fake other products, but often invent new variants, sometimes adding a strong dose of irony, humour, and occasionally even resulting in political statements against monopoly power of international brands.[39] However, if we approach the phenomenon in the governance perspective, it cannot be endorsed as a part of 'official' Shenzhen culture, because government is obliged to regulate and even suppress the deviant activities, even though *shanzhai* can be seen as a huge laboratory and nursing ground for new companies, as early emphasized by the MediaTek CEO, who represents the formal economy in the first place. That means, *shanzhai* as a cultural movement may, in fact, be an important expression of Chinese grassroots level cultural creativity; but as a business model, it is deviant, especially considering the claims of Shenzhen to move up in the ranks of global cities.

That being said, its status as a business model is ambivalent, as the troubles of the WTO demonstrated how to classify the phenomenon.[40] The reason is that most of the IPR violations, considered individually, are below the threshold to legitimize countervailing action in the international domain. This reflects the network structure of *shanzhai* industry, consisting of myriads of small family firms that can be easily shut down and reopened at another place. Even domestic authorities may face insurmountable obstacles to effectively control the structure, while at the same time they are aware that this sector of the economy is indispensable for the majority of urban consumers at the lower end of the income ladder, that is, the migrant workers who toil in the export industry and who populate the urban villages. In other words, migrant lifestyle, urban villages, and consumption of *shanzhai* products appear as an institutional, cultural, and material assemblage that cannot be easily disassembled by political intervention without major ruptures. In the same way as urban villages are a hybrid form of urban settlement between illegal squatting and legally planned urban development, the *shanzhai* industry while achieving substantial societal benefits and continuously upgrading the quality of this special form of urban habitat, is a hybrid form of innovation between illegal pirating and legal catch-up that is continuously upgrading capacities, eventually reaching the cutting edge in certain industries.

Therefore, *shanzhai* gradually achieved a certain degree of legitimacy.[41] Its conceptualization as an expression of Chinese creativity played an important role in this transition, which amounts to a gradual transition from the informal to the formal economy.[42] In the ruthless competition among small-scale *shanzhai* producers, a few of them may upgrade their capacities, become suppliers of companies in the formal economy, and may even grow into original manufacturing. Indeed, one can conceive of some of the lead companies in Shenzhen today, such as in the drone business, as partly being influenced by this specific *shanzhai* culture in the early period of their emergence.

It is crucial to recognize that the two types of entrepreneurship, the modernist and the ritual, often stay in symbiotic relationship. Whereas international IT and electronic brands collaborate with leading OEM companies establishing megafactories, such as Foxconn, many Chinese high-tech entrepreneurs, especially in the early stage of developing their business, rely on the vast networks of flexible SMEs as cooperating producers of parts, gradually grooming some of them to become reliable long-term suppliers and standardizing products. For example, Shenzhen is a globally leading location of drone producers, and in the earlier stages of development, drones were composed of parts which were widely available on the Shenzhen electronics markets. Until today, one of the competitive advantages for electronics and IT start-ups in Shenzhen is that the production and testing of prototypes is very cheap, since large numbers of small-scale producers of parts can easily jump in. That means, if it comes to new companies that can disrupt the established formal sector in certain industries, the combination of formal and informal economy is often the key of success.

A famous example is the mobile phone company Xiaomi which bridges both: On the one hand, it relies on advanced capacities in developing proprietary software and creates new forms of user-generated innovation, and on the other hand it employs an outsourcing strategy of production networks which grew out of *shanzhai*.[43] Similarly, the world-leading drone producer, Dajiang Innovation, combined the proprietary knowledge of its founder with the decentralized *shanzhai* production industry, only gradually 'insourcing' production of crucial components such as cameras. The collaboration with the *shanzhai* network was organized via a system of contractual biddings. In these biddings, some *shanzhai* companies would emerge as reliable suppliers, who however would in turn organize a system of sub-suppliers. This peculiar form of cooperation in networks is called the 'baotuan' 抱团 business model, referring to the flexibility and willingness of small-scale entrepreneurs to share business opportunities in cases when they cannot achieve sufficient scale to fulfil an order, and is most prevalent among Chaoshan people.[44] It bears much resemblance to the notion of 'guanxi qiye' 关系企业 that was deployed in the 1980s to analyse the network patterns in Taiwanese SMEs that, in a similar fashion, sometimes managed to grow into stable and complex patterns of cooperation, achieving economies of scale, strategic coordination, and innovative potential.[45]

An example of such mediating companies that emerged early from that market was founded by a Chaoshan entrepreneur, Shenzhen ZZY Electronic Industries Inc. The company remains 'hidden' in doing without own product brands, but actually expands rapidly internationally in emerging markets, especially with ODM mobile phone manufacturing for Indian telecom firms. This is directly extending on previous *shanzhai* exports to India: Indian telecom firms had noticed this development and had approached the Chaoshan entrepreneur who had established his role as an important middleman. This is exemplary for the developmental pattern of *shanzhai*: In early stages, the company emerged as a major node in arranging decentralized production in the networks of companies that connect with Huaqiangbei market, the key location of *shanzhai* commerce. Then, it moved into ODM without creating large factories of its own, but fully relying on the original *shanzhai* network. Today, the company is moving towards establishing a digital platform for B2B relations that would effectively transform the *shanzhai* network into the digital sphere. Most interestingly, this would imply that digital mechanism of trust formation would substitute for *guanxi*-based mechanisms that drove the original *shanzhai* networks.

An interesting case in point is the ongoing transformation of one of the most famous markets for *shanzhai* products, the Huaqiangbei market, which was established in 1982 and gathers more than 700 retail companies in the electronics industry under one roof. Today, Huaqiangbei gradually changes its nature: One focus is becoming an incubator in the creative hardware business, thereby exploiting the fact that retailers are often directly tied to producers or are simply outlets of factories at other places. Creative hardware makers can rely on this rich source of agile and flexible manufacturing even of single units, such as prototypes. This has also attracted international activists in the creative hardware industry, as organized in the HAX Accelerator incubator, which has various locations in the US and Shenzhen and is a vast networking structure that is grounded in the decentralized network of local manufacturers in Shenzhen.[46]

Throughout the past decades, however, Huaqiangbei was deeply rooted in Chaoshan business and its *guanxi* networks.[47] These were less visible in the atomistic world of its hundreds of small shops than at the place where most of the Chaoshan entrepreneurs at Huaqiangbei chose to live: Futian village, a 20-minute ride away. As we discuss in the next chapter, Futian village is one of the many examples where a native village became a settlement of a subethnic group, thus overlaying different ritual spaces (for a report with pictorial impressions, see endnote[48]). Futian village is a place where Chaoshan people can even live without any workable knowledge of Mandarin, and where they can nurture ties of native place, kinship, and other ways of *guanxi* formation at the many venues that offer an authentic Chaoshan social environment.

The *shanzhai* phenomenon is a paramount example of cultural and ritual entrepreneurship with transformative powers in innovative industries. The gradual attainment of legitimacy was essentially driven by grassroots level cultural entrepreneurship. This was an interactive phenomenon with many other agents jumping on the train, such as academics or artists, and not the least, the consumers themselves who created a *shanzhai* movement on the web. But some producers were also engaged, such as the entrepreneurs who created Huaqiangbei and the real estate investors who realized the potential. Ritual entrepreneurship mattered essentially for the entire organization of the industry. First, *shanzhai* is a reproduction of the traditional form of family based and market-mediated production systems that was technologically enabled by the modularization of key technologies. But these systems can only work if they are grounded in a moral economy of family and networking, and specifically the ritual backing of *guanxi* relations. That was even further strengthened by the role of Chaoshan subculture in stabilizing such networks in an environment that was otherwise characterized by extremely ruthless and volatile competition. Second, and as a consequence, the emergence of stable long-run relationships in the ritual economy created the condition for interactive and open learning in associated companies. Probably, this also implies that eventually the networks become disembedded, as it happens, for example, in the drone industry. But this does not mean that in other industries and product groups new disruptive trends may not emerge from the ritual economy anymore. Currently, the Huaqiangbei Chaoshan entrepreneurs move into the health care and cosmetics sector, reinventing the original structures of their business in another industry context.[49]

5 Ritual as a means of entrepreneurial action: The case of *pencai*

A most important domain of ritual entrepreneurship is tourism. Tourism has attracted much scholarly attention in recent Chinese studies, as this is increasingly focused on cultural legacies, both tangible and intangible, and has to be located in the larger context of locational strategies of cities.[50] The demand for tourism has been exploding with the recent rise to prosperity, and this motivates many municipalities to build on their history. Naturally, this mainly involves artefacts that touch upon aspects of traditional culture. This means however that such projects are not without tension and contradictions. This is quite similar to the situation with *shanzhai*: Culture includes many deviant and non-mainstream phenomena and can become subversive.

One cause for tension is that most of these projects are driven by municipal authorities in cooperation with some entrepreneurs, which might drive a wedge towards the wider population, especially if the project touches upon active local practices, such as when exploiting the touristic potential of a popular temple.[51] This can be most evident when the customs of minorities are involved, which may not really be in charge of the projects. Selling minority culture may not rely at all on grassroots-level dynamics, which might even be deliberately controlled to avoid the emergence of sensitive issues.[52] Similar problems emerge when popular religion is involved, which has been denounced as feudal superstition for long. That means projects may effectively expropriate the original bearers of culture of their own cultural autonomy. This overlaps with the wider context of cultural governance that we explore in Chapter 7.

Yet, at the same time, there is also room for genuine cultural entrepreneurship at the grassroots level. This is most evident in many Shenzhen cases, which therefore highlights differences to many other cases of top-down projects. As we explained in the first section, Shenzhen municipal government is only recently discovering the role of culture in local economic development as leaders previously followed the modernist conceptualization of the place. That means many of the local activities may have first emerged in a different context, as genuine grassroots-level initiatives that involve identity politics of native groups. A fascinating case in point is the 'pencai' 盆菜 ('common pot' or 'big basin dining'), which we can classify as a clear case of ritual entrepreneurship, activating an existing ritual as a means of entrepreneurial pursuits (for pictures, see endnote[53]).

The common pot is a most interesting case of intangible cultural heritage that reveals a wide range of aspects related to the ritual economy. *Pencai* is a dish that is widely familiar in Guangdong but was almost unknown in other parts of China.[54] It became more famous when it was featured in a report in the widely acclaimed CCTV series *A Taste of China* as a local speciality. It had also diffused via emigration to other countries, such as Singapore. In all these places, it has become a festive dish consumed at certain holidays and family events, mostly devoid of ritual meanings, comparable to turkey in Anglo-Saxon countries. In Hong Kong, there are also cheap variants, even as single dishes in small eating outlets. Yet, even today many Chinese in other provinces do not know the dish, and when the original form is described to them, they express bemusement or even find it weird.

This weirdness was also manifest in the first scholarly account of that dining practice by James Watson.[55] Watson met the practice for the first time as a PhD student in Hong Kong, together with his Chinese teacher, who also expressed bewilderment when visiting the New Territories and by happenstance running into a local *pencai* event. The reason for this is that *pencai* violates cultural mainstream rules for cooking, eating, and dining ritual.

The traditional *pencai* is a huge pot filled with various food items. Traditionally, the core ingredient was fat pork. This is what one can still see at certain festive events in Fenghuang village today; but most *pencai* is now offered with expensive seafood as the main ingredient. The rich and various ingredients of the *pencai* are cooked separately before being put into the pot, layer by layer, right before it is offered. In other words, in principle, the various items could be also presented in the standard Chinese way, on separate plates, and allowing for selection by the guests of a meal. Instead, they are deliberately mixed and offered at the centre of the table. Guests are invited to eat from the pot without any rules or constraints. There is no rule of seating guests at the tables, even at serious festive events. As these traditionally involved larger numbers of attendants, another deviation from standard practice comes into play: Guests come and go as they like, take a seat, eat freely, and leave. So, the composition of guests changes during the feast.

When Watson met this dining practice for the first time, it presented a puzzle precisely because he faced the version before commercialization at a festive occasion in the New Territories. The *pencai* was a ritual practice with a strong symbolic significance, tightly connected with core lineage rituals, such as offered by families to the community on the occasion of the birth of a son. What is the origin of the practice? As always in China, there are various myths of origin, which however boil down to certain core elements that relate the practice with traditional high culture, though appearing to be deviant. One version is that when the Song Emperor fled the Mongols to the South, the troops arrived tired and starved at the Pearl River Delta. The villagers rushed ahead to show their solidarity and prepared big basins to feed the troops, filled with most valuable and nourishing food items. Later, the Emperor himself tasted the dish and praised it, ordering his chef to prepare a recipe. These stories are still being told in Shenzhen today. The myth of origin therefore falls in line with other local accounts of migration history of the region, with certain groups arriving in waves over the centuries following cataclysmic political events, with the Song dynasty collapse the most significant one. This migration history establishes a dialectical relationship between local identity and mainstream culture, as local villagers such as the Wen may trace back their origin to elite members of the Song empire. This cultural dialectic is also reflected in the *pencai* myth, with the *pencai* invented locally, but recognized even by the Emperor.

In his research on *pencai*, Watson could unearth the real meaning of the dining ritual. The key are two aspects: one is pork and the other is sharing. In pre-1949 China and until the early 1980s in Maoist China, different from the New Territories already at that time, pork was seen as the most valuable and prestigious food item. Ordinary peasants rarely had the opportunity to eat pork, and often groups of villagers invested together in raising a hog. The pig is an animal of high symbolic value in Chinese imaginaries, symbolizing wealth and prosperity, and in colloquial speech the pig referred to all kinds of material gains. In particular, 'pork' referred to the share that individual peasants would gain from any kind of collective enterprise by lineages, as in the case of a jointly invested hog: 'Pork' is the symbol of joint participation in and sharing of profits, such as dividends.[56] In other words, the *pencai* combines two symbolic acts on one ritual, one is offering pork as a symbol of prosperity to the guests and the second is sharing it freely, without any rules. In other words, *pencai* rituals celebrate prosperity and solidarity in the lineage.

In old China, *pencai* offered by families also served as a marker of household status. The bigger events, though, were mostly sponsored by lineage estates and rich lineage members. Hence, *pencai* feasts were a media of redistribution within the lineage; as for the poor members, these were the rare occasions when they could eat pork at all and get access to high-calorie fat. If one considers the frequency of feasting throughout the lunar year, including the festive occasions of single families, the *pencai* could indeed make a substantial contribution to poor members' welfare. Aside from that, the expression of solidarity enhanced lineage cohesion, not just because of the mere fact of sharing pork, but because of the disruption of etiquette. It is important noticing that this disruption had no carnivalesque meaning, in spite of the *renao* atmosphere created at *pencai* feasts, because the *pencai* was offered at the most solemn ritual occasions. It was an essential part of lineage rituals beyond the prescriptions of Confucian orthodoxy.

This is also evident for the rules that govern *pencai* preparation. Traditionally, like the local lineage idiom, the *pencai* recipes were treated as secret of the individual villages. That is perfectly possible, because the many ingredients could be prepared in a very large number of combinations and variants. These recipes were only transmitted within the male line of the lineage, and only males could take part in preparing the dish. Women were only allowed to cater the dish to the guests, although the sexes could freely intermingle at the tables during the feast.

It is highly significant noticing that the *pencai* survives in Hong Kong until today in this specific meaning of a dining ritual that expresses group identity and cooperation, even in the commercialized environment. In today's affluent society, there is no functional need to offer pork to less affluent people, but what counts is solidarity. Hence, in the New Territories, a new form of *pencai* feasts had emerged such as offering the dish on occasion of political rallies or community events, often of very huge size, with thousands of guests.[57] Against this background, it is highly significant that the practice was prohibited in Maoist China. There are reports that it needed to be revived semi-officially by a rural cadre in 1992 on the occasion of establishing a shareholding cooperative.

Indeed, in Shenzhen, the *pencai* has retained its major ritual functions in many contexts. Apart from *pencai* held at regular occasions of the lunar year and ancestor worship, *pencai* feasts may be held when the shareholding cooperatives distribute their dividends, typically on New Year, when traditionally all dues are settled. This is ominous, because in traditional colloquial, the distribution of dividends is 'dividing the pork equally'. *Pencai* feasts are regularly held when villagers conclude major collective deals with developers, which create a fortune literally overnight for everybody.

The Huang lineage at Xiasha launched a major ritual innovation of the *pencai* and claim that they invented a new form of *pencai*, the 'da pencai', the 'big common pot'.[58] Probably this claim is misleading, as the mega *pencai* already had emerged in Hong Kong previously, as mentioned. But the Huang launched it deliberately as an 'intangible cultural heritage' in Guangdong province, achieving provincial-level status. The *da pencai* feasts at Xiasha are huge indeed, the biggest including 60,000 guests, filling the entire cultural square, on the occasion of the World Huang Convention (for a video clip on *da pencai* feast, see endnote[59]). Hence, *da pencai* is an almost ideal typical manifestation of the ritual economy, combining traditional lineage practice with business goals. Taken together, it is a manifestation of local identity politics, because the strong international presence of Huang naturally also boosts the position of Xiasha community in Shenzhen. This is recognized in a strong symbolic act. At the Xiasha Huang museum, a separate space is devoted to a life-sized bronze instalment of a group of villagers enjoying the *pencai* together, accompanied by explanations and even a recipe. An exact copy of this installation can be also found at the central Shenzhen museum, together with a video show of the Huang ancestral rites.

The *pencai* case shows all essential features of ritual entrepreneurship, both on the individual and the collective level. As we shall see in the next chapter, *pencai* feasts have been launched as central events in creating a global Huang clan movement under the leadership of Huang Yingchao, the Xiasha village head. As they create special moments of effervescence, they express group identity, while being increasingly inclusive in the context of urban villages and the attempts to transform them in major tourism attractions. This is not a contradiction, as the sheer size of the *pencai* demonstrates the status and success of the local lineage. As in Hong Kong, the practices adapt to changing contexts, but keep the original spirit. For example, the big *pencai* events are no longer prepared by the male villagers, but outsourced to restaurants and caterers who are lineage members. As in the traditional *pencai*, these activities strike a balance between local identity and global aspirations of Shenzhen: It is the local custom that becomes globalized as a tourism event too, apart from the continuing observance at more specific ritual occasions that only involve family and lineage.

In sum, the *pencai* is an archetypical case of ritual entrepreneurship. Whereas many villagers just enjoy the ritual, the Huang identify *pencai* as a means of entrepreneurship, contributing to the local strategy of upgrading Xiasha as a site for tourism and leisure. At the same time, it is a medium for creating arenas of Huang business networking in particular, as we analyse in more detail in the next chapter. And as a mode of entrepreneurial action, it is an expression of Huang identity and a status signal in the wider Shenzhen business community. There are plenty of other examples in Shenzhen today, as many villages discover the potential of local rituals for similar goals, reaching from identity politics to tourism projects.

6 Conclusion

This chapter focused on the core agents of the ritual economy: The entrepreneurs. Of course, they are present also in the other chapters, as, for example, ritual entrepreneurs create ritual spaces. But this example also demonstrates an important point: sometimes ritual entrepreneurs are leaders of communities which collectively realize the entrepreneurial function. This point has already been made in the context of cultural entrepreneurship.[60] For example, in a sense the *shanzhai* phenomenon is a collective entrepreneurial movement with many agents involved and no single one emerging as a leader. The same applies for the creation of ritual spaces in many contexts, where this collective process can even be institutionalized, such as when villagers participate in decision-making of a shareholding cooperative. This aspect also includes the economic functions of group identity in creating sustainable business relations. No single Hakka entrepreneur can create, just by individual agency, the commitment to becoming trustworthy and the general recognition of Hakka as being trustworthy. As we elaborate in the next chapter, this is the reason why *guanxi* dynamics and structures often build on an institutional infrastructure that manifests the collective identity of actors, such as Hakka associations in this case.

Ritual entrepreneurship is a conceptual addendum to Collins' framework, but only in focusing on a phenomenon that is already implicit in it. Ritual entrepreneurs are the key actors in mediating between rituals and markets, in both senses of activating ritual for entrepreneurial action, especially in creating trust in networks, and of transforming rituals into economic goods, such as commercializing ritual artefacts. In doing this, ritual entrepreneurs become innovative, again in two senses. They may create new forms of ritual or new arenas of ritual action, and they may build on ritual to launch innovations. The latter establishes the direct connection between the ritual economy and economic structure, technology, and market transformation.

One can approach this phenomenon in terms of the regional innovation systems literature, which has included the aspect of cultural embeddedness. This opens the view on the conditions that create the basis for global competitiveness. Shenzhen has been an incubator of disruptive business models also involving hardware development, such as in the drone industry. This success has been rooted in the strong interaction between decentralized production networks of SME and the large local market potential of low- and low-middle-income migrants aspiring to upgrade their lifestyles at low costs. The model of *shanzhai* handsets has become a reference for other products, such as drones. In this sense, the ritual economy stays at the core of Shenzhen competitiveness as it stands today. Of course, this does not mean that it remains there forever. But we should not limit our view only on the narrow industry contexts here. The ritual economy is manifest in many ways, bridges economy and wider cultural and social contexts, and is therefore innovative on its own, evolving towards new manifestations in other domains. Ritual entrepreneurs drive this evolution.

Notes

1 Florence (2017).
2 O'Donnell and Wan (2016).
3 Much cited is his compilation on the 'Ten Great Concepts of Shenzhen', Wang (2011).
4 There is a fascinating but puzzling installation at the Shekou museum. The installation puts Tiananmen Square and the huge Mao portrait in the background of an altar-like instalment that shows the famous motto of Shenzhen ascribed to Yuan Geng together with a collection of famous Shenzhen company logos.
5 Lao Heng (2018: 264).
6 http://szsb.sznews.com/PC/content/201811/06/content_498078.html, accessed November 26, 2019. There is a substantial literature in China about the various regional business cultures that aim to establish a connection between historical types and current practices; see, for example, Fang and Lin (2011a, 2011b).

7 https://baike.baidu.com/item/%E5%85%89%E6%98%8E%E5%8C%BA/22608759?fromtitle=%E5%85%89%E6%98%8E%E6%96%B0%E5%8C%BA&fromid=4812057; https://mp.weixin.qq.com/s/wP4qWDZye5pKXqFqB3ZI9w, both accessed November 6, 2019.
8 Kearney (2018).
9 https://www.lboro.ac.uk/gawc/world2018link.html, accessed January 20, 2020.
10 Sassen (2018).
11 Wang (2016: 264).
12 For a more detailed discussion of this, see Herrmann-Pillath (2018a).
13 According to our best knowledge, we were the first to introduce this concept; see Herrmann-Pillath et al. (2019).
14 Rea and Volland (2015).
15 Rea (2015).
16 Herrmann-Pillath and Zweynert (2014).
17 As an example for these uses, https://culent.com/definitions/; https://i-lab.harvard.edu/deans-challenge/cultural-entrepreneurship/; accessed February 8, 2017. Some universities offer programs in cultural entrepreneurship, referring to the creative industries. However, even in this context the meaning is fuzzy; see, for example, https://ssir.org/articles/entry/social_or_cultural_entrepreneurship_an_argument_for_a_new_distinction (accessed September 24, 2017), where the term is referred to any kind of activity that triggers cultural change and is referred also to social entrepreneurship.
18 Lean (2015).
19 Rea (2015).
20 Source of data in this paragraph: Shenzhen shi tongjiju (2018: 33, 34, 46).
21 Source of data in this paragraph: Shenzhen shi tongjiju (2018: 10, 144, 196).
22 Source of data in this paragraph: Shenzhen shi tongjiju (2018: 14, 80, 100, 108).
23 Source of data in this paragraph: Shenzhen shi tongjiju (2018: 63, 65).
24 Osburg (2013).
25 Chang (2010).
26 Hakka business culture is discussed by many Chinese researchers; for an overview, see Zhou Li and Gong Dandan (2014).
27 There are also scholarly comparisons; see, for example, http://www.bjqx.org.cn/qxweb/ShowArtd73602ad-b153-4dd6-83a3-0604e9714ece.aspx, accessed November 13, 2019.
28 The deep historical roots are revealed in Yang's (1957) classical paper on reciprocity. These mechanisms have been confirmed in our interviews with Chaoshan entrepreneurs.
29 This congruence between social exchange and exchange with gods has been emphasized by many observers, such as Chang (2010) or Chu (2010).
30 Chu (2010) and Blake (2011). Blake (2011: 102) presents a very relevant argument that the specific role of money in China reflects a 'cash-based social economy', which retains components of the 'tributary mode' as theorized by Gates (1996). We would identify this as 'ritual economy'. Burning money is a frequent practice observable in religious sites in Shenzhen: For example, the Fenghuang temple has several furnaces.
31 This is a core argument in Huang's (1990) seminal theory of involution in the Chinese economy. For a more recent view on the dominance of the family in the traditional economy, see von Glahn (2016).
32 For an excellent overview of the literature, see Seidel (2019). The significance of the phenomenon is reflected in the fact that there is a very detailed and comprehensive entry on Baidu: https://baike.baidu.com/item/%E5%B1%B1%E5%AF%A8/7401, accessed January 20, 2020.

33 https://disnovation.org/shanzhai.php, accessed January 22, 2020.
34 Fu et al. (2013).
35 Brown and Hagel (2005); Booz&Co (2009).
36 On the role of consumer behaviour in *Shanzhai* business, see Qin et al. (2019).
37 Shih et al. (2010).
38 On the wider cultural background, see Boretz (2010).
39 Chubb (2015).
40 Yu (2011).
41 This process is brilliantly analysed as 'institutional entrepreneurship' by Lee and Hung (2014).
42 The Chinese debates are well overviewed in the Baidu entry on *shanzhai*: https://baike.baidu.com/item/%E5%B1%B1%E5%AF%A8%E6%96%87%E5%8C%96, accessed January 20, 2020. It deserves notice that the entry is about '*shanzhai* culture', thus clearly emphasizing the cultural and less the economic dimension.
43 Seidel (2019).
44 https://baike.baidu.com/tashuo/browse/content?id=242a1308b5f4eede411c4569, accessed November 25, 2019.
45 Numazaki (1996), Hamilton (1996).
46 https://hax.co/
47 https://wenku.baidu.com/view/830a2feb18e8b8f67c1cfad6195f312b3169ebdc, accessed November 25, 2019.
48 https://mp.weixin.qq.com/s/4IqcQBXPRi52ciCb3QNkdg, accessed November 26, 2019.
49 https://baike.baidu.com/tashuo/browse/content?id=242a1308b5f4eede411c4569, accessed November 25, 2019.
50 Tim Oakes has pushed this field over the past two decades; see Oakes (1999, 2019).
51 Exemplary studies include Kang (2009) and Bruckermann (2016).
52 Oakes (2017).
53 http://www.sz.gov.cn/cn/zjsz/fwzwhyc/gdsfy/content/post_1325843.html; http://www.sz.gov.cn/cn/zjsz/fwzwhyc/gdsfy/content/post_1325843.html, both accessed January 22, 2020.
54 There is even a useful Wikipedia entry, see https://en.wikipedia.org/wiki/Poon_choi), although it concentrates on Hong Kong. For a scholarly account of recent trends, see Chan (2010).
55 Watson (1987, 2014).
56 For more detail, see Zhou (2014).
57 Chan (2010).
58 For extensive news coverage, see http://paper.oeeee.com/nis/201406/06/226791.html, accessed October 11, 2017; http://szsb.sznews.com/html/2016-11/12/content_3660224.htm, accessed October 12, 2017; http://news.szhome.com/233392.html, accessed October 12, 2017.
59 https://v.youku.com/v_show/id_XMzYwNzg5ODExMg==, accessed November 27, 2019.
60 Culp (2015).

6 Ritual in associational life

1 The public domain between family and state: The transition from Empire to contemporary China

This chapter builds on the chapter on lineages in treating associations as an important part of the ritual economy that transcends kinship. This is an approach that is unusual in contemporary China studies, which mainly approach the topic from the perspective of political science and political sociology. However, this also means that we adopt a narrower approach and confine our discussion on those types or cases of associations that have an explicit ritual dimension. This does not mean that other associations have no ritual aspects, but that we look at those associations that have an origin that is partly rooted in ritual and that eventually contribute substantially to economic organization. Vice versa, this includes associations that have an economic function but combine this with ritual activities that are tied to ritual origin. The paradigmatic cases for the first type of association are the surname associations, and for the second are extraterritorial chambers of commerce ('yidi shanghui' 异地商会); the latter is a variant of native place association that is explicitly focused on business. We use the term 'ritual' here because we treat certain references to origin and purpose as being rooted in traditional aspects of ritual, such as descent in surname associations, and because the practice and activities of certain associations emphasize ritual activities beyond what is universal standard in any association, such as general assemblies of members. The core criterion is whether associations involve ritual expressions of shared identity of members, as assumed in the Collins framework.

The term 'chamber' ('shanghui' 商会) is ambiguous and should not be equated with the Western use of the term. Often, the meaning is just that of an association of businesspeople. For example, in 2016, the Chaoshan Women Chamber of Commerce, 'Shenzhen jin guo chao shanghui' 深圳巾帼潮商会, was inaugurated at Shenzhen and is headquartered there, which has global reach, however. In 2019, it launched a big event exploring the role of female entrepreneurs in the Larger Hong Kong-Shenzhen Bay development. It is mainly a networking arena. Ritual aspects as defined above loom large, when considering that the association has set up subsidiary organizations that concentrate on education (an academy and a committee for education) and a charity.[1] In general, the root term referring to all kinds of associations is 'hui' 会. It is important to note that certain functions can be fulfilled by various *hui*, such as when the functions of a surname association would be also fulfilled by a 'culture study association', such as considered in Section 4, the 'Jiangxia culture associations' that refer to an important location in the migration history of the Huang descent group. In the recent history of associations in China, such terminological variants mattered a lot, because depending on the name, certain legal regulations might apply. For example, newly emerging *shanghui* in Shenzhen were sometimes called 'friendship associations' ('lianyihui' 联谊会), which would not require registration under the umbrella of a government organization. Given the tight regulation of civil society in China today, the designation of an association may easily attract the criticism that it might be 'illegal', thus creating the risk of government intervention. Therefore, the transition to legality may be accompanied by terminological metamorphoses, even though the underlying and evolving social structure remains the same.[2]

Traditionally, Chinese society had a very rich associational life.[3] This also applies for the traditional village which is the structure that underlies our conception of ritual space.[4] We cannot reduce the traditional rural social structure to the elementary categories of kinship and locality exclusively, which points to the social creativity of cultural imaginaries of cooperation and cohesion. Peasants form a wide range of associations with many functions in organizing cooperation for the production of collective and public goods, for example, associations for managing irrigation, which could also transcend village boundaries, such as managing a water reservoir used by several villages.[5] Associations had varying sizes, beginning with the smallest, such as temporary clubs for raising pigs, and as this example also shows, might have specific functions, such as the quite common Qingming associations in which members of a kinship group cooperated in funding and organizing the activities on that holiday. Important associations were the temple associations, which organized funding and management of a temple and which continue to play a role in contemporary China.[6] This already reveals that many associations have a ritual dimension but mainly focus on economic issues in their regular activity. This is because at the end of the day, even purely ritualistic activities require to raise resources or coordinate joint action, hence involve economic decisions and investment. Accordingly, patterns of cooperation that emerge in a ritual, narrow sense can become implicit templates for cooperation in domains which are primarily marked as economic and purely instrumental.[7] Thus, associations are a mode of social relation that is independent from kinship. Yet, one can say that some of their organizational features go back to kinship organization, especially if one considers the separate entities that were created by lineages.

This includes patterns such as rotating leadership, membership by holding shares, or regular supervisory boards, which apply for both lineage estates and many types of associations.[8]

Many traditional associations emerged against the background of migration and sojourning, especially in traditional urban society. This is a context where ritual beyond kinship looms large. In Late Imperial times, large Chinese cities were places where sojourners of diverse origins and social status lived together, such as transport workers or rich merchants from other places.[9] Since the Imperial administration was weak in fiscal and infrastructural terms, urban society mainly organized itself via a plethora of associations with various purposes led by the urban elites, mostly rich merchants. For example, merchant leaders organized firefighting and mobilized shop owners and other businessmen to contribute funds. An important field of activity was philanthropy, such as setting up and managing hospitals. In most of these activities, the Imperial administration was not directly involved, but degree holders mediated between the various groups, thus instilling associational life with the Confucian worldview and ritual meanings. In other words, associations assumed a central role as intermediary level of Imperial governance in late Imperial China, and in turn, ritual was the medium by which the government governed the associational domain, as in the case of governing lineages by public governance of kinship ritual.

In the Late Empire, a dualism of economic associations had emerged as early as in Tang dynasty, when the Imperial government promoted the creation of trade associations in which craftsmen, merchants, and sometimes even beggars were organized along the lines of 'trades' ('hang' 行). Often translated as 'guilds', these were intermediate forms of government-led market organization, such as safeguarding product quality, implementing taxation, and enforcing procurement for the Imperial court. Hence, the Chinese guilds cannot be compared to the corporate organizations in medieval Europe. Especially, the Imperial government actively intervened in any attempts of guilds to limit market access and monopolization.[10] In contrast, merchant associations such as those linked to their native places were driven by grassroots-level initiatives, originally as support organizations for travelling merchants ('huiguan' 会馆). In late Qing China, the organizational forms evolved towards larger diversity and became more autonomous. Merchants established new forms of guilds independent from native place, the 'gongsuo' 公所; within native place associations, trades fellowships emerged, the 'shang bang' 商帮.[11] An intermediate important form of collective organization was the representation of market communities by local leaders, which were located at certain places, but not necessarily controlled by the territorial unit of the village. An important issue was the organization of taxation: Market communities assumed a formal role in dealing with the county magistrate and assuming certain functions as tax collectors and in establishing market order. Associations obtained a double role as representatives of local populace and as stewards of the state.[12] One important factor in the evolution of associations was the competition with the official system of licensed brokers, which was used by the Imperial government since Tang times to control markets while also extracting revenue. In the debates of the times, perhaps counter-intuitively, the merchant associations often claimed to represent the 'public' 'gong' (公 interest), whereas the brokers were denounced as being driven by 'private' 'si' (私 interests).[13]

In the 19th century, this traditional form of associations was supplemented by the modern form of associations. Whereas traditionally merchants and craftsmen were organized in native place associations and guilds, now modern chambers of commerce emerged, moving away from those particularistic ties which represented the new constituency of 'business' beyond the trades. For example, in Hankou, the so-called 'Eight Great Guilds' joined forces and created a Chamber of Commerce in 1898 that represented the interests of the business community in toto.[14] They assumed an important political role in expressing and organizing interests and worldviews of newly emerging groups in Chinese society. Chambers were major political actors in the movements for enhancing provincial autonomy before the fall of the Empire, but they also maintained strong cultural identities tied to ritual notions of rule, such as leaders displaying academic and official titles.[15] Beyond these developments, we should also mention that traditional associations were very important institutions in organizing the life of Chinese sojourners abroad, especially in Southeast Asia.[16] Given the distance to political authorities in the places of sojourning, associations shaped Chinese life in many ways, such as sustaining cultural identity and ties to the homeland, organizing cross-regional trade networks, organizing social support in case of individual and collective mishaps, and governing the settlements of the Chinese ('China towns'). This phenomenon needs emphasis, because these associations often became active in re-establishing ties to the Mainland when China adopted the open-door policies in 1978, and remain important partners for associations in China today, for example, mediated via native place.[17]

We do not need to go into the details of this complex historical transition here, which was never completed, in the sense that the traditional forms of associations were eventually superseded by modern forms. This is a crucial observation in this chapter: In Shenzhen today, we observe the resurgence of certain forms of associations that build on leitmotifs of traditional associations, yet certainly do not follow their template in organizational details and functions. However, whether traditional or not, assessing their nature is difficult as far as their role in societal governance is concerned. This partly reflects the ambivalence of associations in the Chinese public domain across the historical divide of the fall of Empire.[18]

In the 20th century, and especially in the PRC after 1978, the modernization of associational structures took another direction than the one originally emerging in the final decades of the Empire. At that time, the new associational movement was mainly driven by grassroots-level activities, thus counting as the emergence of new forms of civil society and a public sphere. But with the reinstatement of authoritarian government already in the early years of the Republic, new forms of state corporatism emerged that partly reinstated the subordinate role of the emerging civil society vis-à-vis the government, but added modern components, especially the orientation of public interest towards the nation. This orientation towards national interest had also shaped associational activities in the early years of the People's Republic, before all autonomous societal organizations were politically suppressed or transformed into units under the governance of 'United Front' policies and organization.[19]

In various shapes, the conceptual framework of corporatism is the most widely used in studying associations in contemporary China.[20] The central question is how far associations operate independently from government, and whether they mainly express needs, interests, and autonomous actions on the part of the social groups that organize them, or whether they are the means of a government policy to control those groups and apply indirect measures for policy implementation. This is the distinction between societal corporatism and state corporatism, with archetypical examples for the latter in fascist states that refrain from imposing totalitarian control of all sectors of society. In China today, this issue is further complicated by the distinction between party and government, and the difficulty to assess long-term trends, including the regional dimension. In the past two decades, Shenzhen was often conceived as an experimental region with reference to state-society relations and civil society innovations. At the same time, there are also clear regional differences in associational practices which might be traced historically to various factors, such as the subcultural and linguistic variety, the patterns on immigration, and the political tradition of dissent and mobilization in Republican times. Indeed, in many respects, South-Eastern China has always been a region with strong associational life, reflecting often weak government institutions in areas which continued to manifest characteristics of frontier societies, the strong subcultural identities, reflected in linguistic diversity, or the presence of foreigners, especially in the treaty ports.

2 State corporatism versus ritual economy

In this chapter, we confront the corporatist conceptual model with the ritual economy model. To repeat, the argument has only limited reach, yet covers important domains and cases. The corporatist model theoretically requires that we have clear empirical standards to distinguish between state and society. This is even implicit in international standards, as is evident in the troubles in dealing with Chinese trade unions: The ILO establishes the benchmark of tripartite organization, which requires that there are neat institutional barriers between trade unions as representing workers, employers' associations, and the government. But obviously, even if this were formally the case, the CCP encompasses all three sides via overlapping memberships.[21] We will discuss these questions in more detail in the next chapter, focusing on the role of associations in societal and economic governance. In this chapter, we concentrate on ritual aspects. However, it is important to highlight already here that as in the Imperial tradition, ritual partly defines the status relation between government and private sector, especially also in terms of the recognition of a public interest that is represented by associations. Associations gain legitimacy if they pursue a public interest, and they become legally acknowledged if this is also endorsed by the government, and eventually formalized in their registration with the Bureau of Civil Affairs. In this relationship, ritual aspects of associations are important as communicative means to express this orientation towards public interest – as we saw, the Chaoshan Women's association engages in charity, beyond networking and lobbying.

There is an important implication: Ritual aspects may cover a wider range than we considered so far in empirical cases, because it includes political rituals which are mostly cast in the ideology of the Communist Party.[22] For example, the Hunan Chamber of Commerce at Shenzhen highlights the most famous native of Hunan, Mao Zedong, with artefacts and rhetorical references. Compared to other cases, accordingly this association pays more attention to party development and requirements of expressing and performing party ideology, as recently Xi Jinping's ideas. There is less emphasis on specifics of Hunan identity, although this is also celebrated (we come back on this). In the context of associations as intermediate governance institutions, which we explore in the next chapter, this ritualization of ideology and party policies certainly must be included in our analysis. The criterion is whether this type of political ritual is just enforced by superordinate bodies, or whether there are spontaneous and independent activities, such as the explicit reference to Mao Zedong in the case of the Hunan Chamber.

In 2015, the Chinese government changed administrative regulations on associations in a substantial way. Before, there was one clear institutional indicator for supporting the state corporatist model: The principle had applied that only one association can represent one constituency, and that every association should be assigned to one supervising government organization. In the economic domain, this implied that one business association should exclusively represent one industry. This principle was abolished; however, social practice had been undermining its relevance anyway. According to data for the years before the new regulation, in Shenzhen only about 10 per cent of all associations were registered at all.[23] Certainly, many of these were of small size, especially if one considers the seniors' clubs and other associations on the neighbourhood committee level. Yet, at the same time, many organizations may not bother if they were not directly interested in enjoying preferential tax treatment, which requires registration. According to recent data, there are about 800 municipal-level business associations in Shenzhen with roughly 80,000 members, which are registered.[24]

Continuing with a similar dualism in Imperial China, this number includes two different types of associations, using different terms, 'xiehui' 协会 and 'shanghui' 商会, with the former relating to 'trades' ('hangye' 行业), whereas the second represents a business constituency across industries, although this is not always a sharp distinction. One reason for the huge gap between the official number of organizations directly subordinate to government units and the factual number of associations is the distinction between the national level and the local level. Certainly, for national-level organizations and their local branches, this applies almost universally, but on the local level there has always been much leeway. If we look at the business sector, the 'All China Federation of Industry and Commerce' ('Zhonghua quanguo gongshang lianhehui' 中华全工商联合会) is the central unit to which all regional and especially industry-level organizations belong, indicated by the special term 'xiehui'. But on the local level, there are other types of business associations, mostly denoted as 'shanghui', chamber of commerce, which often fall beyond the scope of the national federation. However, there is much ambiguity, since even the Federation is often referred to as 'General Chamber of Commerce' ('zongshanghui' 总商会), such as on the district level in Shenzhen. For many chambers, one cannot unequivocally claim that they are fully controlled by government.

At the end of 2017, there were 617 *xiehui* and 293 *yidi shanghui*, according to the official report of the Department for Social Organizations of the Shenzhen government. Many of them have been founded after 2010.[25] This number apparently does not include other forms that we scrutinize here, such as business-focused surname associations. Indeed, one can roughly say that the *xiehui* are in the domain of industry interest representation tightly combined with government regulation, hence manifesting the state corporatist pattern, whereas many *shanghui* reach into the domain of the ritual economy. One important indicator of this is that *xiehui* exclusively focus on professional information and policy, whereas the *shanghui* often include charity in their profile and other activities related to culture, as in the previously mentioned example of the Chaoshan Women Chamber, and often express ethical commitments of their members: In ideal-typical terms, the *shanghui* mostly are identity-based organizations, whereas the *xiehui* are interest-based. Both, however, assume a public role: This is evident in the regulatory functions of *xiehui*, and calls for ritual confirmation in case of the *shanghui*.

Industry associations as 'hangye xiehui' 行业协会 are involved in various activities. One is dispute resolution among members. In a sample of 265

Shenzhen associations, they managed 1,581 cases within one year in 2018. In the same sample, participation in public events was by 307,000 members.[26] The associations conducted 156 research projects on behalf of the government, and they submitted 1,254 policy initiatives to the government. A special task is to launch initiatives to lower the costs of business. One is to ease up access to loans and lower the interest rate. For example, the Shenzhen restaurant association concluded an agreement with Minsheng Bank that resulted in the release of additional loan facilities. Another policy domain is lobbying for tax reductions, such as the software association that supported new administrative regulations in the software industry that reduced the industry tax burden by an estimated RMB 3 billion in 2017. In the context of 'One belt, one road' policy, associations have also organized trade fairs, such as in the garment industry. Such activities are partly done as contractual work for the Shenzhen government, under the label of 'marketization' of certain government services.[27] However, probably the most essential activity is holding numerous meetings. Take, for example, the Shenzhen Gold & Jewellery association, which is significant as Shenzhen is the prime business location in China for this trade, especially also with reference to external trade. The example is also noteworthy because the trade has a very substantial share of Hunan entrepreneurs, so the Hunan Chamber of Commerce is also engaged in this field. In 2017, the *xiehui* held more than 40 meetings with government bureaus and engaged in more than 60 joint activities with government organizations or other associations.[28] The *xiehui* adopts many paragovernmental functions, including monitoring and identifying criminal activities in the trade and more generally, upgrading standards and improving regulatory conditions.

This is the reflection of their fundamental institutional difference, as mentioned: Whereas the *xiehui* are strictly organized according to industries, most *shanghui* include all industries, but focus on different criteria of membership. Even for the *xiehui*, more than 90 per cent of members are private business, which certainly applies for the *shanghui*. *Shanghui* membership criteria mostly relate to identity-based categories, such as place of origin. An important phenomenon in Shenzhen is the role of extraterritorial chambers of commerce, because they maintain a close relationship with the government of their place of origin. The Shenzhen government has established special channels of communication with those chambers, such as in the context of legal development and enforcement. In a recent meeting with the Department of Justice, eight Chambers were invited, probably representing those with the largest clout: Chaoshan, Hunan, Shandong, Shanxi, Henan, Gansu, Jiangxi, and Jilin.[29] As this list demonstrates, there are also important differences between extraterritorial chambers: 'Chaoshan' is a criterion based on location but is independent from administrative structure. In contrast, for example, the Hunan chamber in Shenzhen was originally the 'Shenzhen Hunan Enterprise Management Association' ('Shenzhenshi Hunan qiye guanli xiehui' 深圳市湖南企业管理协会) that was managed by the representative office of Hunan government in Shenzhen ('Hunan renminzhengfu zhu Shenzhen banshichu' 湖南省人民政府驻深圳办事处). In 2013, this organization was transformed into a chamber of commerce and is now supervised by the All-China Federation of Industries. Hence, although it is based on territorial criteria, it is neither an identity-based association nor originally emerged from grassroots-level activities, such as the Chaoshan associations. We come back to this example in Section 4.

Therefore, the question leads us astray whether China as a whole follows a certain pattern of corporatism. There are domains where the state corporatism paradigm certainly applies, such as trade unions and the national organization of industries. Here, the associations are directly and indirectly tied to government and the CCP and have functions that mainly serve the implementation of government policies. This includes a consultative mode, thus establishing the pattern of 'responsive authoritarianism' which might include the representation of interests of the constituencies.[30] That being said, however, in 2018 even among the *xiehui* only roughly 50 per cent have established a party cell, although this is official policy under Xi Jinping.[31]

At the same time, there are domains of societal corporatism, which might overlap with the former. The associational life in Shenzhen business is bewilderingly complex. For example, subcultural business associations such as the Chaoshan association typically may have a 'youth' branch. At the same time, there is an extraterritorial association of businesspeople from Meixian county in Chaoshan region, which is in fact a Hakka association. This reveals that 'Chaoshan' is a fuzzy territorial criterion and factually refers to subcultural identity (dialect, customs etc.). There are surname associations with specific business associations, such as the Huang Chamber that we meet in the next section. That means, including the whole range of *xiehui*, a single businessperson can be member of several, if not many criss-crossing associations. Many of these associations are not directly controlled by the government.[32] The case of extraterritorial associations is intriguing here, because they might be registered and even endorsed by the government of their place of origin, but not with the local government where they operate. In other words, in Shenzhen they operate as private, though publicly legitimized, organizations. They represent the interests of the private business vis-à-vis Shenzhen authorities, and at the same time, this is endorsed by their native government which pursues regional interests of the native territory (province, city, county) in economic relations with Shenzhen. That means the complex decentralized administrative structure of Chinese 'decentralized' or 'fragmented authoritarianism' finds expression in the hybrid nature of extraterritorial chambers.[33] This complicates the state corporatist paradigm in interpreting Chinese associations.

Although the majority of the *shanghui* represent the interest of their members and are formally independent from any government unit, there are two channels how they can be pulled into the orbit of the state-corporatist regime. The first is via party membership of leaders. This is bolstered by the requirement that has been enforced under Xi Jinping that the associations should set up a party cell, which is led by a party secretary. This does not imply a full transition to the PONGO (party-organized NGO) model, because the original motivation and impetus may be with the constituency, and not with the party. But the party co-opts the organization, and this partly is in the interest of the constituency, especially in business, because the CCP controls crucial resources. The second is the co-optation of leaders into the formal political system, which is independent from party membership, such as becoming a member of the local Political Consultative Conference (PCC) where a certain number of seats is reserved for certain constituencies. Both mechanisms, of course, can work together.

It has been noticed by many observers that businesspeople in China show a strong tendency to assume public office.[34] There are straightforward reasons why this is in their direct interest as businesspeople. For example, PCC membership gives access to government officials and may therefore create insider advantages, such as regarding plans for urban renewal, and offer opportunities to influence policies. Interestingly, the role of associations in lobbying may have been strengthened under Xi Jinping, because individual influence mongering today may easily transgress the red line of corruption, whereas collective representation is much more legitimate.[35] However, empirical research has also provided evidence that aiming at public office may reflect genuine moral and political engagement. This marks the transition to ritual dimensions of associations. Even for the individual leader, striving for public office is often seen as the genuine completion of a lifelong career in business, in the sense of the full development of a moral and civilized person. In other words, the ritual dimension of associations is intimately tied to the views on leadership in business, and hence the personal aspirations of their leaders.[36]

The conceptual linkage is established by status and social capital and the specific symbolic means by which these are signalled. Assuming a leadership position in an association is a signal of social status. Traditionally, and in most associations also today, leaders are expected to sponsor the association financially. These contributions are publicly listed, as is done on the plaques that show the donations to a temple. For example, the journal of the Meixian chamber at Shenzhen presents a list of 346 donors, which details not only cash support, but also other contributions, accumulated since the founding of the association.[37] The smallest donation is RMB 150, the largest is by the chairman, RMB 10,616.000: This is a very substantial amount, and if one considers rank 30 of the list, this still is worth RMB 400,000. The contributions fulfil two functions: One is to get the association running and the other is to signal the wealth and achievement of the businessperson. Hence, we diagnose the characteristic ambivalence of ritual economy activities: The contribution certainly is to the public good, but also meets needs and interests of the sponsor. Leadership positions include important ritual roles such as chairing core events of associations. Many associations have specific ceremonial media, such as their own hymn. Again, this is mostly not the case for industry associations.

The associations formalize a sense of relatedness that is operative in the dynamics of *guanxi* formation. That means associations are arenas of *guanxi* formation, and therefore the internal organization reflects an explicit signalling and ranking of social capital of members. One feature of associations is the proliferation of official functions and titles, certainly far beyond actual needs, which signals internal status and recognition. For example, the Meixian association has a long list of officials, with 'li shi' (directors) numbering 75 which certainly does not reflect actual functional requirements of organizing the association. The much bigger Chaoshan *shanghui* has more than 240 'directors'. The point is to be included in the list as signalling to be a responsible member of the respective business community. This leadership position is a social asset that can be utilized in many contexts to advance individual business interests. One significant aspect is that being a leader also signals certain moral qualities that are recognized by the community. Hence, the moral dimension is expressed in the fact that most associations are active in philanthropy. This is a significant difference to Western NGOs, which specialize functionally, thereby also treating philanthropy and lobbyism separate. In the Chinese case, a business association may also be active in various philanthropic activities and advertises this as a signal that it pursues goals of public interest. Often, this would not necessarily mean that the association directly funds charity, but that it instigates and leads the business community to engage individually in charity or in emergency activities such as disaster relief.

In sum, many associations reflect ritual concerns in terms of manifesting a moral economy of collective leadership and community responsibility, both relative to the constituency and to society at large. This moral economy is certainly less prominent as far as purely functional associations are concerned, such as those representing a specific industry. But they come to the fore in the more generic associations, such as extraterritorial associations in which shared native place is prominent. Shared native place suggests shared identity, if not a sense of relatedness as closeness. This may be reflected in the considerable philanthropic investments of sojourners back home, which might not be visible at the place where they actually live. Therefore, a certain tension may arise: The associations may reflect pure interest group politics in the Shenzhen environment while displaying their ritual roles at the native place. Yet, in the public appearance, the latter are showcased in the media and publications.

As we see, the ritual dimension introduces a new perspective in the duality of state versus societal corporatism, as it highlights the potential role of public mindedness, moral economy, and moral status in explaining the relationship between elites in associations and government. Government does not need to impose certain goals on society, but a core principle of leadership in associations is to identify with the common good and, by implication, with the government. This fits squarely with the Confucian tradition. This tradition is much more salient in those types of associations that explicitly activate imaginaries of belonging and shared identities, such as the surname associations.

3 Surname associations: Descent as frame for networking

As already introduced in Chapter 4, one case where traditional ritual and associations are directly connected is surname associations. Although surname associations are ubiquitous in the Chinese context, they have rarely been subject to more detailed research. In terms of the logic and practice of ritual, however, surname associations are of considerable interest. This is because surname is a category that in principle bridges across most other particularistic ties, especially dialect and region. At the same time, surname is articulated in a way that establishes deep historical connections among people sharing the same surname, thus extending the notion of shared descent beyond genealogy in the narrow sense. This specific logic was explicitly recognized in postcolonial Singapore early on, where the government actively sponsored surname associations under certain conditions, especially engagement in dissemination of Mandarin.[38] Whereas Singapore immigrants were mainly organized in terms of native place and by implication, dialect, surname is a much more inclusive category, and would invoke the cultural unity of the Chinese in terms of shared descent, as we have seen, many surnames reaching back into a distant past of even the origins of Chinese civilization.

In this chapter, we look at one surname association in more detail, which is prominent in the context of one of the urban villages that we studied, the Huang. The Huang are of special interest as they represent a very clear case of how genealogy and cultural descent interact, as explored in Chapter 4. The Huang (Wong) surname belongs to the most frequent in China and globally, probably including more than 25 million people in China and 60 million worldwide.[39] The international surname association, however, does not simply rely on shared surname but on shared descent. This is obvious via the specific terminology of naming the association (see Chapter 4 for more detail) 'World Huang Surname Association' ('Shijie Huang shi zongqinhui' 世界黄氏宗亲会): first, it uses *shi* to refer to surname, which in many uses of the term comes close to 'clan'; second, we find *zong* which goes beyond descent in invoking ritual descent more specifically; and *qin* which signals special emotional closeness of members. Therefore, surname implies both ritual and emotional relatedness.

Theoretically, the Huang surname can be traced back to the Yellow emperor.[40] Then, there is an ambiguity between Huang descent and Han descent in general, as the Yellow Emperor is a mythical ancestor of all Han

Chinese. As such, the annual Grand Rites held at his birthplace do not give a prominent place to Huang surname group but are conceived as a national event (for reports with pictorial impressions, see endnote[41]). Yet, Huang proudly participate and send delegations. As we explain in Chapter 4, the other part of the spectrum is the lineages at certain locations, such as Xiasha. The Xiasha Huang refer to the Yellow Emperor as well, but also to the first 'high ancestor' who can be historically identified and thereby substantiates genealogical claims. This is the Tang official Huang Qiaoshan, married to three wives and siring 21 sons, who form the branches of the Huang surname group as one subgroup of all people sharing the name.[42] In fact, in Huang myths of origin, reference is made to a tribe in the Warring States period in today's Inner Mongolia, thus even suggesting non-Han tribal identity, at least as a subethnic group. However, even in this respect the same applies, as mentioned previously: the notion of cultural descent even overcomes strong subethnic and quasi-ethnic distinctions, such as the differentiation between 'yumin' (Tanka) and Han today: If the Yumin adopt proper rituals and share the same surname, they can change their subcultural ascription in joining the Huang mainstream.[43] In Shenzhen, this transpires in the confusion that is often created regarding the subethnic identification of certain groups. At Longgang, there are two neighbouring Hakka villages, both dominated by Huang, who trace themselves back to different high ancestors, although all of them lead back to Qiaoshan: The Kengzi Huang treat a certain Huang Chaoxuan as their ancestor who lived during the Ming/Qing transition, and who in turn is diffusely related to a Song official who is identified as a Qiaoshan descendant.[44] Accordingly, there are often statements that the Xiasha Huang are also Hakka, which however is elusive. One reason why this distinction is fluid lies in Hakka identity as such, which is even not necessarily based on dialect (see Chapter 7). In fact, the Huang at Shenzhen are a surname group with lineages at many locations, resulting from waves of immigration and local migration within historical Xin'an area, thus creating a web of *guangfu* Huang groups, such as the Huang at Futian village, which we met in Chapter 3, or the Huang at Shanghe village, Bao'an district, whom we will visit in the next chapter.

Considering the origin of the largest Huang branch with Huang Qiaoshan, presumably covering all Shenzhen Huang, obviously the size of the genealogically related group is very large, encompassing more than 11 million individuals, with 3 million only in Guangdong province. However, via the genealogy, all of them could be joined in shared rituals. One of these is the conventions of the World Huang surname association, at which, as we have seen in the previous chapter, the *da pencai* events were held. This association was established in Taiwan in 1980 as an umbrella organization of all national Huang associations worldwide. Hence, this is an example for international impact on the formation of associations in Mainland China: The Shenzhen Huang could just jump on a train running for decades and exploit global networking opportunities. However, this is by no means unique to the Huang. For example, the Yuan surname is said to have settled in the Dongguan area already during the Northern Song times, later migrating to the Shenzhen territory, especially Luohu. Since their origin is said to be at Runan county located in Henan, they trace their origin back to the Western Zhou times, when a fiefdom of this name already existed. Accordingly, the Shenzhen Yuan, together with other Yuan groups, especially in Hong Kong, use the term 'Runan' to refer to their surname. Even though today there is no Yuan ancestral hall in Luohu, the Yuan refer to this in their imaginaries, manifest in the name of their shareholding cooperative 'Shenzhen shi Luohu Runan shiye youxian gongsi' 深圳市罗湖汝南实业股份有限公司, which was established in 1992. The Yuan group at Shenzhen is small (about 400 individuals), but they connect tightly with the Hong Kong Yuan, and reach out globally via the surname association, the Hong Kong-based 'Xianggang Yuan runan tang zongqinhui' 香港袁汝南堂宗亲会.[45]

There is significant networking among local Huang groups across China. As in the case of the Yuan, we need to observe the linkage between genealogy and the history of migration. A core location in Huang history is Jiangxia in Wuhan, where the early tribes first settled when their kingdom was destroyed. Therefore, Jiangxia is also a synonym for Huang (as Runan for the Yuan). Accordingly, when it comes to associations, we also need to include the 'Jiangxia culture' associations at many places in China. These are distinct from lineage organization, in the sense that they directly invoke cultural descent. Therefore, we observe a maze of regionally distributed associations that relate with the surname Huang and the specific descent line which historically runs through the node of Jiangxia. Local Huang groups in Shenzhen may refer to historically closer ancestors: The Huang at Xiasha trace themselves back directly to Huang Siming, who is the ninth-generation descendant to Huang Moutang who is the shared ancestor of Huang in the region, especially the neighbouring Shangsha Huang. Huang Moutang is the 15th-generation descendant of Huang Qiaoshan, and as such part of a 'living memory' in Shenzhen, as his tomb can still be visited and has been declared cultural heritage of the Guangdong province in 2002.[46] Evidently, this system of nested descent also shapes a web of potential relations in the present.

This web is activated in various shared activities. There are important locations such as Huang Qiaoshan's tomb that are the destination of study tours which have the distinct flavour of pilgrimages. Often, delegations of Huang visit other Huang branches and may take part in certain ritual activities. Today, one essential medium for these activities is the internet, both via websites and WeChat. There are portals which gather many independent websites of local Huang and Jiangxia organizations, and which regularly report about ritual events. A not-for-profit company established by Huang in Shenzhen, the Shenzhen Huang Surname Culture Web Technology Company Ltd (深圳·市黄氏文化网络技术有限公司), created a 'shopping mall' on

WeChat offering exclusive services to Huang business against the background of the huge size of the Huang community.[47] For example, the website offers products by Korean Huang companies. Although it is difficult to assess the authenticity of the proclamations, the website claims to establish a 'sharing economy' of the Huang (e.g. no fees for posting an offer) and emphasizes the mutual benefit and concern of all Huang ('mutual help and shared benefit, jointly creating value'; 'huzhu tongxiang, gongchuang jiazhi' 互助同享，共创价值). But in fact, authenticity is not really a central concern here, as we observe the mobilization of ritual context, namely cultural descent, for business.

The Huang have also established a Huang Chamber of commerce which offers various kinds of support for Huang members, such as in recruitment of staff. Via the Chamber of Commerce, the Huang create networks that reach out internationally. One important location is Xiamen, where currently the headquarters of the World Huang Chamber of Commerce is located, together with the headquarters of the World Huang Association, which was moved from Taipei.[48] A beautifully restored temple is devoted to Huang Peisong (who was active in overthrowing Imperial rule and became a Republican military leader) and hosts the offices of the Chamber. The location is significant because it connects to Taiwan, and many visitors from Taiwan visit this place.

If one asks what establishes the shared Huang identity, the answer mainly lies in ritual practices. We should not define this in overly narrow terms, because the activities on WeChat are ritual practices transferred to another context. The Huang websites are mostly similar in content, but all of them converge on raising similar claims on the cultural excellence of Huang.[49] As we discuss in some more detail in the next chapter, one element is the promulgation of 'family customs' 'jiafeng' 家风 or 'jiaxun' 家训, which are norms of proper behaviour in the familial and social context. The hall at Xiamen has a separate room devoted to *jiafeng*, which includes an accessible database on family customs in China for all surnames.

The Huang case shows the complex ramifications of cultural descent and its use in the economic context. There are many other examples, since we observe a revival of surname associations in general. Let us look at the Luo.[50] In Tangnan township, Meizhou prefecture, the Luo are a very large lineage that dominates even the township government. Meizhou is a Chaoshan region where many Luo also have leading government positions. A Luo entrepreneur moved to Shenzhen and slowly developed a business ecosystem centred on a hotel. That means, in the neighbourhood of the hotel, many Luo from his native place set up related business mainly in the service industry. In May 2017, the Luo surname association was founded.[51] This case is interesting, because there is a famous Luo lineage in Longgang belonging to the Hakka group. The former Luo walled village is today the Shenzhen Hakka museum that features the history of the local Luo, which includes very far-reaching relatives, because the Luo emigrated to the Bahamas, among other locations, where one Luo married a former slave. As a consequence, there is even a US news reporter who is apparently African American, but in fact has Luo ancestors.[52] The office of the Shenzhen Luo association is located there. The local museum has all the details about the case, because the American recognized her Hakka ancestry and followed the practice of *xun gen*. As we see, the category of surname is extremely inclusive: For example, the Huang include the Australian politician Penny Wong into their line, who is of mixed descent of a Malaysian Chinese father and an Australian mother.[53]

A central activity of surname associations is the collection and reconstruction of genealogies. The internet is a medium through which the various local initiatives can be connected, and genealogies can be combined, mainly in reconstructing the migration history. Clearly, this history mostly leads back to the Northern origins of the Han civilization. Therefore, surname ritual is deeply imbued by ethnic and national identity. This is a powerful means of driving the inclusiveness of business networks. Via the historical dimension, the local groups at Shenzhen can also establish claims of cultural excellence countering their image as native farmers: For example, at the entrance of the Xiasha Cultural Square, a huge bronze shows the first *jinshi* degree holder of the local Huang branch. All surname groups in Shenzhen highlight the scholarly celebrities in their genealogy, with prominent examples such as the Chen who claim to be genealogically connected to the Song dynasty neo-Confucian scholar Chen Xiang.

To sum up, surname associations are one of the most visible examples for the role of ritual in the traditional meaning in creating social capital that can be mobilized in business, both within the business domain and in relation to the government. They are an associational form between lineage organization and functional associations, and which grows out of a core category of traditional ritual, kinship. Although the huge size of surname groups does not justify the use of 'kinship' here, still it is significant that ritual serves to create relations of trust that ultimately rest on a kinship logic, and after all that logic is not purely artificial, because it is based on descent, often with clear historical evidence. As we have argued in Chapter 4, kinship as cultural descent is manifest in ritual activities which create emotional stances of *qin*, that is, relatedness.

4 Place of origin: Networking arenas and the production of trustworthiness

One of the prominent phenomena of the ritual economy of associations is the role of native place or place of origin. When we use the term 'native place' here, we include many organizational forms that do not refer to the native place of individuals, but to the place of origin of companies or the location of the headquarters. Native place associations in the narrower meaning have a long history in China, and there is rich variety of related organizational forms in Shenzhen today. It must be noticed that native place associations have been under strict control of the CCP as far as national representation is concerned, emphasizing national unity and cultural homogeneity. However, especially in the context of the economy, native place associations flourish, mostly under the label of 'XX chamber of commerce'. The modern term for these organizations is *yidi shanghui*, extraterritorial chambers. The notion of native place is a scalar one, because it can apply with various scope, such as treating a province as a native place or a county in that province, so that there are often various native place associations which an individual can join. At the same time, native place associations are present at different locations, so that a web of potential relationships is created.

If we deal with extraterritorial chambers of commerce, an important difference to genuine native place associations must be emphasized, since membership is limited to entrepreneurs and companies. Indeed, these organizations can be mostly conceived as a framework of collective organization of private businesses. Depending on the size of the local community and the economic position of the place of origin, therefore extraterritorial chambers can have considerable size. For example, Wenzhou in Zhejiang province is famous for being one of the cradles of private business in reform China, and Wenzhou entrepreneurs create associations in all important cities of China and worldwide. Via the Wenzhou chambers, they are connected.[54]

Let us look at the example of Hunan in some more detail, which we met several times already. Hunan entrepreneurs are very active in the Pearl River Delta, and there is a rich associational life that is grounded in native place networks. Hunan people form one of the largest groups in Shenzhen, comparable to Chaoshan people; numbers vary between three and four million. One example for Hunan immigration is You county in Hunan.[55] There is a You chamber of commerce in Shenzhen and a You chamber of commerce in Guangdong province. The county has attracted news interest, because in the past 30 years, before the advent of car calling services, the Shenzhen taxi business was dominated by drivers from You county. This was the result of chain migration. Individuals from You county migrated to Shenzhen in search of opportunities, settling down at one urban village, Shixia, located in the CBD Futian. Historically, Shixia was a multi-surname village, and probably for that reason very receptive to outsiders already in the early years of opening up. Once some You immigrants entered the taxi business successfully, they attracted relatives from their native place to this urban village. This resulted in a growing concentration of taxi drivers from You county in Shixia. At the height of this development, it is said that about 3,000 drivers lived there with their families, making up one-third of the population in that urban village. This massive concentration of people from this specific place of origin triggered the emergence of other You-related businesses, such as restaurants or shops with local specialties. As a result, Shixia or part of Shixia has been nicknamed 'dishi cun' or 'digecun'. However, there are also other urban villages that manifest similar phenomena, such as Dawang village, where it is estimated that about 1,000 driver families live. In this case, the village is almost entirely populated by Hunan people, because the villagers have moved out, mostly to Hong Kong, and only come back at certain ritual occasions.

The Hunan taxi drivers naturally form a network of relations, partly via kinship, but mostly via shared place of origin. Many of the drivers are sojourners in the traditional sense, who, for example, invest back home in building lavish homes while living under modest conditions of the urban village in Shenzhen. That means their social relations in Shenzhen are still under the shadow of the relations in their native place. For example, social status is not primarily determined by their status in Shenzhen, but by the status of the family in You county and their native villages.

The growing presence of You taxi drivers in Shenzhen forms a natural ecosystem of business information which enabled some of them to move into other related service areas and upscale their business. In addition, the strong network ties back to native place also create a flow of business relations and potential for contact that attracts other entrepreneurs from You county. In response to these developments, in 2016 the You Chamber of commerce established a presence in Shenzhen, also endorsed by You county government. Apart from the usual function of business intelligence, social networking, and advertisement, a characteristic feature is philanthropic activity, such as mobilizing members for service in flood relief measures at other places.

We already mentioned the Hunan Chamber of Commerce, which has the province as a reference and originated from a government body, as we saw. Therefore, the Hunan Chamber is less explicit about ritual aspects of Hunan culture as expressing Hunan identity. Yet, the imaginary of 'hometown' ('laoxiang' 老乡) is prominent in many activities of the chamber. A recent example is the 'Returning home' event at Changsha, at which 19 Hunan associations abroad and more than 100 Hunan extraterritorial Chambers in China participated, and which was a major networking arena.[56]

In May 2019, a famous Hunan public business thinker visited the Hunan Chamber, Wu Jiyan.[57] A successful businessman and investor from Hunan, he is an example of cultural and ritual entrepreneurship par excellence, who is engaged in promoting business associations in general and Hunan culture in particular for more than two decades. Culture is an essential concept in *shanghui*: The You chamber explicitly ties up with a 'You culture net' which celebrates local culture. As mentioned previously, the Hunan chamber is less explicit because it puts its Maoist credentials at the forefront. Wu became engaged in the Hunan association issue when in the early 2000s, he launched the first national meeting of local chambers, and he also established the first

Chamber in Chongqing. Later, he became active in masterminding a special ritual framework for the chambers, which builds on an elaborate opinion about their historical background. He explicitly argues that modern Chambers need to cut the relationship with traditional blueprints (which he refers to as 'shangbang') and adopt a modern approach which is defined in the 'small government, big society' model. One activity was to create an oath and a hymn for 'xiangshang' 湘商.[58] That is part and parcel of his effort to create a specific 'xiangshang' culture, especially in the organizational form of 'Associations promoting Xiangshang culture' ('Xiangshang wenhua cujinhui' 湘商文化促进会). This must be seen against the background of current stereotypes of Hunan, which emphasize its role as place of origin of political and military leaders (which is effectively accentuated by the Shenzhen Hunan Chamber). Wu suggests a new, modernist interpretation of *xiangshang* culture, which emphasises innovation, entrepreneurship, and social responsibility. This new view is manifest at the public events of the associations, which reach out also internationally.[59]

As we have already noticed in the context of surname associations, there is an internal contradiction in the cultural claims of associations which are particularistic by definition, but mostly characterize local culture in terms of mainstream values. Apparently, this has been strengthened under Xi Jinping: For example, the official website of the Hunan chamber at Shenzhen mostly highlights the strong interaction with political leaders and its role in mediating between business and politics, of course, as embodied in the party. Yet, at the same time, cultural identity is increasingly invoked: A recent international assembly of Hunan chambers at Yiyang ran under the label of 'Xiangshang', as programmatically established by Wu Jiyan.[60] The Hunan chamber cooperated with the Xiangshan culture association and other associations, including a 'Xiangshang Institute for Advanced Confucian Studies', in celebrating the 400th anniversary of Wang Chuanshan's birthday, a famous Ming dynasty philosopher (original name Wang Fuzhi).[61] These activities join the Confucian revival movement in China, which we look at in more detail in the next chapter.

There are examples of extraterritorial chambers which emphasize the cultural specificity of their native culture. This is most salient in case of the Hakka. The Meixian chamber at Shenzhen adopts a highly traditional frame of presenting its public image, in which much emphasis is laid on one distinct aspect, namely that Hakka businesspeople pay much attention to scholarship. This transpires in using the classical form of a long 'fu' poem to express the spirit of 'Mei merchants'. In this context, it is necessary to consider the relationship between subethnic identity and native place in some more detail. As we have already mentioned, the category 'Hakka' is invoking special features, such as a distinct dialect, a certain cuisine, or traditionally a specific architectural design. In Shenzhen today, being Hakka is of significance because Hakka occupy important positions in government (see next chapter). This has consequences: We learned of examples of local leaders who learn Hakka dialect to smooth interaction with government. But, as we have mentioned in the previous section, this also renders diffuse how to demarcate the Hakka community. One is native place: One is Hakka if one comes from a place that is historically and until today prominent as a Hakka settlement and region. This is especially true for Meixian. The interesting observation, however, is that Meixian is part of the Chaoshan region, so that origin and subethnic identity interfere in complex ways. Meixian origin does not imply Chaoshan identity, but Hakka identity.

Like other native place organizations, the Meixian Chamber emphasizes the role of Meixian people in national politics and history. Its honorary chairman is Ye Xuanping, eldest son of Marshall Ye Jianying, a celebrated leader of the PLA. This highlights the association between business and government, which also ritually asserted: The association joins the Ye family on Qingming in worshipping at the Marshall's tomb. The main function of the association is to launch and sustain an intensive flow of events on different levels and with different scope, including activities outside Shenzhen, especially paying visits to Meixian, such as holding meetings with the Meixian government. The list of events in 2018 includes more than 110 items. One focus is connecting with Meixian associations at other places, including in other countries. Via honorary positions, leading figures are included in the membership of the associations, such as a famous Indonesian business leader.

There are also Hakka associations in Shenzhen which explicitly refer to Hakka identity, hence obliterating reference to a certain native place. The Hakka chamber is a branch of the powerful Guangdong Hakka chamber, which has supported many Hakka-related business endeavours, such as the establishment of the Meizhou Hakka Bank, which is a private bank that mainly concentrates on national and international Hakka private business.[62] With such valuable services, the Hakka associations are also attractive for young generation Hakka businesspeople. In our interviews with second-generation Hakka successors in family business, they often state that their social circles are prominently based on the Hakka Youth Chamber. One reason is that many of them studied abroad and therefore lack own local *guanxi*. If they do not simply want to follow their fathers' tracks, the association is the best choice as a business networking arena.

As a comparison, it is illuminating to consider the Chaoshan case. The Chaoshan chamber of commerce is a very significant organization, although it was only established in 2010.[63] As mentioned previously, Chaoshan immigrants form a very substantial share of Shenzhen population, and they dominate certain industries. The new chamber is not simply an arena of business networking but offers substantial services to the Chaoshan business community. As a registered entity, it has established various subsidiaries, such as a microcredit fund and a venture capital fund. The association has established formal relations with more than 200 Chaoshan organizations worldwide to foster business. There is a sister organization, the Chaoshan Youth Chamber of Commerce. Both organizations, like in the Hakka case, sustain an intense flow of events that often have a ritual nature with specific orientation, such as involving government organizations. The Youth chamber has also established an academy that regularly offers lectures on business topics. The ritual dimension of these organizations comes to the limelight when considering their engagement in topics related to traditional culture. For example, in 2017, the youth chamber created an initiative for the study of ancestral halls.[64] Apparently, this meets a demand: In interviews with second-generation Chaoshan successors of family business, much emphasis was laid on Chaoshan traditions in business relations and family management.

In addition, as mentioned, associations manifest their ritual nature in philanthropic activities. The Youth chamber includes activities that directly support Chaoshan sojourners in Shenzhen. A most interesting example is that it covers medical insurance for the Chaoshan people living at Hubei village. Hubei village can be compared to the previously mentioned case of the 'Hunan village' in being a subunit of an urban village that is exclusively inhabited by Chaoshan people, and the local villagers, the Zhang lineage, have moved away, only leaving an ancestral hall to mark the ritual space. Chaoshan culture, however, has usurped this ritual space entirely in imbuing it with many religious artefacts in the Chaoshan tradition, as we saw earlier (see Chapter 2).

However, the main function of the Chamber is not to implement charity projects on its own but coordinate the activities of its members. This includes the promotion of model companies, often those of leaders of the association. Another important difference to the Hubei case is that many of the projects do not target Shenzhen, but Chaoshan region, which is remarkable because this implies that the audience to which these projects is addressed is not Shenzhen society, as in the traditional pattern of the relations between sojourners and their native place.

If we draw our various examples together, we notice that extraterritorial chambers increasingly bring the notion of local culture to the fore, against the trend to interpret Shenzhen as a place in which a new cosmopolitan culture is emerging. Imaginaries of local culture mostly emphasize history and all kinds of artefacts that have historical origin. In practical terms, native place is a symbolic reference in activities of creating arenas for networking. This must be distinguished from the representation of interests. However, the *shanghui* also fulfil this function: For example, the Hunan Chamber has established internal committees for certain trades in which Hunan business is especially active, such as jewellery, where Hunan business makes a share of more than 30 per cent of the national market, as we saw previously. One of the most essential functions of *shanghui* is to mediate trust relations between members and various audiences. This is where the signalling of moral and political standing achieves direct relevance for business. For example, Chambers often establish relations with banks and mediate loans and other financial contributions to members: The Hunan Chamber operated as a trustee for banks in mediating about 70 billion loan facilities to member companies during its existence, and it has established a financial committee that manages about 23 funds with a total volume of about 30 billion Yuan and is involved in organizing IPOs, among other financial activities.

These activities reveal that there is no contradiction between traditional ritual notions such as native place and functional requirements of modern business. Although one can certainly argue that associations manifest a range of internal governance mechanisms that could work independently from ritual notions, such as reputation, yet the origin and maintenance of the network structure builds on the ritual frames.

5 Conclusion

Ritual entrepreneurship and associations are closely related phenomena. Often, associations are created by the initiative of single individuals adopting leadership roles; however, eventually they are transformed into forms of collective entrepreneurship as embodied forms of business networking. Theoretically, what matters is the distinction between 'interest' and 'identity', which reveals another fundamental difference between Western and Chinese views on associational life that root in diverging theoretical perspectives. In Western economics, associations are exclusively interpreted in terms of 'interest', hence as lobby groups and rent-seeking outfits. This view, however, begs the crucial question on how interests come into being, especially as shared interests.[65] In sociological theory, the point has been made early that collective action cannot be based on shared individual interests alone, because this would automatically trigger all individual disincentives for collective action as scrutinized in the vast literature on Public Choice. There must be an additional force, and on the most abstract level this is to share 'preferences', in the economic jargon, which translates into shared identities.[66] However, there must be a medium through which these shared identities can be created in a dynamic and changing world. This is communication of ideas, again, on the most abstract level, or more concretely, rituals. Whereas Western social theory would emphasize ideas, the Chinese view suggests ritual, and hence vindicates those minority positions in Western theory that emphasize ritual, too, such as our chosen framework, Collins' approach.

In modern Shenzhen, we see these differences in lively detail. Most importantly, 'interest', different from liberal capitalist economies, is not the main domain of self-organizing civil society but is part and parcel of a state-corporatist institutional regime. This is represented by the *xiehui*, which have both functions of representing interests and mediating government policy. The second ideal type form of associations, such as many chambers, are also pursuing the interests of their members, but activate a shared identity which is often not directly related to interest: An extraterritorial chamber does not represent the interest of the native region, whatever that would mean, although home governments try to co-opt these chambers. Interests are embedded in a more fundamental process of expressing shared identity. As stated in Collins' theory, this is mainly based on activating certain emotions of belonging. Evidently, these relate to cultural imaginaries that refer to migration, settlement, and descent. Shared identities emerge from shared narratives about the past, which are triggered by references to certain places or ancestors. These have no relation at all with 'interests' as emerging in the economic domain, in the specific sense. But they enable forms of collective action that support the pursuit of interest.

As we have noticed, associations are a form of societal self-organization that can easily adapt to modern life and to the lifestyles of a younger generation, probably different from kinship-related rituals. This adaptation is often undertaken by ritual entrepreneurs. Hakka identity can be manifest in traditional 'mountain songs' or Hakka rock music elegies, as is well known from the very lively Hakka scene in Taiwan. What song is sung at a future Hakka convention does not change its nature as a ritual.

Notes

1 http://www.chaoshang.org/News/Info-2759.html; http://www.chaoren.com/news/chaoxun/magazine/sdcr/2016-02-25/104354.html, both accessed November 15, 2019.
2 Tao Qing (2007: 2ff).
3 Seminally, Sangren (1984).
4 Tang Tongxue (2010).
5 This is an interesting example, because the institutional constructs that enabled inter-village cooperation in irrigation also shaped marriage relations and therefore kinship alliances; Wu (2014).
6 There is rich anthropological literature on the organization of temples in modern China; see, for example, Pennarz (1992) or Chau (2006).
7 In his study of the emergence of the Huaqiangbei Chamber of Commerce, Tao Qing (2007) systematically refers to metaphors taken from traditional ritual to refer to the processes and organizational features of the Chamber, although these, in their original meaning, do not play any factual role. In doing this, the author suggests this implicit transfer.
8 Sangren (1984) analyses these commonalities in detail.
9 A landmark study of Hankou, which reveals much detail about associational life, is Rowe (1989).
10 Von Glahn (2016: 267, 301).
11 Liu (1988); Von Glahn (2016: 395).
12 On market communities and taxation, see Mann (1987). These patterns have been theorized as 'state brokerage' in Duara (1988).
13 Chan (1988).
14 Rowe (1989: 323f).
15 Bastid-Bruguiere (1980: 563). Chan (1991) reports the fascinating observation about colonial Hong Kong in the late 19th century, when local merchant leaders shot pictures of themselves adorned with the insignia of Imperial officials.

16 Chan (1992).
17 Kuah-Pearce (2011). Cohen (1994) discusses the relationship between periphery and mainland in 20th century Chinese culture.
18 Fewsmith (1983).
19 State corporatism emerged in Republican China and was then also maintained in Taiwan until democratic reforms since the 1980s. For an overview of the transitions in the 20th century, see Bergère (1983).
20 Unger and Chan (2015).
21 Chen (2010) therefore speaks of a 'quadrupartite' structure. In another context, Thornton (2013) uses the term PONGO, 'party organized NGO', for a specific type of NGO that have been instigated by the party.
22 This wider scope of the notion of ritual is adopted in Herrmann-Pillath (2018a).
23 Ma Hong et al. (2013). This corresponds to the national situation at that time. Hsu and Jiang (2015) report that in 2013, there were about eight million unregistered NGOs in China, and only about 500,000 registered with the Ministry of Civil Affairs.
24 Shenzhen shangbao, April 3, 2019.
25 Shenzhen shi shehuizuzhi guanli ju (2018a).
26 Shenzhen shangbao, April 3, 2019.
27 Shenzhen shi shehuizuzhi guanli ju (2018a: 20).
28 Shenzhen shi shehuizuzhi guanli ju (2018b: 135ff)
29 http://www.chaoshang.org/news/info-2651.html, accessed November 4, 2019.
30 Fukuyama (2011). Teets (2013) uses the term 'consultative authoritarianism'.
31 Shenzhen shi shehuizuzhi guanli ju (2018a: 11).
32 Compare Heberer and Schubert (2019).
33 Xu (2011).
34 Li and Liang (2015).
35 Heberer and Schubert (2019).
36 Chen and Lee (2008); Chen and Farh (2010). The management literature on Chinese leadership styles emphasizes the centrality of moral authority and legitimacy.
37 Shenzhen shi meixian shanghui (2019).
38 Chan (2002).
39 https://baike.baidu.com/item/%E9%BB%84%E5%A7%93, accessed March 5, 2019.
40 On Huang genealogy, see http://www.jxhzw.org/hxyy/739.html, accessed March 6, 2019.
41 https://mp.weixin.qq.com/s/4V70HUndktDSxc_CgM7ZSg, accessed March 6, 2019. https://baijiahao.baidu.com/s?id=1629956168823059368&wfr=spider&for=pc&isFailFlag=1, accessed January 21, 2020.
42 With special reference to the Xiasha Huang, see http://www.360doc.com/content/16/0923/21/13888283_593145032.shtml, accessed March 6, 2019.
43 Inazawa (2016).
44 Liu (2002: 56f.).
45 For the Hong Kong Yuan association, see http://www.yuenclansmen.com/. On the shareholding cooperative, see http://www.szlh.gov.cn/qgbmxxgkml/nhjdbsc/jgzn/gfgs/201409/t20140912_10038975.htm; both accessed November 28, 2019.
46 https://szbbs.sznews.com/forum.php?mod=viewthread&tid=1717705&extra, accessed March 6, 2019.
47 http://rhd361.com/special/news?id=2929a6fd4ef941708f551132c2e59183, accessed March 6, 2019.
48 http://blog.sina.com.cn/s/blog_4e9a6f920100ueqr.html, accessed March 6, 2019.
49 For important examples, see http://www.jxhzw.org/ and http://www.ihuang.org/a8-01.htm, both accessed March 6, 2019.
50 Zhou (2003).

51 http://www.360doc.com/content/17/0522/16/36555814_656195153.shtml; http://www.zhlswhw.net/news/?2612.html, both accessed November 25, 2019.

52 On the Hakka Luo, see http://www.zhlswhw.net/news/?2612.html; https://zhidao.baidu.com/question/53430989.html. On the story of Paula Lowe, see http://sz.southcn.com/m/content/2016-09/06/content_155345718.htm, all accessed November 25, 2019.

53 http://www.jxhzw.org/hwhs/1409.html, accessed November 25, 2019.

54 Compare Pieke et al. (2004), who discuss the activities of Fujian people abroad.

55 On the following, see https://xw.qq.com/cmsid/20190717A0RVIZ00; https://baijiahao.baidu.com/s?id=1637831939423809979&wfr=spider&for=pc&isFailFlag=1; http://m.voc.com.cn/wxhn/article/201604/201604071002328093.html; http://www.sohu.com/a/119596061_442221; https://szbbs.sznews.com/thread-3536908-1-1.html?from=threadlink, all accessed November 26, 2019.

56 http://www.szhnsh.com/shxw/show.asp?id=3239, accessed November 26, 2019.

57 http://www.szhnsh.com/shxw/show.asp?id=3256, accessed November 26, 2019. Wu Jiyan (2014) published a book on the conceptual framework of his activities that also includes many original documents. An extensive summary of his thought and activities can be found at Baidu: https://baike.baidu.com/item/%E4%BC%8D%E7%BB%A7%E5%BB%B6 accessed March 26, 2019.

58 See "The manifest of xiang shang", Wu Jiyan's Sina blogsite http://blog.sina.com.cn/s/blog_59bd2c3e0100aa48.html (last accessed March 26, 2019); "The Song of Xiang Shang" is on Baidu Encylopedia, https://wapbaike.baidu.com/item/湘商之歌/19916372?ms=1&rid=8781787220867319695&rt=true&bk_tashuoStyle=topLeft&bk_share=shoubai&bk_sharefr=lemma (last accessed March 26, 2019).

59 'The Association of Promoting the Xiang Shang Culture Sent a Delegation to Celebrate the Inauguration of the Hunan Chamber of Commerce and Hunan Natives Association of Phillippines', Wu Jiyan's Sinablog, December 3, 2017, http://blog.sina.cn/dpool/blog/s/blog_59bd2c3e0102x65i.html, accessed March 26, 2019.

60 https://hnxs.rednet.cn/content/2019/10/29/6172040.html, accessed November 26, 2019.

61 http://www.chinakongzi.org/rw/jiaoliu/201910/t20191008_200918.htm; http://www.hn.xinhuanet.com/2019-10/31/c_1125177273.htm, both accessed November 28, 2019.

62 The chamber website: http://www.zhks.org/; the bank website: http://www.kshbank.cn/ksyhjj.html; accessed November 28, 2019.

63 https://baike.baidu.com/item/%E6%B7%B1%E5%9C%B3%E6%BD%AE%E6%B1%95%E5%95%86%E4%BC%9A; http://www.chaoshang.org/about/index-1.html; http://www.chaoqing.org/Meet/Default-29.html; http://www.chaoshang.org/news/info-2644.html, all accessed November 29, 2019.

64 http://www.chaoqing.org/Meet/Info-1116.html, accessed November 29, 2019.

65 Hay (2011).

66 Barnes (1995).

7 Cultural governance and the ritual affirmation of traditional values

1 Culture and governance in the local state

In the past two decades, China studies have increasingly noticed the growing role of traditional culture in societal governance, dubbed 'cultural governance'.[1] This phenomenon can be approached in various, sometimes complicated, ways, which we disentangle in this chapter and look at how this is manifest in Shenzhen today. There are two basic perspectives.

- The first and direct form is the increasing and explicit support for traditional values and various elements of Chinese cultural tradition by official CCP policies. This includes the much-noticed revival of Confucianism, in both grassroots level versions and intellectual contributions, endorsed by the CCP in various forms.[2]
- The second manifestation is indirect and refers to the patterns of cultural control. This comes along in two versions. One is the control of cultural production in the widest sense, which includes today not only the creative sector, but also economic domains such as tourism. The other is approaching culture as means of governing society, which stands in the tradition of Imperial rule. This would partly correspond to the first form, but allows for wider variation in terms of cultural content. In other, provocative words, Confucian control of culture can combine with non-Confucian cultural content.

The theoretical concept that emerges from this diagnosis is 'cultural governance'. This reflects the ambiguity of the previous, as this can mean both 'governance *of* culture' and 'governance *by* culture', which is not mutually exclusive. As we argue in this book, however, the concept of culture needs to be substantiated by the concept of ritual. That means ritual is a core domain where we can observe cultural governance in action, and ritualization is a form of cultural governance. This does not only include traditional ritual, however, but any form of hybrids and even purely modernist rituals. In our book, we mostly leave the latter aside, but that does not suggest that these are irrelevant. One important corollary of this emphasis on ritual is that we mainly look at phenomena in the public space, and do not discuss beliefs and values in the narrow sense that people might have and endorse. Rituals may be downplayed as mere propaganda, but often public activities are expressions of voluntary actions on the grassroots level or cooperative actions of private and government actors. In cultural governance, ritual entrepreneurs can assume a leading role, co-opted by the government, and act as brokers in civil society.

The concept of cultural governance directly ties up with the notion of 'culturalism' when referring to Imperial rule.[3] In Chinese studies, culturalism refers to a specific form of Imperial governance that was the solution to the huge tension between the size and diversity of the Imperial territory and the weak infrastructural capacity of the Imperial administration. We cannot go in the details here; suffice to say that the Chinese Empire was operating on a very weak fiscal basis by orders of magnitude smaller than comparable regimes in the West, which partly was itself an expression of Confucian commitment to keep the tax burden on the population low.[4] This assessment still applies, even if one considers corruption and irregular extraction from the population.

Against this background, a central pillar of Imperial rule was the cultural control of intermediary elites, especially on the local level. This was mainly implemented by the Civil Service examination system, and was manifest in local rituals, such as the role of the magistrate in lunar year rites.[5] One apparently dysfunctional phenomenon achieves great relevance here: Given the small size of the Imperial bureaucracy, the vast majority of degree holders did not join administration, but obtained special elite status in their local societies, which legitimized their original social status as salient in their capacity to support their male progeny in running for exams. Thus, local landowning elites and rich merchant families were systematically co-opted in the system of Imperial rule. The lineage became one of the core institutions in mediating this role of Imperial culture, especially in South China.[6] The long socialization process in the examination system created a strong shared cultural basis and *esprit de corps* of scholar officials and local gentry.

This stratum of Confucian elites also implemented direct forms of cultural governance, especially in the domain of religion, but also via censorship or editing and launching products of popular culture, such as the various regional operas, thus actively contributing to the dissemination of certain values in the population.[7] This was another building block of culturalism: Confucian and Taoist thinking both supported the idea (contra legalist practices) that society should mainly govern itself based on a set of shared legitimate values. In this sense, familism obtained a pivotal function in political rule, as envisaged by neo-Confucian orthodoxy.[8]

The thesis advanced in this chapter is that the emerging pattern of cultural governance in China today stays in this tradition of culturalism, in the sense of highly significant family resemblances. Of course, this argument needs to take into consideration the simple and 'hard' fact that the infrastructural capacity of the modern Chinese state is much more encompassing than anything that previously existed. But this argument must also recognize that simultaneously the challenges of sheer complexity have grown in tandem: Governing a megacity like Shenzhen under the conditions of the modern technological division of labour, globalization, and overwhelming quantities and flows of information certainly is very different from governing Guangzhou in the 19th century. This is salient in the policy process at the grassroots level: For example, in the debates about the establishment of the Huaqiangbei Chamber of Commerce, government representatives began to support this plan when they realized that more direct supervision and control of companies might be impossible, even if an intermediary organization would be created by the government. In the early 2000s, this would have been a 'zong shanghui' 总商会 under the roof of the Futian district government to which the new Chamber would have been assigned, together with other business associations in the area. But the officials diagnosed that in Futian there were about 46,000 companies and only 0.2 per cent formally under supervision of the Futian government, so that every staff member of the *zongshanghui* would be responsible for 2,000 companies on an average, mostly unknown to her or him. That was deemed infeasible. To the sheer size, add the dynamism and complexity of the rapid urbanization process. When Huaqiangbei was emerging, even most fundamental parameters of development were highly uncertain, such as the property rights structure. Most of the land was already state-owned, but not under the control of the municipal government because the place was occupied by state-owned and military companies active in the first decade of SEZ development. The companies had left, creating a legal limbo, since land use rights were sublet to the private companies now occupying the place. The result was a serious governance issue in the district.[9]

In other words, we surmise that the infrastructural gap in governance may be of similar relevance in Imperial China and China today. This is evident in many recent studies on the fiscal system, in particular. Until most recently, the Chinese central government struggled to contain the centrifugal tendencies in the fiscal system. On the one hand, for decades subordinate governments actively deployed all possible means to create and maintain fiscal resources under their control, partly outside of the formally centralized government budget, such as extra budgetary funds or more recently, local investment vehicles. On the other hand, the local-level governments typically are under severe fiscal stress, because since the 1994 tax reforms, internal fiscal redistribution works in favour of the central level in the first round. This drove the phenomenon that increasingly so-called 'service units' ('shiye danwei' 事业单位) were created which need to fund themselves via user fees and other independent forms of income generation. That means, even within formal government, there is a wide range of organizations that are becoming 'corporatized' in the sense of operating for autonomous revenue generation.[10] In other words, there is the apparently paradoxical phenomenon that growing centralization of government is accompanied by a growing mediatization of governance via the creation of intermediary organizations. Obviously, many of the organizations that we discussed in the previous chapters fall under this category, if only after having been co-opted or perhaps sometimes usurped by the municipal government: The *xiehui* are an example of government-instigated organizations, the shareholding cooperatives of the latter.

That being said, our argument on cultural governance is challenged by a 'legalist' phenomenon of cultural governance that is emerging currently. This is using the internet for directly monitoring and incentivizing or sanctioning individual behaviour, such as via the 'social credit system'.[11] We will not explore this further, because the developments are still open-ended; but we recognize that this is a genuine alternative to the more traditional forms of cultural governance because mediation by communities is lacking. However, it is fascinating that in these political visions, the old legalist forms of directly tying individual and state together in a panopticon of rewards and punishments would be manifest in a modern shape.

Cultural governance is a form of governance that is intimately tied to the internal decentralization and lack of coherence of the Chinese bureaucracy that has inspired notions such as 'fragmented authoritarianism' or 'decentralized authoritarianism'.[12] A pivotal concept is that of the 'local state' which mainly applies for the county level, but also involves various forms of urban management and politics that have emerged during the rapid urbanization process in places like Shenzhen. The local state is a governmental entity with a large leeway of autonomous decision-making, while being subject to tight controls of performance as delivered by its political leaders.[13] It plays a central role in the dynamics of experimental policy design, innovation, and adoption, especially in the economy.[14] By definition, a special zone such as the original Shenzhen has many features of a local state, and the new unified municipality carried on with this framework of partly autonomous policy design and implementation. One salient example for this is the way how shareholding cooperatives are regulated: major elements in their corporate governance structure do not follow national corporate law, and one can certainly argue that they are not corporations in the legal sense. They are institutional hybrids which emerged in the Shenzhen local state as a major economic entity, and are being regulated on the local level with guidance on the provincial level.

The general governance framework has been characterized by Philip Huang as 'contracting out' which has a long tradition in China, complementary to the notion of culturalism. Huang has suggested the term 'centralized minimalism' to catch the continuities across the watershed of the fall of empire.[15] That means a politically and culturally strong centre combines with weak bureaucratic integration and infrastructural capacity. The corresponding governance scheme is out-contracting government functions to intermediate bodies. In Imperial China, this even applied for the magistrate: The *yamen* was mainly funded by private money of the lowest-level Imperial scholar-official.[16] Beyond the *yamen*, there were many entities and individuals who directly worked as mediators of government actions, such as the licensed brokers who operated markets. All this follows the general pattern of out-contracting: Against the Imperial assignment of certain privileges, the entity or individual is obliged to fulfil a certain task for the government. Accordingly, these intermediate bodies were Janus-faced. Vis-à-vis the government, they appeared to be private actors and were therefore often treated with mistrust and contempt (such as the even officially despised *yamen* runners). Vis-à-vis the populace, they represented the government and claimed public legitimacy.

More generally, Huang treats this as the administrative complement to a 'third sphere' as a 'public sphere' that is different from 'civil society' as envisaged in Western discourses.[17] In our terminology, cultural governance creates a specific form of third sphere. This is where the previous hypothesis applies that there might be cultural continuities in form, but not in content. The shareholding cooperatives can be interpreted as a semi-governmental unit that is contracting with government about public policies. In this case, cultural governance relies on traditional values and institutions such as the lineage. But there are many other cases where the entities in the third sphere emerge independently from any reference to cultural tradition, such as the Huaqiangbei Chamber of Commerce that we will briefly analyse in this chapter. Yet, its functions are very similar to the role of traditional intermediary bodies of market regulation. In this sense, the Chamber is also a form of cultural governance, albeit in a modernist form.

When analysing State-society relations in China today, it is essential to distinguish between government and party in the One-Party state. Even when the government pursues a minimalist strategy in administration, the party can reach much farther and deeper into society. Specifically, in an out-contracting framework, the contractor organization may be formally independent, but still may set up a party cell which monitors and influences decision-making even if party members are not the leaders. Party building has been a major policy pursued by Xi Jinping and is very active in Shenzhen, too. Party members should not be simply equated with the same roles in Western democracies, however. Although party membership is voluntary and selective, once an individual joins the party, she or he becomes subject to the nomenklatura system of career development and the disciplinary apparatus of the party. That means every party member is faced with performance evaluations that will impact on her or his further career, both within the party and within her or his work environment, which might not be identical with the organization where the party cell is located (such as a chamber, where the party member is active versus the company where she/he works). Therefore, the party secretary does not only have special authority in the relation to other leaders of an organization, but is also motivated to exert this authority for sake of the goals defined by upper levels of party organization. As we have seen in the case of the Hunan chamber of commerce, therefore cultural governance also includes non-traditional rituals, especially political rituals of the Communist Party, such as studying Xi Jinping's speeches at party congresses. As we noticed, the headquarters of the Fenghuang shareholding cooperative is heavily adorned by the ritual artefacts of party leadership.

In sum, cultural governance in Shenzhen should not be simply reduced to the mobilization of tradition for maintaining social order. Cultural governance is complementary to a specific form of administrative decentralization, if not fragmentation, and mediation between government and other societal domains, such as business or the local communities hosting urban villages. Yet, the strong presence of traditional culture in urban life of a modern metropolis is remarkable, by any means.

2 Revival of traditional culture, hereditization, and Shenzhen identity politics

One characteristic of successful local states is that they develop a shared vision of place and policy approaches that drives experimental designs and mobilizes societal actors. There are many examples for this across China on various levels of administration, reaching from counties to megacities. Accordingly, one key concern for Shenzhen leaders has always been to identify a local culture that defines Shenzhen. Until most recently, this was the radically modernist story 'from fisher village to megacity', also emphasizing the role of Shenzhen as a reform avant-garde, a place where many of institutional innovations in Chinese reforms were initially introduced and tested (see Chapter 5).

The Shenzhen local state faces two major challenges in the domain of culture. One is internal integration and cohesion of a migrant society, the other is the evolving role of a shared cultural space with Hong Kong and the larger Pearl River Delta region. In the first two decades, Hong Kong played an important role in speeding up private business development in Shenzhen beyond the efforts of the government, but today Shenzhen has surpassed Hong Kong in many respects, certainly in technology, being home to several of the Chinese internet behemoths, and has emancipated itself from the Hong Kong cultural scene.[18] This compares with the earlier notion of the Pearl River Delta as 'Greater Hong Kong', which was the leading analytical narrative in the 1990s. The 'Greater Hong Kong' narrative was mainly based on the relocation of manufacturing from Hong Kong to the Pearl River Delta, with the accompanying role of Hong Kong corporations and service providers in supplying the global networking capacities for Pearl River Delta business, and on the cultural forces emanating from the shared use of Cantonese language, which enabled the avid reception of Hong Kong popular culture across the border (Hong Kong TV, Canto-Pop etc.).

This pattern has changed dramatically, although Hong Kong has retained its leading role in specific respects: For example, today many Shenzhen businesspeople have also set up a company registered in Hong Kong in order to be able to activate the rich resources of Hong Kong in services, finance, or global connectivity. Often, the entire business family holds Hong Kong passport, thus enjoying the many advantages that come along with it, especially international travel. Last but not least, in the 'One country, two systems' model, Hong Kong continues to supply the scarce good of rule of law and all kinds of conflict resolution in business, which creates confidence on the part of foreign business partners and thus leverages all kinds of cooperation with Shenzhen companies.

However, in other respects, the narrative of 'Shen Kong' seems to fall apart: For example, the second-generation Shenzhen residents often cannot speak Cantonese fluently, eroding more intensive interaction with native Hong Kong people, and increasingly identify with Shenzhen; however, more young Hong Kongers see the inflow of Mainland Chinese with critical eyes, and the trend is growing to express a genuine Hong Kong identity against the earlier idea of cultural integration in the Pearl River Delta.[19] This trend has recently led into severe political turmoil in Hong Kong, resulting in tighter controls of Shenzhen people commuting to Hong Kong. Many Shenzhen people do not share the political convictions of Hong Kong protesters. It is noteworthy, however, that the New Territories play an ambivalent role.

For many decades, the Hong Kong connection had a strong subcultural dimension which mainly focused on the New Territories, previously an integral part of Xin'an county. In the 20th century, there was continuous immigration into the New Territories, often involving lineages with branches in different regions. As we discussed previously, the New Territories partly preserved traditional lineage structures, and therefore Hong Kong lineages played an important role in reviving ancestral halls in Shenzhen after 1978. After 1949, many inhabitants of Shenzhen villages fled to Hong Kong, later returning as investors, but continuing to stay in Hong Kong. The Wen are an important example, with a major branch in Xintian village stemming from Imperial times: In the first decade, many Shenzhen Wen send their children to the Xintian school, but later dispersed to other places, also related to higher-level education.[20] The new pattern of household settlement with two locations, as mentioned, strengthens this Hong Kong connection of local lineages further. However, this introduces a cultural tension against the background of the growing revival of traditional culture in Shenzhen. In this sense, cultural governance in Shenzhen also affects the future role of New Territory groups in Hong Kong. Lineage members in the New Territories often identify with the Chinese Mainland via their shared reference to the Imperial past in their genealogies and myths of origin.[21] When today Shenzhen bloggers, writers, and journalists explore the local history of the region, they increasingly include the New Territories in terms of the reference to old Xin'an county, the precursor of Bao'an county.

The second challenge to Shenzhen cultural governance, internal integration, is today much more important than the Shen Kong theme. As we stated above, under Xi Jinping culture has become an important policy dimension that touches upon many areas and calls for an integrated approach. This applies for Shenzhen with a vengeance, as Shenzhen (see Chapter 5) aims at becoming a 'global city' where culture is a major factor of competitive advantage. The government issued a master plan for the period until 2020 that reflects this view: This comprehensive view emanates from the distinction between five 'systems' where cultural policy must be designed explicitly: The 'spiritual system' ('jingshen xitong' 精神系统), the 'cultural brand system' ('wenhua pinpai xitong' 文化品牌系统), the 'culture dissemination system' ('wenhua chuangbo xitong' 文化转播系统), the 'culture services system' ('wenhua fuwu xitong' 文化服务系统), and the 'modern cultural industries system' ('xiandai wenhua chanye xitong' 现代文化产业系统).[22] The different entities in the systems would need to be coordinated in creating an integrative Shenzhen culture. This transpires in the many ways how culture is manifest in Shenzhen today. For example, the merger between socialist values and tradition would need to be reflected in corresponding research and publications (system 1) that would be picked up by the media (system 3). These ideas would also influence the design of public spaces which contribute to the face of the city, hence its branding (system 2). Relevant cultural products would be made accessible, for example, via libraries (system 4), and further developed in various ways, such as movies (system 5). There are many examples where one can observe this policy in implementation. One important measure is the flow of events and festivals touching upon many topics, from modern design to Hakka 'mountain songs', which involve public spaces, allow for communicating political messages, and invite for further processing, such as creating and promoting creative products.

More recently, as we noticed many times now, the image of Shenzhen is shifting towards the historical origins of the place, while also enriching modernist views of urban life with traditional culture. Under Xi Jinping, traditional culture has achieved a core status in recent propaganda, in the shape of tying national identity of the modern Chinese state back to its civilizational origins, and in promulgating traditional morality and values.[23] Clearly, this does not mean that Confucianism would be directly communicated as a comprehensive frame of reference, but a socialist amalgam of some traditional and modernist values of the CCP. Yet, this list includes core Confucian values, with a paramount status given to 'filial piety' which combines with the explicit endorsement of the family as a nucleus of society. This selective approach is programmatically reflected in the term 'excellent traditional culture' ('youxiu chuangtong wenhua' 优秀传统文化), where 'excellent' implies that not all of tradition is considered to be worthy of emulation today.[24]

These values are conceived as a response to the perceived decay of morality and public spirit in Chinese society, a view that is widely shared with the public. Accordingly, restoring public morality is a major aim of current public policy. This works together with the rich scene of similar activities on the grassroots level, which however would partly fall out of the party line, such as people engaging in Christian house churches or other autonomous religious movements. Even the Confucian revival movements may contain the seed of dissent, especially when it comes to moral critique of the government. Therefore, promoting a socialist version of traditional culture also aims at fencing in alternative and even deviant grassroots-level initiatives. Interestingly, this is an issue in Shenzhen where the socio-psychology of rapid urbanization has led to feelings of anomy and isolation, which might be overcome in a large diversity of grassroots-level religious activities.[25] When it comes to Confucianism, too, Shenzhen is a place where modernist interpretations of Confucianism have taken root, such as the 'political Confucianism' promoted by the philosopher Jiang Qing.[26]

In sum, the Shenzhen local state has moved towards a growing importance of cultural governance. This ties up with the larger setting of shaping Chinese national identity, which is especially salient in the melting pot of the megacity. However, this should not be simply equated with the cultural variety of place of origin, but mainly with the distinct difference between rural and urban, which is enshrined in the Chinese system of household registration. A major fact about Shenzhen is that despite the abolishment of the rural *hukou* in 2004, the majority of natives were farmers before, and still define themselves as 'villagers', and that the vast majority of migrants are still with their native rural *hukou*.[27] In this sense, the socio-cultural mainstream in terms of practices is rural, though not claiming cultural hegemony, which is defined by elite modernism. Subcultural variety is still mainly shaped by the original duality of urban and rural culture. This poses complex challenges at any attempt of explicitly defining a modernist Shenzhen identity that incorporates tradition, because the latter may still be defined in terms of the 'little traditions' of rural people. In other words, cultural governance cannot just impose any form of 'great tradition', be it classical Confucianism or modernist 'socialist civilization', but must incorporate various forms of local traditions, often of rural origin, but make them compatible with modernist conceptions of urbanity and socialism after all.

One solution of this conundrum is offered by the ritual economy: The tension between urban modernity and rural tradition can be overcome in projects of tourism and leisure, a strategy pursued all over China. This is embedded in a rich array of 'hereditization' measures on all levels of government, thus neutralizing the rural reference in terms of 'local customs' or 'historical sites', often baptized as 'cultural heritage' following the UNESCO template that are transformed into tourist and leisure attractions.[28] The situation in Shenzhen, however, is special because these projects are often, as we have seen, driven by autonomous grassroots-level action which effectively expresses the identity politics of the native population. One important trend in these activities is that emphasizing the historical roots of local culture puts it on equal footing with national culture, since its origins are often claimed to tie up with elite culture in Imperial times. This defines a very different frame as compared, for example, with the situation when 'rural' combines with ethnic minority status.[29] Yet, Shenzhen municipality has adopted a comprehensive organizational framework of recognizing and protecting both tangible and intangible cultural heritage, a policy that is also driven by the competition among lower-level administrations, especially district level, who want to develop locational advantages. One can even say that this level is most significant as far as concrete actions are concerned, whereas the higher-level authorities monitor the process and allocate resources; one institutional lever is the grading and ranking of heritage items, which reaches also beyond the municipal level, and involving experts in the decision-making process.[30]

In China today, hereditization also includes even the creation of quasi-religious places of national worship, such as the memorial and rites devoted to Emperor Shun.[31] We have already mentioned the Grand Rites held for Emperor Huangdi in Chapter 6. In this context, however, there are also areas of potential political tension, since this often implies to focus on Han tradition as Chinese tradition. This is especially salient in minority regions, where hereditization is therefore much more geared to the classical Soviet construction of a multi-ethnic state. That means both minority culture and its relation to Han culture become artificial constructs shaped and monitored by the CCP, and eventually mobilized for tourism and leisure. However, this does not mean that tensions are alleviated, although there is a potential for accommodation of diverse interpretations and views on the same artefacts and practices. This is mostly negotiated between actors on the local level, involving officials, businesspeople, engaged citizen groups, and the wider public.[32] One area where tensions often flare up, and tourism may offer a framework for effectively regulating them, is conflicts over urban renewal where the destruction of old buildings, even though perhaps neglected for long, may stir feelings of loss of identity on the part of the local population.[33]

These constellations look very different in Shenzhen. But there are new sources of tension, since the hereditization of local culture effectively excludes rural traditions of migrants from other places. As we will see in the next section, this is directly reflected in the emerging 'quadrangular' pattern of urban governance in Shenzhen, which still excludes the vast majority of Shenzhen population.

3 The new cultural nexus of power

In further detailing cultural governance in Shenzhen, we start out from the infrastructural gap in developing this megacity; the central facts have already been laid out previously: The extremely rapid growth of the city could not be possibly supported by appropriate measures of infrastructure development fully funded by the municipal authorities. The spread of the megacity took place without a long-term master plan and the corresponding measures of fiscal planning beyond certain core areas and projects. However, at the same time, the growth of Shenzhen obviously took another course than the growth of megacities in other parts of the world: Only in the early stage, the phenomenon of urban villages may appear to be the functional substitute of the formation of slums, but with a very different performance already in the medium term, as the many cases of successful urban renewal projects demonstrate.[34]

One reason for this distinct performance perhaps is simply economic: Different from most megacities in the developing world, Shenzhen soon emerged as a powerful centre of the Chinese export industry, also moving fast into the more advanced electronics sector. Therefore, high growth could be achieved that also allowed for funding urban expansion and upgrading. Still, as explained, the urban villages assumed a central role in resolving the tension between orderly urban growth and sustaining a low wage advantage, because cheap urban living space was arranged.

Behind this works the unique institutional construct of the shareholding cooperatives. In 2017, there were 1,017 shareholding cooperatives, of which 94 were established already in 1992 in the original SEZ and 923 in 2004 with the inclusion of outer rural areas in Shenzhen municipality.[35] As we have seen previously, initially, these emerged as means of local villagers to maintain their control of agricultural land. But many of these soon emerged as a specific form of urban governance because of their control of vast resources generated from land rents.[36] Technically, this meant that the shareholding cooperatives adopted an important function in funding and realizing urban infrastructure, such as in urban renewal measures, in cooperation with urban developers. However, this did not happen without government control. The institutional mechanism behind this is the construct of collective capital. As we have seen in Chapter 4, although the shareholding cooperatives distribute a share of annual profits to the villagers as shareholders, the lion's share would be retained and accumulate as retained profits, thus forming collective assets. These assets are supervised by a specific body, the collective assets management committee. According to the regulations, this body is chaired by the Party secretary. More generally, we have noticed the emergence of managerial and business elite in the villages, who are systematically co-opted by the party and the local government, thus directly creating a channel by which coordination with the municipal government becomes possible.

Now, it is important to recognize that there are different types of shareholding cooperatives emerging path-dependently from the interaction between villagers and municipal administration. One reason is the origin, because some shareholding cooperatives may have been set up by small villages that later would not be transformed into *shequ*: They continue to exist as a transformation of the original collective economy into a new corporate form. Though this can be tied to kinship groups, it is without a clear territorial reference resulting from the continuing control of land. The shareholding cooperative is not representing the *shequ* directly, so there can be several cooperatives within one *shequ* that relate with natural villages and lineages that are part of that *shequ*. In other cases, such as Fenghuang, the shareholding cooperatives have a two-tier structure, thus reflecting the original division between production brigade and production team. Finally, there are the comprehensive village-level shareholding cooperatives. Therefore, there are more shareholding cooperatives than *shequ*, but many of the shareholding cooperatives are identical with *shequ*, and hence are even named 'community shareholding cooperatives' ('shequ gufen hezuo gongsi' 社区股份合作公司). As we have seen, one factor that explains this divergence is the existence of strong local lineages, mostly in single-surname villages. Take the districts to which our most important case studies belong, Futian and Bao'an. In Futian, there are some *shequ* with a shareholding cooperative, but this includes several natural villages where the native population has been mostly dispersed after selling their land rights. In these cases, the shareholding cooperative becomes a form of organizing the economic functions of the *shequ*. In other cases, such as in Xiasha, *shequ*, natural village, and shareholding cooperative are congruent. In Bao'an district, this is the standard case, which reflects different starting conditions as compared to the original SEZ.

The shareholding cooperatives drive a systematic wedge into the structure of urban administration, because there is a fundamental difference between the street committees and the shareholding cooperatives in terms of internal governance and membership. Independent of how one judges the quality of democratic participation at the grassroots level in China, the street committees include all citizens with household registration in an area. Membership in shareholding cooperatives is also based on household registration, but only with reference to the original village population. That means, even if only considering residents with registration, there is a large group with registration which is excluded from participation at the shareholder assembly of the shareholding cooperatives that is effectively congruent with the village assembly. The more significant the investment decisions of the shareholding cooperatives, the more counts the fact that many residents with registration are excluded from participating at the decision-making processes about urban development. That being said, however, it is the developers who often open the planning process to the entire resident population in public consultations. In sum, the emergence of shareholding cooperatives as intermediary hybrids of villages, corporation, and public agent implicitly reinstates an exclusive authoritarian pattern of urban management, even though formally there are direct forms of citizen participation on the lowest level of municipal administration. This is the result of the additional segmentation of the population beyond the distinction of urban *hukou* holders and immigrants with only temporary residence permit.

This institutional wedge has affected the internal governance of urban villages in the past. From the perspective of the majority of immigrants, the relevant authority was the landlords of the villages, organizationally embodied in the shareholding cooperative, and not the municipal administration. For example, initially even the public security may have been formed by villagers in the historical tradition of village militias. This created much tension, if only because of linguistic differences. Hence, many shareholding cooperatives switched to recruiting immigrants for public security to improve communication.[37] As this example shows, there are fundamental differences in terms of governance between urban villages and slums or similar settlements elsewhere, because the original villagers assumed a pivotal role in managing the villages, including general municipal services. Insofar as they did not manage, this created space for entrepreneurs to take private action, such as setting up private schools for migrant children. However, some villages early adopted a more active role, such as opening local public schools for immigrant children.

Today, the *shequ* shareholding cooperatives are intermediate institutions that are tightly monitored by the municipal government, but are not part of the fiscal system. Yet, one cannot simply treat them as 'extra budgetary funds', since they originate with the villagers and since the governing elites play a double role. The shareholding cooperatives have become an essential aspect of the local governance structure in merging the economic and the political domain in a separately corporatized organization. This is most obvious in their role in funding local infrastructure development. Via the CCP institutional channel, the local government can suggest infrastructure projects to the local community which might be funded and implemented via the cooperative. However, since the villagers have a direct stake in the profitability of the cooperative, the leaders need to act as entrepreneurs who can balance these different interests. This includes the long-term perspective and the implicit exchange of business opportunities in the network of companies. That means, even if an infrastructure project appears to be less profitable in the first place, meeting the demands of the local government may open chances for business projects in other areas. Accordingly, the leaders of the shareholding cooperatives typically merge two roles – that of an entrepreneur and that of a local community leader. In both respects, what eventually counts most is their personal networks behind the institutional and organizational structures of the cooperatives and local governments. Therefore, one may equate them with the role of intermediary elites in Duara's model of 'brokerage' (see Chapter 2). In this model, brokers can play different roles, sometimes extracting profits from exploiting special relationship to the state, as in pure tax farming arrangements, and sometimes protecting local society from the grabbing hand of the state: The former creates the pattern of 'entrepreneurial state brokerage', the latter of 'protective state brokerage'. This resulted in what Duara has coined 'the cultural nexus of power'. On the one hand, this is an arrangement of mutual benefit between intermediate elites and the state, but on the other, this is embedded in a larger cultural pattern that shapes the interactions between the various sides. In traditional South China, a central institution in these interactions was the lineage.

The question is how far we can diagnose a modern cultural nexus of power in the institutional construct of shareholding cooperatives. We have argued in Chapter 4 that this emerges from the fusion between lineage and shareholding cooperative at least in the sense of shareholding cooperative retaining a shareholder structure that is still based on lineage membership. For shareholding cooperatives also counting as a manifestation of cultural governance, it is crucial to identify a role in creating and maintaining local cultural patterns that are supportive of the wider political scheme of culture promoted by the CCP. One of the core elements in the traditional imaginary is the role of high ancestors in mediating between local culture, modern national identity, and cultural descent of the Chinese, mostly conceived as Han.[38] Via the genealogy, local lineages connect back to the Imperial tradition, and thereby place themselves firmly also in the modern nation. These historical references build the ground for legitimizing a public role and even authority for the shareholding cooperatives. An excellent example for this mechanism is Hakka local culture in Shenzhen, which we already looked at in the previous chapter.

The 'guest people', on first sight, may appear as a peripheral subcultural group in the context of Pearl River Delta history. In the 19th century, the 'Hakka wars' released the severe tension with other groups in local society. Hakka customs differ in some substantial ways from local mainstream culture, such as regarding gender. Yet, at the same time, we observe today a strong role of Hakka in Shenzhen government. Hakka occupy a significantly stronger share in government positions compared to other groups, especially Chaoshan. It is difficult to present firm empirical evidence on how to explain this. There are many indications for a leading role of Hakka in the early history of reforms, especially Shenzhen, with several CCP leaders, including Deng Xiaoping himself, being Hakka.[39] This role is increasingly recognized publicly. The original SEZ project was proposed and managed in the early years by Yuan Geng, a local Hakka and powerful intelligence official in the CCP. However, it is doubtful whether this alone created strong path dependencies explaining the public role of Hakka.[40]

Instead, in our view, cultural factors loom large. This is also evident from the fact that the previous argument rests upon the basic assumption of how many Hakka factually live in Shenzhen. If we start out from the original native population, this should be a very small number. However, estimates for the entire Hakka population in Guangdong province are about 25 million people. Some observers claim that as a result of migration, now 5 million Hakka concentrate in Shenzhen.[41] That would imply that Hakka even represent the subcultural mainstream in the place, which would naturally result in a relatively high share in public office.

Despite being an apparently peripheral subcultural group, the Hakka claim to be genuine representatives of classical Imperial culture, tracing themselves back to Song times and via genealogies to even earlier times. In assessing this claim, one should notice that the term 'Hakka' only emerged in Qing times, becoming more widely used in the 19th century, mostly also reflecting the sharp divides of the Hakka wars.[42] Hakka started to identify themselves as Hakka in that time and in a more assertive way only in Republican times. In other words, there is a deep contradiction between the genealogical depth of Hakka lineages and the factually very late emergence of this group as a subcultural phenomenon: Hakka never did exist in earlier times, and corresponding claims can only be deduced from the genealogies that connect the Hakka of today with people in the past, who however were not identified as Hakka at that time. Since many of these lineages count Imperial elites of the past as ancestors, this means that Hakka can construct themselves even as representing the Han cultural mainstream. This is reflected, as we saw in the previous chapter, in the distinct role that traditional culture plays in Hakka identity today, especially with reference to education and public-mindedness. In a significant sense, Hakka subculture represents a manifest form of grassroots level Confucianism. This peculiar Confucian stance of Hakka culture explains why there is a strong inclination even of Hakka business families to stay close to the government and, for example, supporting their children to leave business and become an official in the government.

Against this background, the modern cultural nexus of power is deeply embedded in the renaissance of genealogical consciousness among local farmers and their emerging elites. In referring back to high ancestors with public office, the shareholding cooperatives develop a cultural identity of paragovernmental responsibility that easily dovetails with their role in the larger municipality, and which is institutionalized in the mediating function of the shareholding cooperative. Evidently, this requires full endorsement of the genealogical values enshrining this culture. Wen Tianxiang certainly is one of the most significant historical figures in this regard, who increasingly is also seen as a part of Shenzhen history and cultural roots. With the Wen reinstating their historical role as a powerful lineage in the Pearl River Delta, they actively endorse and enrich the CCP shift to cultural governance building on traditional culture. This translates in active strategies to achieve upward social mobility, mainly via education. For example, the shareholding cooperatives, in the tradition of lineage trusts of Imperial times, often offer scholarships to village children to study abroad.

This kind of mainstreaming local culture via reaching into genealogical depth is a widespread phenomenon in Shenzhen today, implying a civilizational continuity between Empire and modern Chinese state. This is obvious in the case of the Huang, too. We already analysed the ritual space of Xiasha. When Xiasha commissioned a plan for the renewal of the urban village, the design company explicitly analysed the cultural dimension in diagnosing the peripheralization of local culture in modern Shenzhen at that time.[43] Thus, the cultural revival became a leitmotif in designing the future development of Xiasha, while also emphasizing its multicultural openness, which interestingly was defined as an amalgam of Chinese subcultures in the first place and in the sense of internationalization in the future. Other examples abound: The model community of Huaide puts much emphasis on the genealogical depth of the Pan lineage, and their ancestral hall is officially declared as an educational basis of the CCP (report with pictorial material in endnote[44]).

That means urban design moved towards mainstreaming local subculture already in the early 2000s. However, this does not include the local culture of the migrants who form the majority of the population. Even in the case of villages such as Hubei village, where none of the original villagers live, the strongly manifest Chaoshan local culture is not included in the discourse on renewal.[45] Hubei reveals another important development in cultural governance: the emergence of a public sphere that is dominated by the educated stratum in society, especially the intellectuals. In the movement of protecting Hubei village against destruction, neither the local Zhang nor the Chaoshan inhabitants raised a voice or were actively included in the process. But there is a very different reason for this. The Zhang had already left the territory, and their original reach as a powerful lineage was wider than this place, which was mainly held as an economic pillar of their local power. Hence, as in other cases, for them the only remaining interest in the area is to keep it as a part of their ritual space, that is, protect the ancestral hall, but not the dilapidated buildings of the 'old village' with allegedly ancient origin. The Zhang gain from urban renewal, and hence would not actively support the preservation movement. At the same time, the preservation movement does mainly emphasize the historical significance of the place, which includes the role of the Zhang. However, this is not about the local people as such, but aims at recovering Shenzhen history as a building block of modern Shenzhen identity. Many of the protagonists in the public sphere are second-generation Shenzhener, who search for defining themselves as Shenzhen citizens. Recovering the ancient history of Shenzhen is a popular topic for Shenzhen journalists, thus enhancing awareness among their readers.

Tellingly, the local culture of the migrants is mostly subject to another form of cultural creativity, namely the activities of artists. But these do not include the aspect of traditional culture, but focus on the contemporary experience of migrant workers in Shenzhen. Increasingly, there is also artistic activity on the part of the migrants themselves.[46] This mainly highlights individual experiences, and therefore confirms the narratives about Shenzhen as a modernist place threatening individuals with a potential loss of identity. As a result, what factually constitutes majority culture in a place like Hubei, namely Chaoshan culture, is not becoming part of Shenzhen mainstream tradition as being co-constructed by municipal actors, native villagers, and the public.

In sum, in the context of urban renewal, we can characterize urban governance as a quadrangle of government, villages, and villager elites, developers, and the public, leaving out the majority of the population living in the urban villages. This quadrangle is a modern cultural nexus of power which centres on a new amalgam of urban elites, mainly composed of property owners, officials, and educated groups. These elites are partly included or co-opted by the CCP and its institutionalized role in certain key entities, such as the shareholding cooperatives. At the core of this quadrangle stands the ritual economy, in the sense of a synthesis of culture and economy.

One litmus test for judging the function and strength of this new nexus is the eruption of conflicts and tensions about the progress of demolition of urban villages that necessarily precedes the renewal projects. The negotiation over prices paid to the villagers is naturally fraught with tension; land transformation is often accompanied with outright violence all over China. Therefore, one factor that explains the acquiescence of the municipal authorities with the current governance scheme probably is that it can retreat to the background, as far as the management of violence is concerned, partly also leaving the dirty work to the developers. A most visible expression is the phenomenon of 'nail households' ('dingzi hu' 钉子户) who resist selling their rights to developers. Often, these are villagers who want to maximize the gains from their privately held housing land (*zhaijidi*) on which they had built multi-storey blocks. Developers sometimes must negotiate with single households one-by-one, and unless all households agree, they cannot proceed. This often results in violent tension, with demolition proceeding nevertheless, finally encircling the 'nail household' and employing many measures to put pressure on the owners, some of them certainly illegal, such as sending thugs to threaten them.[47] However, the shareholding cooperatives can also help smoothen the process and coordinate the transfer of ownership collectively, sometimes putting moral pressure on individuals who resist and might therefore block what other might see as a good bargain. Therefore, the quadrangle indeed appears as a governance structure, even considering the role of quasi-legitimate exertion of violence by the state.

Indeed, the quadrangle could be interpreted as the reflection of the ritual spaces in the political governance structure that integrates economic governance in the form of institutional hybrids and that manages conflicts that emerge in the course of rapid urbanization. By implication, we cannot assert that it takes the same form everywhere, and even must recognize that 'ritual' in the sense of its traditional forms is by no means representing the default setting. The crucial variable is the strength of local communities. If they are weak or even non-existent, the quadrangle implodes to a triangle. But there are also alternative forms, as the important and interesting case of Huaqiangbei demonstrates, the *shanzhai* market.[48] As we said previously, the governance challenge resulted from the highly dynamic but amorphous structure of the place after state-owned factories had left. The newly arriving companies mostly focused on commerce and electronics production. Right from the beginning, Huaqiangbei business evolved a hierarchical structure: On top, an opaque group of large investors referred to as the 'bosses' ('laoban' 老板) controlled most larger investments but stayed in the background, with the second level of the entrepreneurs and managers of larger companies act on behalf of those main investors and majority owners. These companies often adopted the strategy to open commercial sites and malls, initially on the premises of the former factories, which were then divided into a huge number of small shops rented out to the lowest level of the hierarchy – thousands of small retailers and producers, many of them of Chaoshan origin.[49] This situation resulted in a chaotic development of the place with no coordination of area use, such as for commercials or parking. Therefore, Futian government launched a redevelopment initiative and intervened in many ways, such as prohibiting outside advertisement. This raised resistance of the local business community that started to organize itself in the late 1990s in the shape of a loosely knit 'friendship association'.

In this association, only medium-level businesspeople were involved and communicated with the government: The Chaoshan small business entrepreneurs were not included, and probably would not even want to be. The government had set up a regulatory committee, which, however, was overburdened with the complexity of the situation at Huaqiangbei, and therefore created an additional service point with a small budget and employees not being civil servants. Local merchants expressed their concerns mostly in the shape of letters ('gong han' 公函) and started an initiative to create a chamber of commerce. This instigated an intensive discussion within the Futian government and with the business community as this was considered 'illegal'. As mentioned previously, the government initially aimed at creating a state-corporatist structure, which failed. Instead, increasingly the idea won approval that business would establish an autonomous and private ('minjian' 民间) organization, a chamber of commerce, which would represent the Huaqiangbei business community. This chamber would neither specialize on an industry nor be congruent with a *shequ*, but would represent all companies located in this business area.

In fact, the majority of business is not a member of the chamber, mostly the medium-level companies, such as the owners of the shopping malls, which alone make up for 700 companies ('shang chang' 商场).[50] This reflects one of the major functions of the chamber: Different from the villages qua *shequ*, the Huaqiangbei area is entirely shaped by corporate investment activities, and these are mostly done by the medium-level companies who build and rent out the market infrastructure. Hence, decision about parking lots, road building, or location of trees directly affect the interests of these companies and involve government decisions. Much of infrastructure is directly funded by the companies, and the chamber coordinates these business decisions with district government plans.

An important additional function is market supervision and regulation. As we explored in Chapter 5, Huaqiangbei is the domain of *shanzhai* business. However, this is exclusively driven by the third-tier businesses. As said, this also reflects a subcultural diversity: Whereas many of the third-tier business are Chaoshan, the second-tier business comes from many regions, such as Shanghai. The chamber has also the task to communicate and partly even enforce government policy, in the sense that the owners of malls would assume responsibility for proper behaviour of shop owners on their premises. At the same time, however, it is in their interest to keep the traders in business, so that they assume a mediating, brokerage function between the two sides.

The Huaqiangbei example is very different from shareholding cooperatives as far as cultural governance is concerned. The chamber is not a traditional identity-based organization, but a modernist form of business organization. However, it is not simply representing business interests, but also fulfils a public function. One of these functions is to regulate *shanzhai* business culture. But this does not result in a resurgence of traditional culture as a means of governance, but, if at all, the dissemination of mainstream business values as an expression of *shenshang* identity. However, this may be interpreted as another modernist form of cultural governance, which is explicit in the activities of public business intellectuals acting as ritual entrepreneurs, in our sense.

An example for one of them among our interviewees, Lao Heng, was supporting the Huaqiangbei initiative while also being involved in reinventing an almost defunct organization established by the Shenzhen municipal government, a 'General Association of Social Organizations', which was originally designed after the state-corporatist model of the Federation of Industries and Commerce. At the same time when the Huaqiangbei chamber was created, also involving Lao Heng's contribution, this association was re-established as a private 'minjian' association offering networking services and lobbying for the vast domain of the budding Shenzhen civil society. If we turn attention to Lao Heng's ideas and driving values, we notice that despite his theorizing about modernist Shenzhen business culture, he is also deeply rooted in traditional scholarship. One of his activities is to offer consultancy to family business, especially second-generation successors. The guiding principles are derived from Confucian conceptions of family and morality, and in seminars the young entrepreneurs would read the classics. After promoting the concept of *shenshang* 'Shenzhen merchant' in the 2000s, now Lao Heng actively endorses and promotes the movement of Confucian education, even including the radical variant of taking children out of regular schools. Education in 'national learning' becomes a central medium by which children can grow both intellectual and moral qualities. This example reveals that the apparent conflict between modernism and tradition is much less sharp as we might imagine, this revealing the synthetic powers of ritual also in modern Chinese society.[51]

4 Governing public morality: The revival of Confucian beliefs and practices

As we have already pointed out, a central concern of the revival of tradition is the restoration and strengthening of public morality. One value that stands out is filial piety and more generally, family values. Public morality is the object of many measures, from small to big. An example for smaller actions is the promulgation of public contracts for civic responsibility, such as the publicly displayed plaque at the central park of Huaide village which promotes standards of proper behaviour in society. An example for the latter is large public events that are devoted to celebrating historical examples of virtue and moral excellence. In between are numerous other activities, often organized on 'cultural squares' that are overseen by ancestral halls, such as, during one of our field visits, when on the Huanggang and Shuiwei cultural square parents together with kids performed a dance devoted to family values.

In the context of lineages, the centrepiece is the family customs or family rules ('jiafeng' 家风, 'jiaxun' 家训). Traditionally, lineages had also obtained important functions in conflict resolution and jurisdiction when it came to civil affairs. This is no longer the case today; yet, there is an intensive promotion of family rules, endorsed even by Xi Jinping himself. Modern family rules do not fall back on old lineage morality, yet they have a distinctly conservative taste and emphasize the proper role of the family in maintaining social order. In our cases, shareholding cooperatives such as the Fenghuang cooperative actively support lecture series and other activities devoted to family rules.[52] In the first decades of urban village development, observers often pessimistically commented on the corrosive effects of sudden wealth and prosperity on the young generation.[53] However, given the deep genealogical identities of the local lineages, the farmers paid much attention to education. For example, before the quality of the local schools improved, many Wen sent their children to the school at Xintian in the New Territories. Most of the lineage-based shareholding cooperatives offer scholarships for bright students to increase the number of 'degree holders' among the local community.

The revival of family rules should not be simply regarded as a local nativist phenomenon, but is part and parcel of the general revival of 'guo xue' 国学, national learning, in China, which is strongly endorsed and promoted by neo-Confucian academics, and is becoming gradually institutionalized in many forms.[54] It is important to note that such activities address the wider public, that is, includes the immigrant population. This is bolstered by many other activities, for instance, the Fenghuang branch of the Women's federation that targets immigrant women with many activities, such as education, counselling, etc. In 2003, Fenghuang village set up the 'Second Women school' that is devoted to educating young women to become proper household heads and wives, and which mainly targets migrants.[55] The curriculum includes various topics, reaching from legal knowledge to hygiene and even cosmetics. Interestingly, this initiative is seen as a part of the 'two innovation' ('liang xin' 两新) policy that the Shenzhen government launched in 2006 and that mainly aims at bridging between companies and party: The school offers free training in computer schools for workers in local companies, combined with its curriculum. This reflects a wider trend all over China and has deep historical roots in the Confucian literature, going back to texts on 'Admonishing women' ('nüjie'女诫) in Han times.[56] The previously mentioned family performance at Huanggang cultural square took place in front of a building where the liaison offices of Zhuang clans in other Chinese cities are located. That means family rules are not local rules in the first place but have a potential reach far beyond a local lineage. This can be studied for our Huang case. The modern family rules are often created based on older material, such as using Huang Qiaoshan's poems and biography in extracting the major elements of the rules. In the end, this does not result in anything that is specific to the family, since all values and behavioural standards just reflect generic ones, such as courage, trustworthiness, or filial piety. Yet, the claim is always made that the family, that is, in this case the Huang, excels in representing those values. But these values are also communicated towards the wider public, and then they are just an example for values shared by the Chinese in general. Similar cases are easily identified, such as the Pan at Huaide village who proclaim that endorsement of *jiafeng* is a central concern of CCP cadres' engagement in society.[57]

The public role of Huang values is salient in recent activities devoted to Huang Shu (report with pictorial material in endnote[58]). Huang Shu is a legendary example of filial piety who lived in the 4th century (Dong Jin dynasty) and who moved from Jiangxia to the Pearl River Delta. His tomb is located in Shajing, Bao'an district. Bao'an district government defined a focus on cultural activities surrounding Huang Shu, including a special tradition of a local Lion's Dance (an officially recognized 'intangible cultural heritage item'), and another 'old village', Shanghe, in Xin'an neighbourhood. Shanghe is an urban village where another Huang lineage is located with an independent ancestral hall. Local villagers count roughly 2,000 people; the entire population is about 60,000. Huang Shu is declared an important personality in the long history of old Xin'an, and Xin'an neighbourhood is today the location of a festival devoted to Huang Shu and filial piety. The festival is part of a district strategy in strengthening 'culture' ('wenhua qiang shequ'), which is neatly defined in *guoxue* terms, symbolized in the numerous actors dressed in Han garments. Central activities address children, for example, with calligraphy lessons, but also ritual performances referring to filial piety.

Thus, family rules may just be interpreted as manifesting core values in what constitutes traditional morality. Therefore, schools are an important environment where this is also activated. Shenzhen is a place where many private or quasi-private schools operate. That means they are under the auspices of the municipal educational bureau but are funded by private or semiprivate entities. This includes shareholding cooperatives in cooperation with large developers, which often take an active role in establishing schools in their condominiums and core areas of investment, and includes international schools and experimental schools, with some of them catering to the local wealthy who want to send their children abroad. One feature of these schools is that they increasingly offer education in *guoxue*.

One prominent example is the Wen Tianxiang elementary school in central Futian district, which explicitly claims to combine modern education with national learning, and which is located at Gangxia, one of the urban villages that belongs to the Wen clan.[59] This school is public, but managed by an educational corporation that founded the famous Nanking experimental school. A strong signal was sent in dressing the new pupils in Han garment when the school was inaugurated. The leaders of the school explicitly emphasize Wen Tianxiang as a role model for the children. Such initiatives are supported by a wide range of government and coordinated NGO actions that aim at the moral education of children: For example, a book series was edited in Futian district that can be used in schools for teaching purposes. Schools respond with a flurry of related activities, such as celebrating a 'festival of national learning' (report with pictorial material in endnote[60]). The Fenghuang public school at Fenghuang village follows this approach, even introducing 'da guo xue', building on a long tradition going back to its founding time in 1890. This school originally accepted locals only, but today mostly receives migrant children. Apart from *guoxue*, the children learn about local Wen culture, beginning with Wen Tianxiang, even including features such as Wen rural life and agriculture.[61] That means what appears to be a rural 'little tradition' on the surface is being transformed into a local 'great tradition' that ties up with mainstream culture and the revival of traditional morality under the auspices of the CCP. The Wen Tianxiang memorials are officially designated 'educational sites' even of the Communist party, receiving groups on an almost daily basis.

These activities should not be seen as being limited to the domain of local rural culture, because the revival of traditional learning is a distinctly urban phenomenon all over China. In their magistral study of the Confucian revival in China, Billioud and Thoraval include many examples from Shenzhen.[62] Beyond the scope of publicly registered private schools, there is the revival of 'traditional schools' ('sishu' 私塾), in which children are educated in the classics and Confucian morality.[63] Sometimes, parents may even take children out of the formal track of public education and opt for home education, which includes similar types of initiatives. This is also the case for the *sishu* in Shenzhen that Billioud and Thoraval introduce. Beyond this specific and rather extreme phenomenon, there is the wave of 'classics reading seminars' and related activities, often instigated by scholars from Taiwan and Hong Kong.

One example is the initiative to establish halls of worship for Confucius ('kongshengtang' 孔圣堂), which is supported by the Confucius Academy in Hong Kong that actively promotes the formation of Confucianism as a Chinese religion (which is so far not recognized as such, and also not widely practiced).[64] The leader of that movement in China even talks about a 'Shenzhen model' of Confucian revival when the *Kongshengtang* at Donghu park was inaugurated. On October 28, 2018, the hall was the location of the 'Ninth Confucian Culture festival' that was also sponsored by the business community (interestingly, including the 'Guangdong High Tech Industry Chamber of Commerce', i.e. a modernist outfit) (report with pictures in endnote[65]). There are two remarkable observations about this event, which featured many performances of traditional music and dances. The first is that beyond these festive events, an authentic 'Grand Rite' was conducted by a leading figure in the Confucian movement, worshipping the Master in a proper ceremony. The second is that political leaders attended and gave speeches, including the vice-chairman of the People's Consultative conference and a former vice-mayor of Shenzhen. The event also established direct connection to business in invoking the model of the 'Confucian entrepreneur', even endorsed by song performances of business leaders and involving representatives of Hong Kong business.

Indeed, one observation is that educational activities often address the business community: activists are often ritual entrepreneurs, like Lao Heng whom we meet previously. This includes consultancy, especially in the context of family business. In family business, traditional values have direct implications for business, especially in the context of business succession. Business succession is a major challenge to the Chinese economy today and increasingly in Shenzhen too, especially in the subcultural contexts, Hakka and Chaoshan. Filial piety can be invoked as committing the second generation to continuing the family business, and stability of marriage relations is an important factor in stabilizing the leadership structure of family business as well. Therefore, promoting traditional morality becomes a concern of the business community. The associations adopt an active role here, such as the Hakka Youth chamber which organizes conferences about the succession issue – intergenerational tension and gender issues – collaborating with various culture-related associations.[66] Many ritual entrepreneurs jump on this train, such as the founders of the 'Academy of Bright Virtue' ('Mingde shuyuan') established in 2017 and headquartered in Shenzhen, and already with several branches in various big cities. This is an outfit focusing on executive education, mixing standard approaches such as team-building exercises with *guoxue* classes in an elegant environment.[67]

To summarize, cultural governance increasingly emerges as a cultural nexus of power that even stands in the tradition of pre-Imperial times in including a revival of traditional Confucian values, though always in tandem with socialist core values. However, there is no tension here, as both are compatible to a large degree. In addition, this does not contradict the interests of the business community who are mostly concerned about a stable social environment, and who increasingly recognize the business potential of culture in a global city. One important social domain where this will further unfold in the future is the growing clout of family business in the economy. Family business leaders worldwide tend towards social conservativism, as family tradition and continuity are a core dimension of their corporate culture.

5 Conclusion

Cultural governance in Shenzhen manifests what in China studies has been sometimes labelled 'neoliberal governmentality': Social control and conservative values are in the interest of business and political elites, and at the same time the market operates as a disciplinary power of its own that interplays with the revival of tradition.[68] However, in our view, this analysis does not fully catch the phenomenon, as it overlooks, at least in the Shenzhen case, the fact that the revival of tradition is partly driven by grassroots-level activities and identity politics, combining with the emergence of economic interests in the context of land utilization. In other words, cultural governance cannot be simply explained as a top-down process of imposing control on society.[69] What we observe can best be understood in terms of Migdal's 'state in society' approach, as a result of complex interactions at the interface between formal government and numerous groups in society, on which the government and the party need to rely to pursue their original goals, eventually co-opting and accommodating many forces that originally may have operated in a subversive way.[70] The urban villages are a material expression of this process in the urban reality of Shenzhen.

This process goes hand in hand with the transformation of the native rural society, which in Shenzhen involves the emergence of a new stratum of economic elites, originally as landlords, but increasingly as entrepreneurs, including a phenomenon well known all over China, the hybrid figure of businessperson and local leader, sometimes combining the roles of entrepreneur, head of shareholding cooperative, and lineage head, thus personifying the ritual economy in the strict meaning. But cultural governance need not be confined to this explicit role of local lineage ritual. Increasingly, many forms of ritualistic assertions of traditional values are reinvented, often in the context of tourism and leisure activities, but also as grassroots-level initiatives, sometimes even subversive, such as when parents send their children to private *guoxue* schools instead of the public schools. Yet, even this subversive activity contributes to the strengthening of traditional values that undergirds the new cultural nexus of power.

This cultural nexus of power is not the same as the old one, as it includes entirely new social formations. In the quadrangle, particularly salient are the developers and the public. Ideal typically, one might equate developers with 'entrepreneurial brokers' and village leaders as 'protective brokers'. However, the latter may only be true when lineages operate in a way that internally traditional governance mechanisms constrain their behaviour.[71] Otherwise, we indeed diagnose a neoliberal governmentality scheme in the collusion between developers and village leaders.[72] In this sense, the ritual economy may work as a protective belt against the final usurpation of Shenzhen society by global capitalism and its value system. Yet, the core contradiction that emerges in the ritual economy is that between local elites and migrant population in the urban villages, often without *hukou*. We diagnosed that the quadrangle reveals a white spot here, systematically created by the wedge between the formal institutions of *shequ* and the shareholder structure of cooperatives in combination with the household registration system. This dilemma can only be resolved by the government in designing inclusive institutions, as envisaged in the rich debates and initiatives on strengthening civil society in Shenzhen in the 2000s, which have been muted recently. Indeed, the newest development plan for urban villages emphasizes inclusive governance, aiming at a less confrontational imposition of modernist urbanization on Shenzhen populace.

In the context of Collins' approach, the Chinese case introduces new perspectives, since Collins does not put much emphasis on the public governance of ritual. This may reflect the long tradition of sociology in assigning ritual to the domain of religion, and not to the domain of the state. The origin of this tradition may be traced to Max Weber. Our theoretical résumé in the next chapter starts out from his contribution to sociology and China studies.

Notes

1 Perry (2013), Oakes (2017).
2 For a survey of this, including examples from Shenzhen, see Billioud and Thoraval (2015).
3 Levenson (1968), Townsend (1992).
4 Brandt et al. (2014).
5 Elman (1991).
6 Faure (2007).
7 Naquin and Rawski (1987).
8 Ebrey (1991).
9 Tao Qing (2007: 313).
10 Wong and Bird (2008), Wong (2009). On the investment vehicles, see Feng (2013). On centralization after 1994, see Mertha (2005).
11 Kramer (2020).
12 Xu (2011).

13 The concept originated in Oi (1992, 1995), who used the term 'local corporatism'. On the relationship between autonomy and performance evaluation, see Heberer and Schubert (2012). The archetypical structure is the county, but in the course of reforms and urbanization, many counties evolved into cities. In addition, Shenzhen emerged as a SEZ, which even formally recognizes rights of autonomy while keeping performance standards tight.
14 Heilmann (2008).
15 Huang (2008, 2019). The concept of contracting ('cheng bao' 承包) was already emphasized by Herrmann-Pillath (1991).
16 Watt (1972, 1977).
17 Huang (1993).
18 Ching (2008).
19 O'Donnell and Wan (2016).
20 Watson (2010).
21 In the wake of the communist riots of the 1960s, the British government also relied on the conservative groups in the New Territories. After handover, the CCP continued with this political strategy.
22 http://www.sz.gov.cn/wtlyjnew/ztzl_78228/tszl/whcy/whcyflfg/201803/t20180323_11587297.htm, accessed November 24, 2019.
23 Walton (2018).
24 Kubat (2018).
25 Fan and Whitehead (2011).
26 Billioud and Theraval (2015: 152).
27 Bach (2017).
28 Oakes (2019).
29 Oakes (2017).
30 http://www.gdupi.com/Common/news_detail/article_id/5570.html; http://www.sz.gov.cn/wtlyjnew/xxgk/zcfgjzcjd/whscsp/201810/t20181026_14340567.htm; http://www.sz.gov.cn/wtlyjnew/ggfw/whl/whycb/, all accessed December 12, 2019.
31 McNeal (2011).
32 Kang (2009).
33 Zhou (2018).
34 Wang (2016: 4ff) offers a comprehensive discussion of possible functional equivalences and their eventual failure to catch the reality of urban villages.
35 Cha (2018).
36 Po (2008, 2012), Shi et al. (2018).
37 Wang (2016: 77ff).
38 Cohen (2017), Trémon (2014).
39 Erbaugh (1992).
40 For example, on occasion of the 40th anniversary of reforms, lists of business leaders have been published, and Hakka proudly notice the significant role among them: http://www.sohu.com/a/284819253_366506, accessed November 22, 2019. However, there is considerable ambiguity in public debates about subethnic identities, which might also reflect sensitivity of the topic. For example, even for Yuan Geng, sometimes it is claimed that he is *guangfu* origin, see http://bbs.tianya.cn/post-free-5960713-1.shtml, accessed November 10, 2019.
41 https://mp.weixin.qq.com/s/QTpZvmfDonVzMxpsOW8m0w, accessed December 12, 2019.
42 Cohen (1996).
43 Shenzhen shi Futian zhengfu (2007).
44 https://baijiahao.baidu.com/s?id=1638196969069147679&wfr=spider&for=pc, accessed January 22, 2020.
45 O'Donnell (2019).

46 The blog by Mary-Ann O'Donnell reports about such activities, especially in the context of her own art gallery and meeting ground for the interested public, Handshake 302, which concentrates on urban villages and is now forced to move, as evictions proceed in Baishizhou, where it is located; see https://shenzhennoted.com/czc-special-forces/. Wang (2016: 144f) points out that many young musicians live in urban villages and create rock music and songs about the life there.
47 Wang (2016: 118ff).
48 On the following, see Tao Qing (2007).
49 https://baike.baidu.com/tashuo/browse/content?id=242a1308b5f4eede411c4569
50 The website of the chamber: http://www.szhcc.com.cn/index.asp
51 http://blog.sina.cn/dpool/blog/s/blog_662ebc110102wv4o.html?type=-1, accessed December 2, 2019.
52 http://www.oeeee.com/html/201804/01/594442.html; http://www.oeeee.com/html/201807/20/678823.html, accessed December 2, 2019.
53 Chan et al. (2009).
54 One intellectual leader is Chen Lai of Tsinghua University; Chen (2015).
55 Fenghuang cun zhi, various items.
56 Ke (2016). For reports about 'morality schools' for women, see https://www.scmp.com/news/china/society/article/2131731/rise-morality-schools-chinese-women-sparks-outcry. Increasingly, these schools are attracting criticism in China, because many of them are set up by individuals who are not qualified at all and employ even physical punishments of young girls; see https://news.sina.cn/sh/2018-12-22/detail-ihqhqcir9126208.d.html?vt=4&pos=108&his=0, accessed November 29, 2019.
57 https://baijiahao.baidu.com/s?id=1638196969069147679&wfr=spider&for=pc, accessed January 22, 2020.
58 http://www.sznews.com/news/content/2018-12/09/content_21266623.htm, accessed January 22. 2020.
59 http://wb.sznews.com/PC/content/201710/31/c213775.html accessed January 21, 2020.
60 http://www.sznews.com/news/content/2019-03/25/content_21499085.htm; http://epaper.gmw.cn/gmrb/html/2019-08/29/nw.D110000gmrb_20190829_1-08.htm accessed January 21, 2020.
61 https://baike.baidu.com/item/%E6%B7%B1%E5%9C%B3%E5%B8%82%E5%87%A4%E5%87%B0%E5%AD%A6%E6%A0%A1/18214008?fr=aladdin, accessed January 21, 2020.
62 Billioud and Thoraval (2015: 61ff, 111ff, 152ff).
63 As an example from Beijing, see http://english.cctv.com/2016/11/08/VIDEjBBGBGTru10ylo0SHg7W161108.shtml, accessed November 29, 2019.
64 Sun (2013: 88ff).
65 https://new.qq.com/rain/a/20181101B06KRF, accessed November 29, 2019.
66 http://zhks.org/article.aspx?aid=914, accessed November 29, 2019.
67 http://www.mingdeshuyuan.com/gxg.html, accessed November 29, 2019.
68 Sigley (2006).
69 In a similar vein, see Trémon (2015).
70 Migdal (2001).
71 Tsai (2002, 2007).
72 Kan (2019).

8 Theoretical résumé

Towards a global social science

1 Max Weber as point of departure

In this chapter, we draw theoretical conclusions while also condensing the results of our research on Shenzhen. We start out from considering one of the most intriguing issues in social and economic history, the emergence of 'the West' and the failure of China to develop capitalism. Today, this seems a moot question, as China has eventually emerged as a world economic power. But in reflecting on the Shenzhen case, we realize that it is of continuing relevance, since just claiming that China has become 'capitalist' cannot neutralize the many doubts and questions about the nature of her current economic system and the terms of its relationship with the political system.[1] Weber had introduced the view that for understanding this relationship, culture may be an important factor, and claimed that this explains differential development in China and the West in early modern times. In many respects, the arguments about long-run limitations of development in China today show family resemblances with the analysis of the past.[2]

That the Weber hypothesis is still relevant today has been made abundantly clear in P. C. C. Huang's prolific writings about interpreting the current conditions in China and re-evaluating their historical background. Huang refers to Max Weber as one core reference.[3] Weber left a mark on Chinese studies with his book on the ethics of world religions which treats Confucianism and Daoism extensively, building on the state of sinology of his time.[4] Obviously, this reference is seriously deficient because in the past century our picture of Imperial history has drastically changed, including three veritable revolutions:

First, and literally, the discovery of the 'medieval economic revolution' which established a fully fledged market economy in China with many institutional and organizational innovations that caused China to become the most prosperous and powerful economy in the world at that time;

Second, the recognition of the prowess and rich results of Chinese science as collected and evaluated in the monumental work by Joseph Needham;

Third, the new view on the maturation and growth of the economy under Qing rule, resulting in a strong growth of population and increasing social differentiation.[5]

These large-scale historical developments belie Weber's view on China as a stagnating society, which reflects the Western perception that emerged after the Opium wars. Previously, European enlightenment scholars had viewed China as the pinnacle of civilizational achievements, such as Quesnay in France and Wolff in Germany, mainly receiving the accounts of Jesuit scholars living in China and working at the Imperial court.[6] Clearly, these shifting judgements reflected less the real situation in China than the conditions in Europe: The enlightenment scholars used China as a foil on which they criticized the conditions in the Ancien Régime, and the intellectuals of the 19th century saw China as the counter pole to Western ascension to world power, in all senses, military, economic, and civilizational, especially with reference to the achievements of Western science. Weber developed a fully fledged sociological theory condensing the latter view because he defined China as the opposite of the West in a fundamental sense, namely representing the case of ultimate 'irrationality'.[7] This view resulted from projecting his narrative of the rise of capitalism onto China. This narrative is grounded in a specific conception of what 'rationality' means, and is highly relevant when reflecting our research on Shenzhen today.

Although Weber clearly said that historical facts may be much more murky and ambivalent, in following his methodology of constructing and analysing ideal types, he approaches Western civilization in terms of what became a standard view in modern sociology, that is, the thesis of increasing functional differentiation of the spheres of value, such as the economy, religion, or erotic life; this functional differentiation came about via rationalization, first emerging in the sphere of religion.[8] This is where Weber's 'protestantism hypothesis' is truly significant, less as a historical account, but making the fundamental point that increasingly religion was conceived as an inner state of beliefs that a person holds, thus freeing the external word of any metaphysical burden, more mundanely expressed in magical beliefs. That means the individualization and interiorization of religion paved the way for pursuing the Western mission of rationally approaching and handling the world, both in the economy and in science. This process is often described as 'disenchantment', although Weber did not use that term often.[9] But in our context, it is relevant because Weber claimed that the irrational status of Confucianism is manifest in being enclosed in the 'enchanted garden', the 'Zaubergarten' of magic, entangled in a rich variety of ritual practices that were conceived as causally affecting the world. In Weber's view of rationalization, the status of ritual is the crucial litmus test: Since Confucians believed that ritual has transformative powers in the relationship between humans and the world, Weber judged them as being stuck in a magical worldview. In other words, the polar opposition between China and the West is the opposition between Confucian ritualism and Protestant anti-ritualism.[10]

As we saw in Chapter 2, Weber's view reflects the 'excarnation' of Western societies in conceiving the obliteration of ritual in religious practices as a most essential expression of rationalization. There are two more specific developments which define this process, according to Weber. The first is the emergence of rational bureaucracy, literally as a machinery of governing society according to principles of instrumental and formal rationality, the latter enshrined in law, and the second is the institutions of capitalism that insulate the economic value sphere from the rest of society, such as accounting or the corporation as a rationally designed organization. Both rely on each other in a substantial way, as capitalist business requires rational governance, and rational governance can reckon with a rationally predictable economic machine. This is the 'stahlharte Gehäuse', the 'iron cage' of modern man and modern capitalism.

As Huang emphasises, in this picture formal rationality looms large. Indeed, although Weber refers to substantive rationality too, he eventually does not approach this as an ideal type of the same analytical status than formal rationality in the context of capitalism. This directly affects Weber's interpretation of Chinese law and legal practice, which has been extensively studied by Huang. Weber interprets Western law as embodying formal rationality, whereas Chinese legal practice is seen as fundamentally irrational and arbitrary as 'Khadi Justiz' (kadi justice). However, as we know today, this view seriously distorts Chinese realities, since the judicial process was shaped by synthesizing legal norms and contextualized moral considerations, institutionalized in the widespread practice of mediation. Huang suggests approaching this as an ideal type of substantive rationality, in which formal law was intrinsically combined with moral considerations of the peculiar context of a case and the individual constellations of the various affected parties, including the community of which they are members. This kind of contextualization has been highlighted in recent research on legal disputes about land in Qing China, to name an example that is also relevant for our reflection of land ownership in Shenzhen today.[11]

Regarding the economy, we can diagnose a similar misconception. For a long time, Western historians of China did follow Weber in projecting the notion of 'capitalism' on China, and thereby misconceiving the role markets factually played in shaping Chinese society and political governance. Weber was already aware of the commercial culture of China but downplayed its significance because it was not capitalist. That means we meet the same phenomenon: Weber treats capitalism as an ideal type, but not the market economy. In the longue durée of historical comparisons, this omission matters, because the more recent research on economic history of China has shown that this market economy was highly developed and operated with a high level of efficiency.[12] This has been synthesized into a grand picture stating that China did not 'fail' in terms of culture and institutions, but efficiently adapted to her economic conditions.[13] This analysis can be interpreted as proceeding in substantive terms, too: Formally, China did not move to the standards of rationalization that emerged in the West, such as unifying monetary systems or creating a unified commercial codex, and so on. But that does not imply that there was a lost historical opportunity to China, because allegedly her institutions were 'irrational'.

Weber's view on capitalist rationality can be put in critical perspective if we consider Polanyi's analysis of capitalism as a utopia imagined by Western political economy which is projected on real-world societies and aims at subordinating them to the logic of markets.[14] Accordingly, one might even conclude that it is capitalism that amounts to an 'irrational' project. Weber claimed another polarity in the comparison between the West and China, namely between 'adaptation' and 'transformation'. Again, he seems to include a hidden value judgement, which is that transformation is progressive, and therefore 'rational'. But that is by no means warranted, as Polanyi's dystopian view on capitalist transformation shows. If the new view on China's market economy of the past is right, this system was rationalized in enabling a highly efficient use of resources and a deep division of labour, both among people and across localities and regions. In comparison, capitalism might be seen as utopian, hence irrational belief in the transformative powers of economic action that eventually fails to create sustainable societies, as the Western drama of two World Wars demonstrated, in Polanyi's eyes.

This fundamental shift of perspective also affects the interpretation of the cultural aspects of capitalism: Despite Weber's talk about the iron cage, he did not delve deeply into the effects of capitalism on the human side of the economy, especially the psychological side of subordinating social relations to the economic logic and its pathologies. It is highly significant in our context that the other great sociologist of Weber's times, Durkheim, highlighted these effects in his work on suicide and anomie in modern societies. As we already pointed out, Durkheim is also the scholar who developed a view on ritual that is polarly opposed to Weber. For Weber, ritual is atavistic magic, whereas for Durkheim ritual generates emotional forces grounding emphatic and solidary social relations in communities.

Accordingly, the concept of ritual economy that emerged in China studies has a deeper significance in these Weberian reflections about global history. The ritual economy is the market economy created, enacted, and maintained by rituals and ritual frames of action. Then, ritual may emerge as the ideal-typical counterpart to the form of rationality in capitalism that emerged in the West.[15] Ritual becomes the core of the alternative ideal type of substantive rationality in institutionalizing the market economy. Starting out from this complete analytical duality, we can approach many facts about China in new light, following the precedents set by P. C. C. Huang in numerous contributions.

Yet, there remains a deep methodological trouble that we already sketched in Chapters 1 and 2, which has been elaborated in detail by one of us in the earlier work on ritual and economy in China.[16] This is the problem of reverse or multiplex orientalism, resulting from the fact that a Weberian view on modernity has been imported to China and has shaped the way how most Chinese intellectual elites perceive Chinese realities, thereby, at least partly, confirming these modernist views and even translating them into transformative actions. As a consequence, the original view seems to be vindicated. The domain of religion is one where this issue is most relevant, since the Weberian view on the Chinese 'Zaubergarten' is directly affirmed by Chinese views on the 'superstition' reigning in the vibrant and vast sphere of popular religion. This influences even the interaction between interview partners and researchers, as the former are aware of the problematic status of many of their practices in Chinese modernist thinking, as conventionally represented by the CCP. That means the Weberian view on the irrationality of ritual, mutatis mutandis, inheres the attitudes that Chinese actors may have towards ritual, at least in the context of communicating publicly about it, as in interviews with researchers. This is why research on Chinese ritual, as we discussed in Chapter 2, is a difficult subject, and why, in a place like Shenzhen, modernism as an attitudinal stance may shape the way how ritual is represented in society.

2 Ritual, rationality, and the state

Turning to Shenzhen, we can now see why the Weberian conundrum is highly relevant for appreciating the case and drawing theoretical consequences for general social science. Shenzhen is often represented as an artificial megacity emerging from nowhere. But it has never been designed according to a rational master plan. The growth of Shenzhen was an evolutionary process of adaptation and selection of alternatives in a highly uncertain and open environment, involving many different actors, who even did not interact in an arena that was designed according to rationally conceived procedures of discourse and decision-making. Yet, the city emerged as one of the great success stories of Chinese transition, development, and modernization.

As we have seen, one of the major explanations for this success is the role of historical background conditions, and specifically the role of existing villages and their people in driving urban change. One most essential factor in the success of Shenzhen was the accommodation of extremely large and rapid inflows of migrants and their integration in an emerging social and economic fabric of Shenzhen. This happened in the urban villages. Urban villages defy any kind of 'rational design', as they embody decentralized decisions of millions of individuals, and in this sense embody the logic of markets driving migration. Accordingly, they were initially denounced as unruly and chaotic, that is, 'irrational' forms of urban development. But this was proven wrong, not only because they produced sizable economic gains for many parties involved, but also because the urban villages turned out to be resilient structures capable of innovation and change, epitomized in autonomous projects of urban renewal and change. Granted, this also required the constant monitoring and guidance by the municipal authorities, but there was always a strong role of village communities and their entrepreneurial leaders.

Weber's view on bureaucracy had also influenced modernist conceptions of state, bureaucracy, and societal governance by law. In the context on developing countries, this often proved to be a fatal misconception, as most states lack the capacity to build, enact, and maintain such structures, as Migdal has masterfully diagnosed in his 'state-in-society' approach.[17] The Weberian rational state is nothing but the ideal-typical sublimation of a very specific historical case limited to Western Europe and North America. However, it is important to avoid the conclusion that its existence might depend on a certain level of economic prosperity. We need to recognize that it is a culturally contextualized phenomenon in the first place. There are many other variants of institutionally relating states and their societies, with China being a most important case in point, historically and perhaps also today.

It must be noticed, however, that the tradition of rational projection of the state on society is not strange to China. In fact, it has been claimed that China was the first place in the world where the modern state in this Weberian sense emerged, precisely with the establishment of Empire under the Qin.[18] This defines the long legalist tradition of rule in China: In this sense, Weber was also wrong in simply defining China as the antipode of the West, because both poles have always been present in China, too, and their tension even defined the evolution of the Chinese body politic.[19] Out of this tension, Chinese 'minimalist governance' emerged, which is manifest in a strong role of self-governance, which Weber also noticed, but counted as backward and mired in tradition, and only as a phenomenon of rural society: Weber did not yet know how self-organization also shaped the megacities of Qing dynasty China.[20]

If we strip Confucian thinking of some of its distinctively Chinese social-conservative elements (such as in the context of gender), we might identify it as the view that government rests on three poles – the state, the civil society, and the family. The Confucian view thematized the mutual support and even interpenetration of the three domains in their being grounded in a form of ethical life, as conceived in Hegel's 'Philosophy of Law' ('Sittlichkeit').[21] Ethical life embodies what Huang approaches as substantive rationality compared to the formal logic and markets and law, which only represents an incomplete stage of the emergence of civil society ('bürgerliche Gesellschaft'). Hegel thought that civil society, if only based on the abstract logic of market contractualism and rational rule of law, would be deeply pathological, thus factually anticipating Polanyi's interpretation of capitalism. But he did not recognize the role of ritual, himself being part of the Protestant tradition in European intellectual history. Confucians believed that ethical life is embodied in the proper enactment of ritual. Unfortunately, Hegel probably also influenced Weber in maintaining the same view on China as the ultimate counter pole of Western, which means, Protestant achievements in the unfolding of the rationality of 'world spirit'.[22] Yet, Hegel also recognized a point that is essential in overcoming the cultural bias in which he was himself implicated. He refuted Kant's belief – deeply influential until today – that ethics could be grounded in principles of formal rationality alone (the 'categorical imperative'). Instead, he argued that it must be grounded in historically evolved and embodied forms of life of real communities, the 'Sittlichkeit'. It is not far to go claiming that this corresponds to a type of substantive rationality.[23]

To a considerable extent, the notion of 'cultural governance' corresponds to this most general philosophical perspective, as it aims at embedding state-society relations in an ethical framework that is itself not simply moral in nature, but extends towards broader aspects of culture, especially in terms of history. In Shenzhen, this juncture is embodied in the architectural pattern of cultural squares, which often evoke the history of Shenzhen in Imperial times and establish contexts of public morality in thematizing lineage traditions that implicitly activate Confucian imaginaries about a good society. This is an essential point: Hegelian 'Sittlichkeit' seems to inhere ritual practices and their artefactual embodiments. Some of the festivals that take place on cultural squares therefore fulfil the function of creating the 'as if' of a 'harmonious society', such as living the ideal of a harmonious family as a core cultural vision in Chinese society.[24]

In this sense, there is a deep connection between the philosophical dimensions of rationality and the question of how to conceive and evaluate the modernist transformation of Shenzhen. On first sight, the phenomenon of urban villages seems to embody the 'irrationality' of local culture as opposed to modernist and capitalist transformational design. But in fact, it emerges as a frame of Hegelian 'Sittlichkeit' that embeds and even enables the pursuit of such designs, while also transforming them. The development of Shenzhen must be conceived as a culturally embedded evolutionary process in which both decentralized market dynamics and cultural frames have played an essential role, constantly monitored by the local state, which mainly intervenes in two forms, one is direct planning and the other is establishing lines of communication and negotiation with the various societal actors, such as co-opting village leaders in formal political institutions or the CCP. In this sense, ritual is a form of rational government.

3 Ritual, the new cultural nexus of power, and evolutionary urban development

Indeed, one remarkable observation is that despite starting out from a massive mobilization of resources, Shenzhen swiftly embarked on an interactive pattern of balancing planned design and grassroots-level initiative, of which the cultural squares are a visible expression. Therefore, the urban villages do not match any other existing category of 'unplanned' development in developing country megacities. As we have seen, the shareholding cooperatives have emerged as the institutional and organizational crystallization of this interactive pattern, being institutional hybrids in two basic senses: First, they embody a hybrid conception of ownership, and second, they are arenas of negotiating various interests, though excluding the non-*hukou* majority population.

Regarding ownership, economists normally maintain a Weberian rationalist stance in demanding clear-cut, precise, and formalized property rights.[25] Accordingly, they typically have argued that the fuzzy property rights structure reigning in China for decades would eventually jeopardize growth. This never happened, although some economists might argue that China could have achieved even better with a much-improved property rights structure, or that crisis looms in the future. But the economist's perspective overemphasizes formal rationality in relation to substantive rationality. Regarding the latter, we must recognize that ownership is a very complex institution that does not only affect market transactions and allocation, but also involves many external effects, distributional issues, and requires legitimacy beyond delivering economic performance.[26] Solving these complex trade-offs in terms of strictly rationalized property rights might eventually fail to achieve the desired goals. Instead, a fuzzy structure allows for continuous renegotiation and adaptive efficiency.[27] The shareholding cooperatives represent such a fuzzy structure, resulting in a complex role in balancing business operations with the provision of public goods and keeping control of land despite nationalization in terms of fiduciary management of land for the municipal government, though informally.

The same applies for their governance structure vis-à-vis the government. The core organizational feature is the management committee of collective assets, which in a purely formal sense are not owned by anybody. But this is the channel where the CCP is most influential, yet mediated via local constellations of informal power, if the party secretary is simultaneously village head and lineage leader. We have analysed this in terms of a new 'cultural nexus of power'. This nexus is the real antipode to the Weberian rational state, as it fundamentally contextualizes the mechanisms of governance, different from the Weberian de-contextualized bureaucracy which only acts on clearly defined rules, to which the single cases are subsumed.

In approaching Shenzhen development as an evolutionary process of state-society interactions that are mediated by cultural contexts, we need to recognize that these contexts are multidimensional and deeply shaped by status distinctions across various groups in Shenzhen society: This is what we have called the new cultural nexus of power. As we have studied in detail, there are various arenas in which the corresponding interactions unfold: Apart from the shareholding cooperatives, often formalized as *shequ* management, a most important and rich domain is associational life. Business associations in Shenzhen are arenas in which state-society relations are enacted and result in contextualized action patterns. We cannot simply approach this in terms of another 'either-or' defined in Weberian categories: Either as representing business interests or being instruments of the state in governing business. Instead, they are the arenas where these two aspects are continuously assembled and reassembled in contextualized patterns of joint understanding and resulting action.

A policy domain where this is directly visible is urban renewal. As has been argued by Daniel Wang, Shenzhen represents an important case for discussing competing, if not conflicting, views on the city and urbanism.[28] There is a strong tradition of rationalist urban design, which has also deeply influenced socialist urban construction, with the classical manifestation of Haussmann's radical redesigning of Paris, which had many followers in maintaining the belief that optimizing cities must follow comprehensive and detailed forms of planning beyond the outlay, perhaps even of basic forms, of the design of buildings. Stalinist architecture is a socialist expression of this approach, which partly survives in the monumental shape of literally capitalist districts in places such as Beijing and Shanghai and their large-scale block design. However, if one considers the Chinese experience, the result has been deeply problematic, even when considering mere engineering criteria.[29]

In the 1960s, the radical critique of this urban rationalism was launched with Jane Jacob's work on the modern city as a living organism, which has also inspired many alternative design experiments, and certainly motivated much caution with urban renewal projects. Until today, socialist China has been slow in receiving this alternative view, presumably because there is a natural affinity between urban rationalism and authoritarian politics. After all, Jacobs emphasizes grassroots-level initiatives and civic activism. Yet, this perspective can be projected on the case of urban villages, which represent a very specific version of grassroots-level initiative, shaped by the local rural society.

The philosopher and urbanist Richard Sennett distinguishes between 'ville' and 'cité' as two fundamentally different ways to look at a city: The *ville* is the domain of physical architecture and design, and the *cité* is urban life.[30] Rationalist approaches in the Haussmann tradition typically centre on the *ville* and ignore the *cité*. In Shenzhen, this dualism is deeply ingrained in its embodied social structure: The modernist areas where the educated and middle-class people work and live, and the urban villages. Hence, even in the official population statistics of Shenzhen, the image of the city appears to be reduced to the *ville* as its modernist part. But the *cité* includes the urban villages in a very essential way, even when considering the upper social classes. One reason why the Shenzhen public is so concerned about urban renewal today is that most Shenzheners have the experience of once living in an urban village, with Baishizhou being a primordial example.[31] Even the Chaoshan real estate billionaire once lived there. If upward social mobility is part of the Shenzhen success story, urban villages are an essential part of it, too.

For understanding the Shenzhen *cité*, the cultural nexus of power is a powerful analytical lens by which we discern how culture or, more specifically, ritual has become an important element of defining Shenzhen identity beyond modernist utopia. This nexus is increasingly merging modernist and ritual aspects of life in the *cité*, embodied in projects of urban renewal that aim at protecting certain forms of life in urban villages via careful transformation of their architectural substance, especially if this can become part of hereditization strategies. As we have shown, this nexus involves the public, but still excludes migrants, a fact which demonstrates the embodiment of power relations in status hierarchies that are partly institutionally enshrined in the *hukou* system.[32] However, the frame of cultural governance also offers alternative ways of integration and overcoming status differences. This is possible because the revival of cultural traditions of rural Shenzhen is compatible with the life-world of many rural migrants coming from other places. In important cases, this goes beyond general notions such as similar stances towards kinship relations or religious practices. Think of the Chaoshan people: They include elites with *hukou* and low-status migrants without *hukou*, yet they share the life-world as defined by native place, often with a very concrete meaning: That is, both the rich and the poor originally coming from the same village in Chaoshan area.

In this sense, the revival of cultural traditions in the emergent scheme of cultural governance is a form in which the grassroots-level life-world becomes accommodated in the new cultural nexus of power. Ritual becomes an important medium of the emerging Shenzhen identity, beyond the modernist credo.

4 Ritual in a global social science

To a certain extent, our analysis of the Shenzhen case is a form of grounded theorizing, as we develop our theoretical conceptions in constant interaction with the empirical data. In doing this, we always start out from theoretical concepts that often are specific to Chinese studies, such as the specific concepts of extended kinship. This follows a methodology that was seminally suggested by Daniel Little.[33] He argued that adequate theorizing in the social sciences cannot build on truly general and abstract theoretical concepts, but must start out from and aim at theories of medium range specific to certain times and places. Obviously, this again reflects the Weberian topic of rationality: Leading philosophies of science think that it is possible to define generic criteria of what constitutes a good theory, a reliable method of empirical testing, and workable criteria of choosing among different theories. Science as a rational project embodies universal standards of rationality.

In comparison, in theories of medium range there is a strong interaction between theory design and what is regarded to be fact on the ground on first sight. Take, for example, our treatment of kinship. For a long time, anthropologists thought that there are universal criteria of what constitutes kinship. This uncritically accepted vision was exploded in the 1980s.[34] Today, and in the Chinese case, we need to pay attention to the contextualized ways how kinship is performed in different societies. That means we need to recognize the specific ways how terms that we relate to 'kinship' in our theory are used in China, and how these indigenous concepts relate with practices. In this view, a concept such as the 'lineage' is a theoretical term of medium range in Chinese studies and is not an empirical fact that can be subsumed to a generic and theoretical concept of 'lineage' in anthropological theory. An essential component of this methodological stance is that the researcher must also heed attention to the indigenous theories about extended kinship, that is, its conceptual representations by the actors themselves.

As we have argued in Chapter 2, 'ritual' has a similar methodological status, although it is much wider in terms of semantics than 'lineage'. For developing a theory of ritual, the Chinese case is very important, because since earliest times the Chinese have developed indigenous theories of ritual beyond ritual practices.[35] These theories can be productively connected to general theories in the social sciences that also refer to ritual. In this book, we have chosen Randall Collins' theory as a rallying point for our ideas and thoughts. Collins' theory is generic, but we claim that at the end of the day further vindication must build on extensions and ramifications that involve medium-range theoretical concepts. Kinship ritual in China is a case in point, or networking á la *guanxi*.

In fact, our argument is very simple: Collins' theory, though being intended as a generic theory, at the same time is congenial to the indigenous Chinese view on ritual, at least as far as the practices and their ordinary life interpretations are concerned. Let us summarize the most significant results.

- In many forms, we identified social circles and artefactual arenas in which ritual activities create events of effervescence that bolster the shared identity of a social group. These are, for instance, the ritual spaces of original villages that are reconstituted via the renovation of ancestral halls, the erection of temples, or the festive activities at these places, such as the *pencai* events; the meetings of chambers of commerce that are held on auspicious days, such as New Year, and that evoke the shared memories of native place; or the pilgrimages of surname groups to certain sacred places, such as tombs of high ancestors. It is essential to recognize that these activities often are expressions of identity politics involving manifest economic and political interests, the pursuit of which requires a degree of solidarity and of communal support for strong leadership, as in the case of advancing the interests of the village community via shareholding cooperatives vis-à-vis municipal government and developers.

- The ritual activities are closely related to the expression of a superior moral status, thus legitimizing the pursuit of interests by reference to common good, if only in the sense of maintaining proper social order. This is salient in the strong emphasis on moral qualities, such as trustworthiness of a group, its public spirit, or the engagement in charities. Many rituals directly involve moral discourses, such as in the context of the *guoxue* revival. Although all these discourses eventually tie back to a universal ethical background of Chinese tradition, such as invoking Confucianism, they are often cast into the language of particularism, such as being communicated as values of a subethnic group (e.g. Hakka) or a surname (e.g. Huang). This connection is often established via a central ritual object, namely the genealogy and the reference to high ancestors, such as almost ideal-typically in the Wen Tianxiang case. The ancestor and the physical genealogy and its various artefactual representations are approached as embodying moral excellence, which emanates to the entire group.
- There is a tight and deep relationship between ritual and market. In practical terms, this emerges from the fact that many ritual activities are hereditized and become assets in business projects of tourism, leisure, and urban development. But the relationship has much farther scope. One simple but very essential point is the creation of trust among market agents via ritual activities, such as signalling trustworthiness in displaying religious beliefs in Buddhism. The trust-building functions of networking rely on the ritual nature of *guanxi*. In many respects, ritual creates the assets, goods, and services that are traded on markets. In this regard, however, many relevant phenomena fall outside the scope of the traditional rituals mostly considered here, such as luxury consumption and its relationship to status rituals. But this omission only further strengthens our argument, because there is much scope for its extension.

As we see, Collins' theory can make sense of many phenomena that we observe in Shenzhen. On the one hand, this may be conceived as demonstrating its validity as a theory. But on the other hand, this also shows that indigenous conceptions of ritual have the status of a proto-theory that already anticipates many core ideas that are fully elaborated analytically in Collins' approach, as we have shown for the practice of *guanxi*. The conclusion to be drawn is that Collins' theory is a general conceptual frame that can integrate local and indigenous conceptions of ritual in a way such that a theory of intermediate reach and scope can be constructed, a theory of Chinese ritual. We think that this is what should be conceived as a 'theory' in a global social science, in the sense of empirically testable hypotheses.

Interestingly, following the debates over the Historical School in Germany in the early 20th century, German economists developed a similar methodological and epistemological position under the shadow of Weber's approach to ideal types.[36] Contra Weber, they argued that general theory can never have empirical reference, but only if combined with concepts of medium range, thus distilling more abstract concepts from historically and regionally specific data, which do not raise claims on generalization beyond this reference. Weberian ideal types appear to be incoherent theoretical constructs, because they confound these two levels. This is what led to the Weberian conundrum with China.

The theory of ritual is an excellent example for this two-level methodology. There are various approaches that allow for building a general theory of ritual, such as Collins'. But they can only become empirically meaningful if they relate systematically with forms of ritual that are specific to certain societies. Otherwise, ritual may emerge as covering almost everything, thus become almost devoid of meaning. In the Chinese case, we have rich empirical and indigenous conceptual materials that allow for distilling a theoretical concept of ritual with medium range from it. Shenzhen is our laboratory for testing this theory, and thereby contributing to the emergence of a truly global social science.

Notes

1 Naughton (2017).
2 This is salient in Brandt et al. (2014), where the essential difference only seems to be the much larger infrastructural power of the modern Chinese state, whereas many other elements appear similar, such as institutional weaknesses, corruption, or an authoritarian ideology.
3 Huang (2015, 2019).
4 Weber (1991).
5 The authoritative assessment of Weber's China scholarship is the edited volume of Schluchter (1983) with contribution of the world's finest China scholars. Yet, the volume does not yet fully cover insights that have been generated by new research since it had been published, such as the rise of the 'California school' dealing with the comparative history of capitalism from the perspective of China studies (Wong 1997; Pomeranz 2000).
6 On the potential impact of that constellation on Western intellectual history, see Mungello (1999: 59ff).
7 Schluchter (1983), Lai (2015).
8 This view is developed in his extremely influential 'Zwischenbetrachtung' that follows the Confucianism book.
9 Joas (2017).
10 Seligman et al. (2008) emphasize this essential opposition in their foundational work on ritual.
11 See various contributions to the important volume of Zelin et al. (2004).
12 The rich literature on this was launched with Elvin's (1973) seminal book on the medieval economic revolution. Some observers have dubbed this as a 'Smithian economy', for example, Arrighi (2007), but this also implies a distinction to

capitalism, as Adam Smith did not yet fully anticipate its emergence, and hence an implicit value judgement.

13 A classic on this is Chao (1986).
14 Polanyi (1944).
15 This is clearly indicated in the title of Chwe's (2001) book 'Rational Ritual'. Here, ritual is a form of rationality in game theory.
16 Herrmann-Pillath (2017).
17 Migdal (2001).
18 Bünger (1983).
19 MacCormack (2006).
20 The classical work on this is Rowe's (1989) comprehensive and detailed study of Hankou.
21 For a lucid analysis of the relevance of Hegel today, see Taylor (2015). One of us has developed the application on China in more detail elsewhere; Herrmann-Pillath (2015).
22 Schluchter (1983).
23 For a related and comprehensive view, see Menke (2015).
24 Sangren (2013).
25 Stiglitz (2013).
26 Kennedy (2013).
27 Ho (2013).
28 Wang (2016).
29 See the analysis of 'superblocs' in World Bank (2014: 142ff).
30 Sennett (2018).
31 Wang (2016) gives a lively description of his own experience.
32 Zhang (2018).
33 Little (1992). Herrmann-Pillath (2018a) offers a more comprehensive and analytical discussion.
34 Schneider (1984).
35 Seligman et al. (2008).
36 This reference if fully explored in Herrmann-Pillath (2015, 2018a).

References

Alesina, A. and Giuliano, P. (2015) 'Culture and Institutions', *Journal of Economic Literature*, 53(4): 898–944.

Arrighi, G. (2007) *Adam Smith in Beijing. Lineages of the Twenty-First Century*, London und New York: Verso.

Bach, J. (2017) '"They Come in Peasants and Leave Citizens": Urban Villages and the Making of Shenzhen,' in O'Donnell, M. A., Winnie, W. Y. W., and Jonathan P. G. B., eds. *Learning from Shenzhen: China's Post-Mao Experiment from Special Zone to Model City*, Chicago: The University of Chicago Press, pp. 138–170.

Baker, H. D. R. (1977) 'Extended Kinship in the Traditional City', in Skinner, G. W., ed., *The City in Late Imperial China*, Stanford, CA: Stanford University Press, pp. 499–518.

Baker, H. D. R. (1979) *Chinese Family and Kinship*, London: Macmillan.

Barbalet, J. (2020) 'The Analysis of Chinese Rural Society: Fei Xiaotong Revisited', *Modern China*, 16, doi: 10.1177/0097700419894921.

Barnes, B. (1995) *The Elements of Social Theory*, Princeton, NJ: Princeton University Press.

Bastid-Bruguiere, M. (1980) 'Currents of Social Change', in: Fairbank, J. K. and Liu, K.-C., eds., *The Cambridge History of China, Volume 11: Late Ch'ing, 1800–1911, Part 2*, Cambridge: Cambridge University Press, pp. 535–602.

Béland, D. and Cox, R. H., eds. (2011) *Ideas and Politics in Social Science Research*, Oxford: Oxford University Press.

Bennett, J. (2010) *Vibrant Matter: A Political Ecology of Things*, Durham, NC: Duke University Press.

Bergère, M.-C. (1983) 'The Chinese Bourgeosie, 1911–37', in Twitchett, D. and Fairbank, J. K., eds., *The Cambridge History of China, Volume 12: Republican China 1912–1949, Part 1*, Cambridge: Cambridge University Press, pp. 722–825.

Beugelsdijk, S. and Maseland, R. (2010) *Culture in Economics. History, Methodological Reflections, and Contemporary Applications*, Cambridge: Cambridge University Press.

Bian Yanjie (2018) 'The Prevalence and Increasing Significance of *guanxi*', *The China Quarterly*, 235: 597–621.

Billioud, S. and Thoraval, J. (2015) *The Sage and the People: The Confucian Revival in China*. Oxford and New York: Oxford University Press.

Blake, C. F. (2011) *Burning Money. The Material Spirit of the Chinese Afterworld*, Honululu: University of Hawai'i Press.

Boldyrev, I. and E. Svetlova, eds. (2016) *Enacting Dismal Science: New Perspectives on the Performativity of Economics*, New York: Palgrave MacMillan.

Booz&Co (2009) *Shanzhai. A Chinese Phenomenon*, Bejing: Booz&Co.

Boretz, A. (2011) *Gods, Ghosts, and Gangsters. Ritual Violence, Martial Arts, and Masculinity on the Margins of Chinese Society*, Honululu: University of Hawai'i Press.

Brandt, L., Ma, D. and Rawski, T. G. (2014) 'From Divergence to Convergence: Reevaluating the History Behind China's Economic Boom', *Journal of Economic Literature*, LII(1): 45–123.

Bray, D. (2013) 'Urban Planning Goes Rural: Conceptualising the "New Village"', *China Perspectives*, 2013(3): 53–62.

Brown, J. S. and Hagel III, J. (2005) 'Innovation Blowback: Disruptive Management Practices From Asia', *McKinsey Quarterly*, http://www.mckinsey.com/insights/innovation/innovation_blowback_disruptive_management_practices_from_asia.

Bruckermann, C. (2016) 'Trading on Tradition: Tourism, Ritual, and Capitalism in a Chinese Village', *Modern China*, 42(2): 188–224.

Brumann, C. (1999) 'Writing for Culture: Why a Successful Concept Should Not Be Discarded', *Current Anthropology*, 40, Supplement, S1–S28.

Bünger, K. (1983) 'Das chinesische Rechtssystem und das Prinzip der Rechtsstaatlichkeit', in Schluchter, W., ed., *Max Webers Studie über Konfuzianismus und Daoismus. Interpretation und Kritik*, Frankfurt a.M.: Suhrkamp, pp. 134–173.

Burt, R. S. (1992) *Structural Holes. The Social Structure of Competiton*, Cambridge, MA und London: Harvard University Press.

Burt, R. S. (2002) 'The Social Capital of Structural Holes', in Guillén, M. F., Collins, R., England, P. and Meyer, M., eds., *The New Economic Sociology. Developments in an Emerging Field*, New York: Russell Sage Foundation, pp. 148–192.

Callon, M. (2007) 'What Does It Mean to Say That Economics is Performative?', in MacKenzie, D., Muniesa, F. and Siu, L., eds., *Do Economists Make Markets? On the Performativity of Economics*, Princeton, NJ and Oxford: Princeton University Press, pp. 344–357.

Campagnolo, G., ed. (2016) *Liberalism and Chinese Economic Development. Perspectives from Europe and Asia*, Abingdon and New York: Routledge.

Carsten, J. (2004) *After Kinship*, Cambridge: Cambridge University Press.

Cha Zhenxiang 查振祥 (2018) 'Report About the Transformation and Development of 1017 Shareholding Cooperatives in Shenzhen' 深圳市1017家社区股份合作公司转型发展研究, in Chen Shaobing陈少兵, ed., *Shenzhen Economic Development Report 2018*, 深圳经济发展报告2018, pp. 260–268.

Chan, A., Madsen, R. and Unger, J. (2009) *Chen Village. Revolution to Globalization*, Berkeley, Los Angeles, London: University of California Press.

Chan, S. C. (2001) 'Selling the Ancestors' Land. A Hong Kong Lineage Adapts', *Modern China*, 27(2): 262–284.

Chan, S. C. (2002) 'Interpreting Chinese Tradition: A Clansmen Association in Singapore', *New Zealand Journal of Asian Studies*, 5(1): 72–90.

Chan, S. C. (2010) 'Food, Memories, and Identities in Hong Kong', *Identities*, 17(2–3): 204–227.

Chan, W.-H. (2010) 'Women's Food and Women's Work in Lineage Land', in: Siu, H.-F. and Chan, W.-H., eds., *Merchant Daughters: Women, Commerce, and Regional Culture in South China*, Hong Kong: Hong Kong University Press, pp. 84–107.

Chan, W. K. (1991) *The Making of Hong Kong Society. Three Studies of Class Formation in Early Hong Kong*, Oxford: Oxford University Press.

Chan, W. K. K. (1992) 'Chinese Business Networking and the Pacific Rim. The Family Firm's Roles Past and Present', *Journal of American-East Asian Relations*, 1(2): 171–190.

Chang, X. Q. (2010) *Guanxi or Li shang wanglai? Reciprocity, Social Support Networks, & Social Creativity in a Chinese Village*, Taipei: Ariti Press.

Chao, K. (1986) *Man and Land in China: An Economic Analysis*, Stanford, CA: Stanford University Press.

Chau, A. Y. (2006) *Miraculous Response. Doing Popular Religion in Contemporary China*, Stanford, CA: Stanford University Press.

Chau, A. Y. (2011) 'Modalities of Doing Religion and Ritual Polytropy: Evaluating the Religious Market Model from the Perspective of Chinese Religious History', *Religion*, 14(4): 547–568.

Chau, A. Y. (2012) 'Efficacy, Not Confessionality: On Ritual Polytropy in China', in Bowman, G., ed., *Sharing the "Sacra": The Politics and Pragmatics of Intercommunal Relations Around Holy Places*, Oxford: Berghahn, pp. 79–96.

Chau, A. Y. (2013) 'Actants Amassing (AA): Beyond Collective Effervescence and the Social', in Hausner, S. L., ed., *Durkheim in Dialogue: A Centenary Celebration of The Elementary Forms of Religious Life*, London: Berghahn Books, pp. 206–230.

Chau, A. Y. (2014) 'Household Sovereignty and Religious Subjectification: China and the Christian West Compared', *Studies in Church History*, 50: 494–506.

Chau, A. Y. (2019) *Religion in China. Ties that Bind*, Cambridge and Medford: Polity.

Chen, F. (2010) 'Trade Unions and the Quadripartite Interactions in Strike Settlement in China', *The China Quarterly*, 201: 104–124.

Chen Lai 陈来 (2015): 中华文明的核心价值。国学流变与传统值观, Zhonghua wenming de kexin jiazhi. Guoxue liubian yu chuantong zhiguan, Beijing: Sanlian shudian.

Chen, C.-C., Chen, X.-P. and Huang, S. (2013) 'Chinese *guanxi*: An Integrative Review and New Directions for Future Research', *Management and Organization Review*, 9(1): 167–207.

Chen, C.-C. and Farh, J.-l. (2010) 'Developments in Understanding Chinese Leadership: Paternalism and Its Elaborations, Moderations, and Alternatives', in Bond, M. H., ed., *The Oxford Handbook of Chinese Psychology*, Oxford: Oxford University Press, pp. 599–622.

Chen, C.-C. and Lee, Y.-T. (2008) 'Introduction: The Diversity and Dynamism of Chinese Philosophies on Leadership', in Chen, C.-C. and Lee Y.-T., eds., *Leadership and Management in China. Philosophies, Theories, and Practices*, Cambridge: Cambridge University Press, pp. 1–30.

Chen, F.-m. C. and Myers, R. (1976) 'Customary Law and the Economic Growth of China During the Ch'ing Period, Parts I and II', *Modern China*, 3(4): 1–32, 3(5): 4–27.

Chen, Y. and Li, S. X. (2009) 'Group Identity and Social Preferences', *American Economic Review*, 99(1): 431–457.

Cheung S.-K. 张少强 (2016) 管治新界。地权，父权与主权 Guangzhi xinjie. diquan, fuquan yu zhuquan, *Governing the New Territories: Territorial Power, Patriarchal Power, and State Power*, Hong Kong: Chonghwa.

Ching, M. B. (2008) 'Where Guangdong Meets Shanghai: Hong Kong Culture in a Transregional Context', in Siu, H. F. and Ku, A., eds., *Hong Kong Mobile: Making a Global Population*, Hong Kong: Hong Kong University Press, pp. 45–62.

Chu, J. Y. (2010) *Cosmologies of Credit: Transnational Mobility and the Politics of Destination in China*, Durham, NC: Duke University Press.

Chubb, A. (2015) 'China's Shanzhai Culture: 'Grabism' and the Politics of Hybridity', *Journal of Contemporary China*, 24(92): 260–279.

Chun, A. J. U. L. (2000) *Unstructuring Chinese Society: The Fictions of Colonial Practice and the Changing Realities of "Land" in the New Territories of Hong Kong*, Amsterdam, The Netherlands: Harwood Academic.

Chung, H. and Unger, J. (2013) 'The Guangdong Model of Urbanisation: Collective Village Land and the Making of a New Middle Class', *China Perspectives*, 2013(3): 33–42.

Chwe, M. S.-Y. (2001) *Rational Ritual. Culture, Coordination, and Common Knowledge*, Princeton, NJ: Princeton University Press.

Clarke, D. C. (2014) 'China's Stealth Urban Land Revolution', *American Journal of Comparative Law*, 62(2): 323–366.

Clart, P. (2012) 'Chinese Popular Religion', in Nadeau, R., ed., *The Wiley-Blackwell Companion to Chinese Religions*, Oxford: Wiley-Blackwell, pp. 219–235.

Cohen, M. L. (1970) 'Developmental Process in the Chinese Domestic Group', in Freedman, M., ed., *Family and Kinship in Chinese Society*, Stanford, CA: Stanford University Press, pp. 21–36.

Cohen, M. L. (1990) 'Lineage Organization in North China', *Journal of Asian Studies*, 49(3): 509–534.

Cohen, M. L. (1992) 'Family Management and Family Division in Contemporary Rural China', *The China Quarterly*, 130: 357–377.

Cohen, M. L. (1994) 'Being Chinese: The Peripheralization of Traditional Identity', in Tu, W., ed., *The Living Tree. The Changing Meaning of Being Chinese Today*, Stanford, CA: Stanford University Press, pp. 88–108.

Cohen, M. L. (1996/1960) 'The Hakka or "Guest People": Dialect as a Sociocultural Variable in Southeast China', in Nicole, C., ed., *Guest People: Hakka Identity in China and Abroad*, Washington: University of Washington Press, pp. 36–79.

Cohen, M. L. (2017) 'High Ancestors among the Hakka Chinese: Past and Present, Rural, Urban, and Global', *Global Hakka Studies* 2017/5: 1–40.

Collins, R. (2005) *Interaction Ritual Chains*, Princeton, NJ: Princeton University Press.

Constable, N. (1996) 'Introduction: What Does It Mean to be Hakka? In Constable, N., ed., *Guest people: Hakka identity in China and abroad*, Seattle: University of Washington Press, pp. 3–35.

Culp, R. (2015) 'Local Entrepreneurs, Transnational Networks: Publishing Markets and Cantonese Communities within and across National Borders', in Rea, C. G. and Volland, N., eds., *The Business of Culture: Cultural Entrepreneurs in China and Southeast Asia, 1900–65*, Vancouver: UBC Press, pp. 181–206.

D'Adderio, L. (2011) 'Artifacts at the Centre of Routines: Performing the Material Turn in Routines Theory', *Journal of Institutional Economics*, 7(2): 197–230.

Dai, W. and Zhang, X. (2014) 当代中国宗族复兴研究:回顾与反思 (Dangdai Zhongguo zongzu fuxing yanjiu: huigu yu fansi), 普阳学干 *Puyang xuegan*, 2: 9–14.

DiMaggio, P. (2011) 'Cultural Networks', in Scott, J. and Carrington, P., eds., *The Sage Handbook of Social Network Analysis*, Los Angeles, CA: Sage, pp. 286–301.

Duara, P. (1988) *Culture, Power, and the State. Rural North China, 1900–1942*, Stanford, CA: Stanford University Press.

DuBois, T. D. 2005. *The Sacred Village: Social Change and Religious Life in Rural North China*, Honolulu: University of Hawai'i Press.

Durkheim, È. (1915) *Elementary Forms of Religious Life*, London: Allen & Unwin.
Eberstadt, N. (2011) 'The Global War Against Baby Girls', *The New Atlantis*, http://www.thenewatlantis.com/publications/the-global-war-against-baby-girls.
Ebrey, P. B. (1991) 'The Chinese Family and the Spread of Confucian Values', in Rozman, G., eds., *The East Asian Region. Confucian Heritage and Its Modern Adaptation*, Princeton, NJ: Princeton University Press, pp. 45–83.
Ebrey, P. B. and Watson, J. L. (1986) 'Introduction', in Ebrey, P. B. and Watson, J. L., eds., *Kinship Organization in Late Imperial China, 1000–1949*, Berkeley, Los Angeles and London: University of California Press, pp. 1–15.
Elias, N. (1969b/1989) *Die höfische Gesellschaft: Untersuchungen zur Soziologie des Königtums und der höfischen Aristokratie*, Frankfurt: Suhrkamp.
Elman, B. (1991) 'Political, Social, and Cultural Reproduction via Civil Service Examinations in Late Imperial China', *The Journal of Asian Studies*, 50(1): 7–28.
Elvin, M. (1973) *The Pattern of the Chinese Past*, Stanford, CA: Stanford University Press.
Erbaugh, M. (1992) 'The Secret History of the Hakkas: The Chinese Revolution as a Hakka Enterprise', *The China Quarterly*, 132: 937–968.
Fan, L. and Whitehead, J. D. (2011) 'Spirituality in a Modern Chinese Metropolis', in Palmer, D. A., Shive, G. and Wickeri, P. L., eds., *Chinese Religious Life*, Oxford and New York: Oxford University Press, pp. 13–29.
Fang Xiuwen 防秀文 and Lin Feng 林锋 (2011a) *Zhonghua shangye wenhua shilun, Vol. 1: Zhonghua shange wenhua tan yuan*, 中国商业文化史论, 第一卷, 中华商业文化探源, Beijing: Zhongguo jingji chubanshe.
Fang Xiuwen 防秀文 and Lin Feng 林锋 (2011b) *Zhonghua shangye wenhua shilun, Vol. 2: bianyi de chuantong shangye wenhua*, 中国商业文化史论, 第二卷, 变异的传统商业文化, Beijing: Zhongguo jingji chubanshe.
Faure, D. (2006) *China and Capitalism. A History of Business Enterprise in Modern China*, Hong Kong: Hong Kong University Press.
Faure, D. (2007) *Emperor and Ancestor: State and Lineage in South China*, Stanford, CA: Stanford University Press.
Fei, X. (1947) *Xiangtu Zhongguo*, Shanghai (Translation by Gary Hamilton and Wang Zheng, *From the Soil. Foundations of Chinese Society*, Berkeley: University of California Press, 1988).
Feng, X. (2013) 'Local Government Debt and Municipal Bonds in China: Problems and a Framework for Rules', *Copenhagen Journal of Asian Studies*, 31(2): 23–53.
Fewsmith, J. (1983) 'From Guild to Interest Group. The Transformation of Public and Private in Late Qing China', *Comparative Studies in Society and History*, 25: 617–640.
Florence, E. (2017) 'How to be a Shenzhener: Representations of Migrant Labour in Shenzhen's Second Decade', in O'Donnell, M. A., Wong, W. W. Y. and Bach, J. P. G., eds., *Learning from Shenzhen: China's post-Mao Experiment from Special Zone to Model City*, Chicago, IL: The University of Chicago Press, pp. 86–106.
Frank, R. H. (1985) *Choosing the Right Pond: Human Behavior and the Quest for Status*, New York and Oxford: Oxford University Press.
Freedman, M. (1967) *Chinese Lineage and Society*, London: Athlone Press.
Fu, W., Diez, J. R. and Schiller, D. (2013) 'Interactive Learning, Informal Networks and Innovation: Evidence from Electronics Firm Survey in the Pearl River Delta, China', *Research Policy*, 42(3): 635–646.
Fukuyama, F. (2011) 'The Patterns of History', *Journal of Democracy*, 23(1): 14–26.

Gates, H. (1996) *China's Motor: A Thousand Years of Petty Capitalism*, Ithaca, NY and London: Cornell University Press.

Geertz, C. (1963) *Peddlers and Princes: Social Change and Economic Modernization in Two Indonesian Towns*, Chicago, IL: The University of Chicago Press.

Geertz, C. (1973) *The Interpretation of Cultures*, New York: Basic Books.

Glaeser, E., Huang, W., Ma, Y. and Shleifer, A. (2017) 'A Real Estate Boom with Chinese Characteristics', *Journal of Economic Perspectives*, 31(1): 93–116.

Goffman, E. (1967) *Interaction Ritual: Essays on Face-to-face Behavior*. New York: Anchor Books.

Gold, T., Guthrie, D. and Wank, D., eds. (2002) *Social Connections in China. Institutions, Culture, and the Changing Nature of Guanxi*, Cambridge: Cambridge University Press.

Goody, J. (1983) *The Development of the Family and Marriage in Europe*, Cambridge: Cambridge University Press.

Goossaert, V. and Palmer, D. A. (2011) *The Religious Question in Modern China*, Chicago, IL: Chicago University Press.

Granovetter, M. (1985) 'Economic Action and Social Structure: The Problem of Embeddedness', *American Journal of Sociology*, 91(3): 481–510.

Granovetter, M. (2005) 'The Impact of Social Structure on Economic Outcomes', *Journal of Economic Perspectives*, 19(1): 33–50.

Greenhalgh, S. (2012) 'Patriarchal Demographics? China's Sex Ratio Reconsidered', *Population and Development Review*, 38(Supplement): 130–149.

Greenhalgh, S. and Winckler, E. A. (2005) *Governing China's Population: From Leninist to Neoliberal Biopolitics*, Stanford, CA: Stanford University Press.

Gui, H. (2014) 礼与生命价值。家庭生活中的道德，宗教与法律 *(Li yu shengming jiazhi. Jiating shenghuo zhong de daode, zongjiao yu falü)*, Beijing: Commercial Press.

Guo, M. and Herrmann-Pillath, C. (2019a) 'Exploring Extended Kinship in 21st century China: A Conceptual Case Study', *Journal of Current Chinese Affairs*, doi: 10.1177/1868102619845244.

Guo, M. and Herrmann-Pillath, C. (2019b) 'Lineage, Food and Ritual in a Chinese Metropolis', *Anthropos*, 114: 195–207.

Hall, D. L. and Ames, R. T. (1998) *Thinking from the Han. Self, Truth, and Transcendence in Chinese and Western Culture*, New York: SUNY Press.

Hamilton, G. G. (1996) 'The Organizational Foundations of Western and Chinese Commerce: A Historical and Comparative Analysis', in Hamilton, G., ed., *Asian Business Networks*, Berlin: Springer, pp. 43–58.

Hang, M. (2006) *"Villages" in Shenzhen: Persistence and Transformation of an Old Social System in an Emerging Mega City*, PhD dissertation, Bauhaus University Weimar, https://d-nb.info/1115337211/34.

Hase, P. H. (1990) 'A Village War in Sham Chun', *Journal of the Royal Asiatic Society Hong Branch*, 30: 265–281.

Hay, C. (21011) 'Ideas and the Construction of Interests', in Béland, D. and Cox, R. H., eds., *Ideas and Politics in Social Science Research*, Oxford: Oxford University Press, pp. 65–82.

He, S. (2019) 'Three Waves of State-Led Gentrification in China', *Tijdschrift Voor Economische En Sociale Geografie*, 110(1): 26–34.

He, S. and Xue, D. (2014) 'Identity Building and Communal Resistance against Landgrabs in Wukang Village, China', *Current Anthropology*, 55: S126–S137.

Heberer, T. and Schubert, G. (2012) 'County and Township Cadres as a Strategic Group. A New Approach to Political Agency in China's Local State', *Journal of Chinese Political Science*, 17, 221–249.

Heberer, T. und Schubert, G. (2019) 'Weapons of the Rich: Strategic Behavior and Collective Action of Private Entrepreneurs in China', *Modern China*, 45(5): 471–503.

Heilmann, S. (2008) 'From Local Experiments to National Policy: The Origins of China's Distinctive Policy Process', *The China Journal*, 59: 1–32.

Herrmann-Pillath, C. (1991) *Institutioneller Wandel, Macht und Inflation in China: Ordnungstheoretische Analysen zur Politischen Ökonomie eines Transformationsprozesses.* Baden-Baden: Nomos.

Herrmann-Pillath, C. (2012) 'Institutions, Distributed Cognition and Agency: Rule-following as Performative Action', *Journal of Economic Methodology*, 19(1): 21–42.

Herrmann-Pillath, C. (2013) 'Performativity of Economic Systems: Approaches and Implications for Taxonomy', *Journal of Economic Methodology*, 20(2): 139–163.

Herrmann-Pillath, C. (2015) *Wachstum, Macht und Ordnung. Eine wirtschaftsphilosophische Auseinandersetzung mit China*, Marburg: Metropolis.

Herrmann-Pillath, C. (2017) 'Performativity, Performance and Politics: Towards an Evolutionary Taxonomy of Economic Systems', *Schmollers Jahrbuch*, 136(3): 257–284.

Herrmann-Pillath, C. (2018a) *China's Economic Culture: The Ritual Order of State and Markets*, Abingdon and New York: Routledge.

Herrmann-Pillath, C. (2018b) *Is Shenzhen Emerging as a Global City with Distinct Cultural Roots? Report of Pilot Study Prepared for China Development Institute, Shenzhen*, doi: 10.13140/RG.2.2.29694.84806.

Herrmann-Pillath, C. and Boldyrev, I. (2014) *Hegel, Institutions and Economics: Performing the Social*, Abingdon and New York: Routledge.

Herrmann-Pillath, C., Feng, X. and Guo, M. (2019) 'Entrepreneurs and Ritual in China's Economic Culture', *Journal of Institutional Economics*, doi: 10.1017/S1744137419000201.

Herrmann-Pillath, C. and Zweynert, J. (2014) 'Institutionentransfer durch kulturelles Unternehmertum', in Apolte, T., ed., *Transfer von Institutionen*, Berlin: Duncker & Humblot, pp. 85–112.

Hirsch, F. (1976) *The Social Limits to Growth*, London: Routledge & Kegan Paul.

Ho, P. (2001) 'Who Owns China's Land? Property Rights and Deliberate Institutional Ambiguity', *The China Quarterly*, 166: 394–423.

Ho, P. (2013) 'In Defense of Endogenous, Spontaneously Ordered Development: Institutional Functionalism and Chinese Property Rights', *The Journal of Peasant Studies*, 40(6): 1087–1118.

Hofstede, G., Hofstede, G. J. and Minkov, M. (2010) *Cultures and Organizations. Software of the Mind*, New York: McGraw Hill.

Hopkins, E. and Kornienko, T. (2004) 'Running to Keep the Same Place: Consumer Choice as a Game of Status', *American Economic Review*, 94(4): 1085–1108.

Hsu, C. L. and Jiang, Y. (2015) 'An Institutional Approach to Chinese NGOs: State Alliance versus State Avoidance Resource Strategies', *The China Quarterly*, 221: 100–122.

Hu, B. (2007) *Informal Institutions and Rural Development in China*, Abingdon und New York: Routledge.

Huang, P. C. C. (1990) *The Peasant Family and Rural Development in the Yangzi Delta, 1350–1988*, Stanford, CA: Stanford University Press.

Huang, P. C. C. (1993) '"Public Sphere" / "Civil Society" in China? The Third Realm between State and Society', *Modern China*, 19(2): 216–240.

Huang, P. C. C. (2008) 'Centralized Minimalism: Semiformal Governance by Quasi Officials and Dispute Resolution in China', *Modern China*, 34(1): 9–35.

Huang, P. C. C. (2015) 'Morality an Law in China, Past and Present', *Modern China*, 41(1): 3–39.

Huang, P. C. C. (2019) 'Rethinking "the Third Sphere': The Dualistic Unity of State and Society in China, Past and Present', *Modern China*, 45(4): 355–391.

Huang, W. (2017) 'The Tripartite Origins of Shenzhen: Beijing, Hongkong, and Bao'an', in O'Donnell, M. A., Wong, W. W. Y. and Bach, J. P. G., eds., *Learning from Shenzhen: China's post-Mao Experiment from Special Zone to Model City*, Chicago, IL: The University of Chicago Press, pp. 65–85.

Hutchins, E. (1995) *Cognition in the Wild*, Cambridge and London: MIT Press.

Iannaccone, L. R. (1991) 'The Consequences of Religious Market Structure: Adam Smith and the Economics of Religion', *Rationality and Society*, 3(2): 156–177.

Iannaccone, L. R. (1998) 'Introduction to the Economics of Religion', *Journal of Economic Literature*, 36(3): 1465–1495.

Inazawa T. (2016) 'Gendai chūgoku no 'yumin' to sōzoku. Guangdong shū tōbu Shanwei no jirei kara' (The Lineages of Fisher People in Contemporary China: The Case of Shanwei in Northern Guangdong Province), in Segawa, M. and Kawagusa K., eds., *"Sōzoku" to chūgoku shakai* (Lineage and Chinese Society: Its Transformations and the Current State of Anthropological Research), Tokio: Fukyo Publishing, pp. 197–232.

Jackson. M. O. (2014) 'Networks in the Understanding of Economic Behaviors', *Journal of Economic Perspectives*, 28(4): 3–22.

Jacobs, J. B. (1982) 'The Concept of Guanxi and Local Politics in a Rural Chinese Cultural Setting', in Greenblatt, S., Wilson, R. W. and Wilson, A. A., eds., *Social Interaction in Chinese Society*, New York: Praeger, pp. 209–236.

Joas, H. (2017) *Die Macht des Heiligen. Eine Alternative zur Geschichte der Entzauberung*, Berlin: Suhrkamp.

Jones, E. L. (2006) *Cultures Merging. A Historical and Economic Critique of Culture*, Princeton, NJ: Princeton University Press.

Kan, K. (2019) 'A Weapon of the Weak? Shareholding, Property Rights and Village Empowerment in China', *The China Quarterly*, 237: 131–152.

Kang, X. (2009) 'Two Temples, Three Religions, and a Tourist Attraction: Contesting Sacred Space on China's Ethnic Frontier', *Modern China*, 35(3): 227–255.

Kawagusa, Y. (2016) 'Sōzoku keisei, henhō soshite genzai. Guangdong shū Zhujiang delta no itsu sōzoku no jirei kara' (Formation, Transformation and Current Status of Lineages: A Case in Guangdong Province Pearl River Delta), in Segawa, M. and Kawagusa, Y., eds., *"Sōzoku" to chūgoku shakai. Sono henhō no jinreigaku kenkiū no genzai* (Lineage and Chinese Society: Its Transformations and the Current State of Anthropological Research), Tokio: Fukyo Publishing Inc., 2016, pp. 263–309.

Ke Qianting 柯倩婷 (2016) 训诫女人：儒家女教的知识生产与话语机制, xunjie nüren: rujia nüxiao de zhishi shengchan yu huoyu jizhi, 妇女研究论丛, 3(135): 15–24.

Kennedy, D. (2013) 'Some Caution about Property Rights as a Recipe for Economic Development', in Kennedy, D. and Stiglitz, J. E., eds., *Law and Economics with Chinese Characteristics. Institutions for Promoting Development in the Twenty-First Century*, Oxford: Oxford University Press, pp. 187–213.

King, A. Y.-c. (1994) 'Kuan-hsi and Network Building: A Sociological Interpretation', in Tu, W., ed., *The Living Tree. The Changing Meaning of Being Chinese Today*, Stanford, CA: Stanford University Press, pp. 109–126.

Kipnis, A. (2017) "Urbanization and the Transformation of Kinship Practice in Shandong", in Santos, G. D., and Harrell, S., eds., *Transforming Patriarchy: Chinese Families in the Twenty-First Century*, Seattle: University of Washington Press, pp. 113–128.

Kramer, S. (2020) 'China's Social Valorization System, guoxue, and the Individual Self-cultivation Narrative', in Kramer, S. and Ludes, P., eds., *Collective Myths and Decivilizing Processes*, Berlin-Munster-Wien-Zurich-London: LIT, pp. 29–52.

Kroker, E. (1959) 'The Concept of Property in Chinese Customary Law', in Brown, R. A., ed., *Chinese Business Enterprise, Vol. IV*, London and New York: Routledge, pp. 370–386.

Kuah-Pearce, K. E. (2011) *Rebuilding the Ancestral Village. Singaporeans in China*, Hong Kong: Hong Kong University Press.

Kubat, A. (2018) 'Morality as Legitimacy under Xi Jinping: The Political Functionality of Traditional Culture for the Chinese Communist Party', *Journal of Current Chinese Affairs*, 47(3): 47–86.

Lagerwey, J. (2010) *China. A Religious State*, Hong Kong: Chinese University Press.

Lai, J. (2015) '"Patrimonial Bureaucracy and Chinese Law: Max Weber's Legacy and Limits', *Modern China* 41(1): 40–58.

Lai, Y., Chan, E. H. W. and Choy, L. (2017) 'Village-Led Land Development under State-Led Institutional Arrangements in Urbanising China: The Case of Shenzhen', *Urban Studies*, 54(7): 1736–1759.

Lai, Y., Wang, J. and Lok, W. (2017) 'Redefining Property Rights over Collective Land in the Urban Redevelopment of Shenzhen, China', *Land Use Policy*, 69, 485–493.

Lai, Y., Zheng, X., Choy, L. H. T. and Wang, J. (2017) 'Property Rights and Housing Prices: An Empirical Study of Small Property Rights Housing in Shenzhen, China', *Land Use Policy*, 68, 429–437.

Landa, J. T. (1994) *Trust, Ethnicity, and Identity. Beyond the New Institutional Economics of Ethnic Trading Networks, Contract Law, and Gift-Exchange*, Ann Arbor: University of Michigan Press.

Landa, J. T. (2016) *Economic Success of Chinese Merchants in Southeast Asia*, Berlin, Heidelberg: Springer.

Landes, D. S. (2006) 'Why Europe and the West? Why Not China?', *Journal of Economic Perspectives*, 20(2): 3–22.

Lao Heng 老亨 (2018) *Shenshang jian shi* 深商简史 *1978–2018*, Shenzhen: Shenzhen baoye chubanshe.

Lean, E. (2015) 'The Butterfly Mark: Chen Diexian, His Brand, and Cultural Entrepreneurism in Republican China', in Rea, C. G. and Volland, N., eds., *The Business of Culture: Cultural Entrepreneurs in China and Southeast Asia, 1900–65* Vancouver: UBC Press, pp. 62–91.

Lee, C.-K. and Hung, S.-C. (2014) 'Institutional Entrepreneurship in the Informal Economy: China's Shan-Zhai Mobile Phones', *Strategic Entrepreneurship Journal*, 8(1): 16–36.

Levenson, J. R. (1968) *Confucian China and Its Modern Fate. A Trilogy*, Berkeley: University of California Press.

Li, X.-H. and Liang, X. (2015) 'A Confucian Social Model of Political Appointments among Chinese Private-Firm Entrepreneurs', *Academy of Management Journal*, 58(2): 592–617.

Liang, Y. (2014) 'Morality, Gift and Market: Communal Temple Restoration in Southwest China', *The Asia Pacific Journal of Anthropology*, 15(5): 414–432.

Lin, N. (2001) *Social Capital. A Theory of Social Structure and Action*, Cambridge: Cambridge University Press.

Little, D. (1992) *Understanding Peasant China. Case Studies in the Philosophy of Social Science*, New Haven, CT und London: Yale University Press.

Liu, K.-C. (1988) 'Chinese Merchants Guilds. An Historical Inquiry', *Pacific Historical Review*, LVII: 1–23.

Liu Lichuan 刘丽川 (2002) *Shenzhen kejia yanjiu* 深圳客家研究, Haikou: Nanfang chubanshe.

Lu, Y., Johnson, B. and Stark, R. (2008) 'Deregulation and Religious Market in Taiwan: A Research Note', *Sociological Quarterly*, 49: 139–153.

Ma, E. X. and Blackwell, A. (2017) 'The Political Architecture of the First and Second Lines', in O'Donnell, M. A., Wong, W. W. Y., and Bach, J. P. G., eds., *Learning from Shenzhen: China's post-Mao Experiment from Special Zone to Model City*, Chicago, IL: The University of Chicago Press, pp. 124–137.

Ma Hong, Luo Siying and Guo Feng 马宏，罗思颖， 郭峰 (2013) '2012 nian Shenzhen shehui zuzhi fazhan baogao' 2012 年深圳社会组织发展报告, in Zhang Xiaoru 张骁儒, ed., *Shenzhen shehui fazhan baogao (2012–2013)* 深圳社会发展报告, Beijing: Shehui kexue wenxian chubanshe, pp. 187–196.

MacCormack, G. (2006) 'The Legalist School and its Influence upon Traditional Chinese Law', *Archiv für Rechts- und Sozialphilosophie / Archives for Philosophy of Law and Social Philosophy*, 92(1): 59–81.

Madsen, R. (1984) *Morality and Power in a Chinese Village*, Berkeley, Los Angeles and London: University of California Press.

Mann, S. (1987) *Local Merchants and the Chinese Bureaucracy, 1750–1950*, Stanford, CA: Stanford University Press.

Mao, N. and Gu, B. (2019) 'Study of the Protection and Renewal of Urban Villages in Emerging Cities: The Example of Hubei Ancient Village in Shenzhen', *Journal of Architectural Conservation*, doi: 10.1080/13556207.2019.1678258.

McCleary, R. M. and Barro, R. J. (2019) *The Wealth of Religions: the Political Economy of Believing and Belonging*, Princeton, NJ: Princeton University Press.

McNeal, R. (2011) 'Moral Transformation and Local Identity: Reviving the Culture of Shun at Temples and Monuments across China', *Modern China*, 41(4): 436–464.

Menke, C. (2015) *Kritik der Rechte*, Berlin: Suhrkamp.

Mertha, A. C. (2005) 'China's "Soft" Centralization: Shifting *Tiao/Kuai* Authority Relations', *The China Quarterly*, 184: 791–810.

Migdal, J. S. (2001) *State in Society: Studying How States and Societies Transform and Constitute One Another*, Cambridge and New York: Cambridge University Press.

Mungello, D. E. (1999) *The Great Encounter of China and the West, 1500–1800*, Lanham, MD: Rowman & Littlefield.

Naquin, S. and Rawski, E. (1987) *Chinese Society in the Eighteenth Century*, New Haven, CT und London: Yale University Press.

Naughton, B. (2017) 'Is China Socialist?', *Journal of Economic Perspectives*, 31(1): 3–24.

Nissim, R. (2016) *Land Administration and Practice in Hong Kong*. Fourth Edition. Hong Kong: Hong Kong University Press.

Numazaki, I. (1996) 'The Role of Personal Networks in the Making of Taiwan's *Guanxiqiye* (Related Enterprises)', in Hamilton, G. G., ed., *Asian Business Networks*, Berlin und New York: Springer, pp. 71–86.

O'Donnell, M.-A. (2017) 'Heroes of the Special Zone: Modeling Reform and Its Limits', in O'Donnell, M. A., Wong, W. W. Y. and Bach, J. P. G., eds., *Learning from Shenzhen: China's post-Mao Experiment from Special Zone to Model City*, Chicago, IL: The University of Chicago Press, pp. 124–137.

O'Donnell, M.-A. (2019) 'Heart of Shenzhen: The Movement to Preserve "Ancient" Hubei Village', in Banajeree, T. and Loukaitou-Sideris, A., eds., *The New Companion to Urban Design*, London: Routledge, pp. 480–493.

O'Donnell, M.-A. and Wan, V. Y. (2016) 'Shen Kong: Cui Bono?', in Bolchover, J. and Hasdell, P., eds., *Border Ecologies: Hong Kong's Mainland Frontier*. Berlin and Boston: De Gruyter, pp. 35–47.

Oakes, T. (1999) 'Eating the Food of the Ancestors: Place, Tradition, and Tourism in a Chinese Frontier River Town', *Ecumene*, 6(2): 123–145.

Oakes, T. (2017) 'Happy Town: Cultural Governance and Biopolitical Urbanism in China', *Environment and Planning A*, 51(1): 244–262.

Oakes, T. (2019) 'Making Cultural Cities in China: Governance, State-Building, and Precarious Creativity', *Environment and Planning A: Economy and Space*, 51(1): 8–86.

Oi, J. C. (1992) 'Fiscal Reform and the Economic Foundations of Local State Corporatism in China', *World Politics*, 45(1): 99–126.

Oi, J. C. (1995) 'The Role of the Local State in China's Transitional Economy', *The China Quarterly*, 144: 132–149.

Orenstein, M. A. (2011) 'Three Models of Contemporary Capitalism', in Birdsall, N. and Fukuyama, F., eds., *New Ideas on Development after the Financial Crisis*, Baltimore, MD: John Hopkins University Press, pp. 29–49.

Osburg, J. (2013) *Anxious Wealth: Money and Morality among China's New Rich*, Stanford, CA: Stanford University Press.

Parish, W. and Whyte, M. (1978) *Village and Family in Contemporary China*, Chicago, IL: Chicago University Press.

Pennarz, J. (1992) *Mazu, Macht und Marktwirtschaft. Die religiöse Organisation im sozialen und ökonomischen Wandlungsprozeß der ländlichen Gesellschaft Taiwans*, München: Anacon.

Perry, E. (2013) 'Cultural Governance in Contemporary China: "Re-Orienting" Party Propaganda', Boston: Harvard-Yenching Working Paper Series 2013.

Pieke, F. N., Nyíri, P., Thunø, M. and Ceccagno, A. (2004) *Transnational Chinese. Fujianese Migrants in Europe*, Stanford, CA: Stanford University Press.

Pinch, T. and Swedberg, R., eds. (2008) *Living in a Material World: Economic Sociology Meets Science and Technology Studies*, Cambridge: MIT Press.

Po, L. (2008) 'Redefining Rural Collectives in China: Land Conversion and the Emergence of Rural Shareholding Co-Operatives', *Urban Studies*, 45(8): 1603–1623.

Po, L. (2012) 'Asymmetrical Integration: Public Finance Deprivation in China's Urbanized Villages', *Environment and Planning A*, 44(12): 2834–2851.

Polanyi, K. (1944/2001) *The Great Transformation: The Political and Economic Origins of Our Time*. Boston: Beacon Press.

Pomeranz, K. (2000) *The Great Divergence. China, Europe, and the Making of the Modern World Economy*, Princeton, NJ und Oxford: Princeton University Press.

Potter, S. H. and Potter, J. (1990) *China's Peasants: The Anthropology of a Revolution*. Cambridge und New York: Cambridge University Press.
Prosterman, R. (2013) 'Rural Land Rights in China', in Kennedy, D. and Stiglitz, J. E., eds., *Law and Economics with Chinese Characteristics. Institutions for Promoting Development in the Twenty-First Century*, Oxford: Oxford University Press, pp. 214–235.
Qi, Xiaoying (2013) 'Guanxi, Social Capital Theory and Beyond: Toward a Globalized Social Science', *The British Journal of Sociology*, 64(2): 308–324.
Qin, Y., Shi, L. H. Stöttinger, B. and Cavusgil, E. (2019) 'Neither an Authentic Product nor a Counterfeit: The Growing Popularity of Shanzhai Products in Global Markets: Consumers' Motives of Buying Shanzhai vs. Counterfeit Products', *Canadian Journal of Administrative Sciences / Revue Canadienne Des Sciences de l'Administration*, 36(3): 306–321.
Rauch, J. E. and Casella, A., eds. (2001) *Networks and Markets*, New York: Russell Sage Foundation.
Rea, C. G. (2015) 'Enter the Cultural Entrepreneur', in Rea, C. G. and Volland, N., eds., *The Business of Culture: Cultural Entrepreneurs in China and Southeast Asia, 1900–65*, Vancouver: UBC Press, pp. 9–33.
Rea, C. G. and Volland, N., eds. (2015) *The Business of Culture: Cultural Entrepreneurs in China and Southeast Asia, 1900–65*, Vancouver: UBC Press.
Riskin, C. (1975) 'Surplus and Stagnation in Modern China', in Perkins, D., ed., *China's Modern Economy in Historical Perspective*, Stanford, CA: Stanford University Press, pp. 49–84.
Rowe, W. T. (1989) *Hankow. Conflict and Community in a Chinese City, 1796–1895*, Stanford, CA: Stanford University Press.
Sahlins, M. (2013) *What Kinship Is - and Is Not*, Chicago, IL: The University of Chicago Press.
Saich, T., Hu, B. (2012) *Chinese Village, Global Market. New Collectives and Rural Development*, New York: Palgrave Macmillan.
Sangren, P. S. (1984) 'Traditional Chinese Corporations: Beyond Kinship', *The Journal of Asian Studies*, XLIII(3): 391–415.
Sangren, P. S. (2013) 'The Chinese Family as Instituted Fantasy: Or, Rescuing Kinship Imaginaries from the 'Symbolic'', *Journal of the Royal Anthropological Institute* (N.S.), 19: 279–299.
Sassen, S. (2018) *Cities in a World Economy*. Fifth Edition. Thousand Oaks, CA: SAGE Publications.
Schein, E. H. (2017) *Organizational Culture and Leadership*. Fifth Edition, Hoboken: Wiley, 2017.
Schmidt-Glintzer, H. (1983) 'Viele Pfade oder ein Weg? Betrachtungen zur Durchsetzung der konfuzianischen Orthopraxie', in Schluchter, W., ed., *Max Webers Studie über Konfuzianismus und Daoismus. Interpretation und Kritik*, Frankfurt a.M.: Suhrkamp, pp. 298–341.
Schneider, D. (1984) *A Critique of the Study of Kinship*, Ann Arbor: University of Michigan Press.
Searle, J. R. (1995) *The Construction of Social Reality*, New York: Free Press.
Searle, J. R. (2010) *Making the Social World. The Structure of Human Civilization*, Oxford: Oxford University Press.
Segawa, M. and Kawagusa, Y., eds. (2016): *"Sōzoku" to chūgoku shakai. Sono henhō no jinreigaku kenkiū no genzai*, Tokio: Fukyo Publishing Inc.

Seidel, J. (2019) *Innovation Networks in the Informal Economy: The Case of Shanzhai 山寨 Innovation*, Master thesis Leiden University, https://openaccess.leidenuniv.nl/handle/1887/77288.

Seligman, A. B., Weller, R. P., Puett, M. J. and Simon, B. (2008) *Ritual and Its Consequences: An Essay on the Limits of Sincerity*, Oxford and New York: Oxford University Press.

Sennett, R. (2018) *Building and Dwelling: Ethics for the City*, London: Penguin.

Shenzhen shi Bao'an qu 深圳市宝安区 (2018) 宝安2017年股份合作公司换届集体资产管理委员会任命办法》, 中共深圳市宝安区街道工作委员, 2018年2月28日.

Shenzhen shi Futian zhengfu 深圳市福田政府and Zhongguo chengshi guihua sheji yanjiu yuan, Shenzhen fenyuan 中国城市规划设计研究院， 深圳分院 (2007) Shenzhen shi Futian Xiasha shequ gaizao zhuanxiang guihua, 深圳市福田下沙社区改造专项规划, Shenzhen.

Shenzhen shi guihua he guotu ziyuan weiyuanhui 深圳市规划和国土资源委员会 (2018) Shenzhen shi chengzhong cun (jiu cun) zongti guihua (2018–2025) 深圳市城中村（旧村）总体规划(2018–2025)(征求意见稿).

Shenzhen shi meixian shanghui 深圳市梅县商会 (2019) Shenzhen meishang huikan 深圳梅商会刊 6, 2018/12.

Shenzhen shi shehui zuzhi guanli ju 深圳市社会组织管理局, ed. (2018a) 2017–18 Shenzhen shi hangye xiehui fazhan baogao 2017/18 深圳市行业协会发展报告, Shenzhen.

Shenzhen shi shehui zuzhi guanli ju 深圳市社会组织管理局, ed. (2018b) 2017 深圳市行业协参与行业治理案例报告. Shenzhen.

Shenzhen shi tongjiju (2018) Shenzhen tongji nianjian 2018 深圳市统计局深圳统计年鉴2018, Beijing: China Statistics Press.

Shi, L., Lamb, Z., Qiu, X. Cai, H. and Vale, L. (2018) 'Promises and Perils of Collective Land Tenure in Promoting Urban Resilience: Learning from China's Urban Villages', *Habitat International*, 77: 1–11.

Shih, W., Chie, C.-F. and Wang, J.-c. (2010) *Shanzhai! MediaTek and the "White Box" Handset Market*, HBS case study 9–610–081.

Shue, V. (1988) *The Reach of the State. Sketches of the Chinese Body Politic*, Stanford, CA: Stanford University Press.

Sigley, G. (2006) 'Chinese Governmentalities: Government, Governance and the Socialist Market Economy', *Economy and Society*, 35(4): 487–508.

Siu, H. F. (1989) *Agents and Victims in South China. Accomplices of Rural Revolution*, New Haven, CT und London: Yale University Press.

Siu, H. F. (1995) 'Community Festivals in Post-Mao South China: Economic Transformation and Cultural Improvisation', in *China Review 1995*, Hong Kong: Chinese University Press, Chapter 16.

Siu, H. F. and Chan, W.-H. (2010) 'Introduction: Gender, Regional Culture, and Women's Positioning', in Siu, H.-F. and Chan, W.-H., eds., *Merchant Daughters: Women, Commerce, and Regional Culture in South China*, Hong Kong: Hong Kong University Press, pp. 7–28.

Skinner, G. W. (1964/1965) 'Marketing and Social Structure in Rural China, Parts I-III', *The Journal of Asian Studies,* 24(1): 3–43, 24(2): 195–228, 24(3): 363–399.

Stacey, J. (1983) *Patriarchy and Socialist Revolution in China*, Berkeley, Los Angeles, London: University of California Press.

Stafford, Ch. (2000) 'Chinese Patriliny and the Cycles of Yang and Laiwang', in Carsten, J., ed., *Cultures of Relatedness: New Approaches to the Study of Kinship*, Cambridge: Cambridge University Press, pp. 35–54.

Steffen, M. A. (2017) 'The Value of Emptiness: Zhengzhou's Empty Houses and the PRC's Housing Bubble', http://www.meganasteffen.com/the-value-of-emptiness.

Stephenson, B. (2015) *Ritual: A Very Short Introduction*, Oxford: Oxford University Press.

Stewart, A. (2013) 'The Anthropology of Family Business: An Imagined Ideal', in Melin, L., Nordqvist, M. and Pramodita, S., eds., *SAGE Handbook of Family Business*, Newbury Park, CA: Sage Publications.

Stiglitz, J. (2013) 'Creating the Institutional Foundations for Market Economy', in Kennedy, D. and Stiglitz, J. E., eds., *Law and Economics with Chinese Characteristics. Institutions for Promoting Development in the Twenty-First Century*, Oxford: Oxford University Press, pp. 71–111.

Storr, V. H. (2004) *Enterprising Slaves and Master Pirates: Understanding Economic Life in the Bahamas*, New York: Peter Lang.

Sun, A. (2013) *Confucianism as a World Religion. Contested Histories and Contemporary Realities*, Princeton, NJ: Princeton University Press.

Sutton, D. S. (2007) 'Ritual, Cultural Standardization, and Orthopraxy in China: Reconsidering James L. Watson's Ideas', *Modern China*, 33(1): 3–21.

Tabellini, G. (2008) 'Institutions and Culture', *Journal of the European Economic Association*, 6(2–3): 255–294.

Tan Tongxue 谭同学 (2010) *Qiao cun you dao. Zhuanxing xiangcun de daode quanli yu shehui jiegou*, 桥村有道。转型乡村的道德权利与社会结构，Beijing: San lian shudian.

Tang, B. (2015) '"Not Rural but Not Urban": Community Governance in China's Urban Villages', *The China Quarterly*, 223: 724–744.

Tao Qing 陶庆 (2007) Fujie de xiandai 'shangren buluo'. Zouchu zhuanxing qi shehui chongjian de hefa hua weiji 福街的现代商人部落. 走出转型期社会重建的合法化危机, Beijing: Social Science Academic Press.

Taylor, C. (2007) *A Secular Age*, Cambridge, MA: Belknap.

Taylor, C. (2015) *Hegel and Modern Society*. Cambridge: Cambridge University Press.

Teets, J. C. (2013) 'Let Many Civil Societies Bloom: The Rise of Consultative Authoritarianism in China', *The China Quarterly*, 213: 19–38.

Thornton, P. M. (2013) 'The Advance of the Party: Transformation or Takeover of Urban Grassroots Society?', *The China Quarterly*, 213: 1–18.

Townsend, J. (1992) 'Chinese Nationalism', *The Australian Journal of Chinese Affairs*, 27: 97–130.

Towse, R. (2010) *A Textbook of Cultural Economics*, Cambridge and New York: Cambridge University Press.

Trappel, R. (2011) 'Agrarian Change in China: The Commodification of Collective Land', in Alpermann, B., ed., *Politics and Markets in Rural China*, Abingdon und New York: Routledge, pp. 15–29.

Trémon, A.-C. (2014) 'La figure du fondateur comme incarnation du public. Mutations de l'ancestralité en contexte urbain (Delta des Perles, Chine)', *Civilisations*, 63(1 & 2): 123–142.

Trémon, A.-C. (2015a) 'Local Capitalism and Neoliberalization in a Shenzhen Former Lineage Village', *Focaal*, 71: 71–85.

Trémon, A.-C. (2015b) 'Heterotopic Sites, Monochronous Urbanization. Saving Space in a Former Village of Shenzhen (1979–2015)', *Quaderni historici*, 149(2): 439–468.

Tsai, L. L. (2002) 'Cadres, Temple and Lineage Institutions, and Governance in Rural China', *The China Journal*, 48: 1–28.

Tsai, L. L. (2007) *Accountability without Democracy, Solidary Groups and Public Goods Provision in Rural China*, Cambridge: Cambridge University Press.

Tuan, Y.-F. (1977) *Space and Place. The Perspective of Experience*, Minneapolis and London: University of Minnesota Press.

Turner, V. (1967) *The Forest of Symbols: Aspects of Ndembu Ritual*, Ithaca, NY: Cornell University Press.

Unger, J., und Chan, A. (2015) 'State Corporatism and Business Associations in China: A Comparison with Earlier Emerging Economies of East Asia', *International Journal of Emerging Markets*, 10(2): 178–193.

Veblen, T. (1899/1965) *The Theory of the Leisure Class*, New York: Kelley.

Von Glahn, R. (2016) *The Economic History of China: From Antiquity to the Nineteenth Century*, Cambridge: Cambridge University Press.

Walton, L. (2018) 'The "Spirit" of Confucian Education in Contemporary China: Songyang Academy and Zhengzhou University', *Modern China*, 44(3): 313–342.

Wan Yan 万妍 (2017) 中国社会文脉下的城市建成空间变迁——以深圳白石洲塘头村为例, Master thesis, Shenzhen University

Wang Jingsheng 王京, ed. (2011) *Shenzhen shi da guannian* 深圳十大观念, Shenzhen: Shenzhen baoye jituan chubanshe.

Wang, X. (2015) '都市乡民' 与乡土传统文化的复活 ('dushi xiangmin' yu xiangtu chuantong de fuhuo, 'Urban Peasants' and the Revival of Rural Tradition), 学海 *Xuehai*, 2: 59–66.

Wang, D. W. D. (2016) *Urban Villages in the New China: Case of Shenzhen*, New York: Palgrave Macmillan.

Watson, J. (1975): *Emigration and the Chinese Lineage*, Berkeley, Los Angeles and London: University of California Press.

Watson, J. L. 1985(2003) 'Hereditary Tenancy and Corporate Landlordism in Traditional China: A Case Study', in Watson, J. L. and Watson, R. S., eds., *Village Life in Hong Kong: Politics, Gender, and Ritual in the New Territories*, Hong Kong: The Chinese University Press, pp. 145–167.

Watson, J. L. (1987) 'From the Common Pot: Feasting With Equals in Chinese Society', *Anthropos*, 82: 389–401.

Watson, J. L. (2004) 'Presidential Address: Virtual Kinship, Real Estate, and Diaspora Formation—The Man Lineage Revisited', *Journal of Asian Studies*, 63(4) 893–910.

Watson, J. L. (2010) 'Forty Years on the Border: Hong Kong/China', *ASIANetwork Exchange*, XVIII(1): 10–23.

Watson, J. L. (2014) 'Meat: A Cultural Biography in (South) China', in Klein, J. A. and Murcott, A., eds., *Food Consumption in a Global Perspective. Essays in the Anthropology of Food in Honour of Jack Goody*, New York: Palgrave MacMillan, pp. 25–44.

Watson, R. S. (1985) *Inequality among Brothers. Class and Kinship in South China*, Cambridge: Cambridge University Press.

Watson, J. and Rawski, E., eds. (1988) *Death Ritual in Late Imperial and Modern China*, Berkeley: University of California Press.

Watt, J. R. (1972) *The District Magistrate in Late Imperial China*, New York und London: Columbia University Press.

Watt, J. R. (1977) 'The Yamen and Urban Administration', in Skinner, G. W., ed., *The City in Late Imperial China*, Stanford, CA: Stanford University Press, pp. 353–390.

Weber, M. (1991) *Die Wirtschaftsethik der Weltreligionen: Konfuzianismus und Taoismus, Schriften 1915–1920*, Studienausgabe, Tübingen: Mohr.

Wei, S.-J. and Zhang X. (2011) 'The Competitive Saving Motive: Evidence from Rising Sex Ratios and Savings Rates in China', *Journal of Political Economy*, 119(3): 511–564.

White, H. C. (2008) *Identity & Control: How Social Formations Emerge*, Princeton, NJ: Princeton University Press.

Williamson, C. G. (forthcoming 2020) *Urban Rituals in Sacred Landscapes. Country Sanctuaries and Civic Transformation in Hellenistic Asia Minor*, Religions of the Graeco-Roman World, Leiden: Brill.

Wong, C. P. W. (2009) 'Rebuilding Government for the 21st Century: Can China Incrementally Reform the Public Sector?', *The China Quarterly*, 200: 929–952.

Wong, C. P. W. and Bird, R. M. (2008) 'China's Fiscal System: A Work in Progress', in Brandt, L. and Rawski, T., eds., *China's Great Economic Transformation*, Cambridge: Cambridge University Press, pp. 429–466.

Wong, R. B. (1997) *China Transformed: Historical Change and the Limits of European Experience*, Ithaca, NY: Cornell University Press.

Wong, S. W. (2015) 'Land Requisitions and State-Village Power Restructuring in Southern China', *The China Quarterly*, 224: 888–908.

Wong, S.-l. (1985) 'The Chinese Family Firm: A Model', *British Journal of Sociology*, XXXVI(1): 58–72.

World Bank (2014) *Urban China. Toward Efficient, Inclusive, and Sustainable Urbanization*, Washington, DC: World Bank.

Wu Chongqing 吴重庆 (2014) *Sun cun de lu: hougeming shidai de ren gui shen* 孙村的路。后革命时代的人鬼神, Beijing: Falü chubanshe.

Wu Jiyan 伍继延 (2014) *Zai shang yan shang? Xiang shang wenhua yu xiandai shanghui* 在商言商？湘商文化与现代商会, Peking: Zhongguo shehui chubanshe.

Xu, C. (2011) 'The Fundamental Institutions of China's Reforms and Development', *Journal of Economic Literature*, XLIL(4): 1076–1151.

Yang, C. K. (1961) *Religion in Chinese Society: A Study of Contemporary Social Functions of Religion and Some of Their Historical Factors*, Berkeley: University of California Press.

Yang, F. (2006) 'The Red, Black and Grey Markets for Religion in China', *Sociological Quarterly*, 47: 93–122.

Yang, F. (2011) 'Market Economy and the Revival of Religions', in Palmer, D., Shive, G. and Wickeri, P. L., eds., *Chinese Religious Life*, Oxford: Oxford University Press, pp. 209–226.

Yang, L.-s. (1957) 'The Concept of 'Pao' as as Basis for Social Relations in China', in Fairbank, J. K., ed., *Chinese Thought and Institutions*, Chicago, IL: Chicago University Press, pp. 291–309.

Yang, M. M.-h. (1994) *Gifts, Favours and Banquets: The Art of Social Relationships in China*, Ithaca, NY: Cornell University Press.

Yang, M. M.-h. (2007) 'Ritual Economy and Rural Capitalism with Chinese Characteristics', in Held, D. and Moore, H., eds., *Cultural Politics in a Global Age: Uncertainty, Solidarity and Innovation*, Oxford: Oneworld, pp. 226–232.

Yao, S. (2002) *Confucian Capitalism. Discourse, Practice, and the Myth of Chinese Enterprise*, London and New York: Routledge.

Yu, P. K. (2011) 'TRIPS Enforcement and Developing Countries', *American University International Law Review*, 26(3): 727–782.

Yue, Y. (2014) 'Holding Temple Festivals at Home of Doing-gooders: Temple Festivals and Rural Religion in Contemporary China', *Cambridge Journal of China Studies*, 9(1): 48–95.

Zelin, M. (2004) 'Managing Multiple Ownership at the Zigong Saltyard', in Zelin, M., Ocko, J. K., and Gardella, R., eds., *Contract and Property in Early Modern China*, Stanford, CA: Stanford University Press, pp. 230–268.

Zelin, M. (2009) 'The Firm in Early Modern China', *Journal of Economic Behavior & Organization*, 71: 623–637.

Zelin, M., Ocko, J. K. and Gardella, R., eds. (2004) *Contract and Property in Early Modern China*, Stanford, CA: Stanford University Press.

Zhai Xuewei 翟学伟 (2011) *Zhongguo ren de guanxi yuanli. Shikong zhixu, shenghuo yunian ji qi liubian*, 中国人的关系原理。时空秩序，生活欲念及其流变，Beijing: Peking University Press.

Zhang, C. (2018) 'Governing Neoliberal Authoritarian Citizenship: Theorizing Hukou and the Changing Mobility Regime in China', *Citizenship Studies*, 22(8): 855–881.

Zhang Shuguang 张曙光, ed. (1996) *Zhongguo zhidu bianqian de anli yanjiu* 中国制度变迁的案例研究, Shanghai: Shanghai renmin chubanshe.

Zhang, J. and Peck, J. (2014) 'Variegated Capitalism, Chinese Style: Regional Models, Multi-scalar Constructions', *Regional Studies*, doi: 10.1080/00343404.2013.856514.

Zheng, Z. (2001) *Family Lineage Organization and Social Change in Ming and Qing Fujian* (trans. Michael Szonyi), Honolulu: University of Hawai'i Press.

Zhou Hua 周华 (2014) *Zongzu bian gongsi. Guangzhou zhangban cun cunmin zuzhi jiegou de bai nian yanbian,* 宗族变公司。广州长湴村村民组织结构的百年演变. Beijing: Contemporary China Publishing House.

Zhou Jianxin 周建新 (2018) *Dongdang de weilongwu. Yige kejia zu de chengshihua zaoyu he wenhua kangzheng* 动荡的围龙屋。一个客家族的城市化遭遇与文化抗争，Guangdong: Guangdong renmin chubanshe.

Zhou Li 周琍，Gong Dandan 龚丹丹 (2014) 'Jin shi nian kejia shangren yanjiu zongshu 近十年客家商人研究综述', *Journal of Gannan Normal University*, 2014(1): 26–29.

Zweynert, J. (2009) 'Interests versus Culture in the Theory of Institutional Change?', *Journal of Institutional Economics*, 5(3): 339–360.

Index

For Product Safety Concerns and Information please contact our EU
representative GPSR@taylorandfrancis.com
Taylor & Francis Verlag GmbH, Kaufingerstraße 24, 80331 München, Germany

www.ingramcontent.com/pod-product-compliance
Ingram Content Group UK Ltd.
Pitfield, Milton Keynes, MK11 3LW, UK
UKHW022130190926
475702UK00013B/1727
* 9 7 8 0 3 6 7 5 6 3 7 2 1 *